LEARNING THE VIRTUAL LIFE

Digital technologies have transformed cultural perceptions of learning and what it means to be literate, expanding the importance of experience alongside interpretation and reflection. *Learning the Virtual Life* offers ways to consider the local and global effects of digital media on educational environments, as well as the cultural transformations of how we now define learning and literacy.

While some have welcomed the educational challenges of digital culture and emphasized its possibilities for individual emancipation and social transformation in the new information age, others accuse digital culture of absorbing its recipients in an all-pervasive virtual world. Unlike most accounts of the educational and cultural consequences of digital culture, *Learning the Virtual Life* presents a neutral, advanced introduction to the key issues involved with the integration of digital culture and education. This edited collection presents international perspectives on a wide range of issues, and each chapter combines upper-level theory with "real-world" practice, making this essential reading for all those interested in digital media and education.

Peter Pericles Trifonas is a professor at the Ontario Institute for Studies in Education, University of Toronto.

LEARNING THE VIRTUAL LIFE

Public Pedagogy in a Digital World

Edited by Peter Pericles Trifonas

 Routledge
Taylor & Francis Group

NEW YORK AND LONDON

KH

First published 2012
by Routledge
711 Third Avenue, New York, NY 10017

Simultaneously published in the UK
by Routledge
2 Park Square, Milton Park, Abingdon, Oxon OX14 4RN

Routledge is an imprint of the Taylor & Francis Group, an informa business

© 2012 Taylor & Francis

Library of Congress Cataloging in Publication Data
Learning the virtual life : public pedagogy in a digital world / [edited by] Peter Pericles Trifonas.
    p. cm.
    Includes bibliographical references and index.
    1. Internet in education. 2. Internet literacy. 3. Digital media—Social aspects.
    4. Information society—Social aspects. I. Trifonas, Peter Pericles, 1960–
    LB1044.87.L4385 2011
    004.67'8071—dc23
    2011026621

ISBN: 978-0-415-89204-9 (hbk)
ISBN: 978-0-415-89208-7 (pbk)
ISBN: 978-0-203-81882-4 (ebk)

Typeset in Bembo and Stone Sans
by EvS Communication Networx, Inc.

Printed and bound in the United States of America on acid-free paper
by Walsworth Publishing Company, Marceline, MO.

SUSTAINABLE
FORESTRY
INITIATIVE

Certified Sourcing
www.sfiprogram.org
SFI-00555
The SFI label applies to the text stock.

5/1/13

To Gunta,

Amidst the struggle between Love and Fate,

Fate always finds a way to reunite those presumed lost
in the ravishes of time to Love

CONTENTS

PREFACE

Learning the Virtual Life:
Public Pedagogy in a Digital World

Digital culture has become an undeniably integral part of how we learn to read and engage with others and the world around us. Digital technologies have transformed cultural perceptions of learning and what it means to be literate, expanding the importance of experience alongside interpretation and reflec tion. *Learning the Virtual Life: Public Pedagogy in a Digital World* offers ways to consider the local and global effects of digital media on educational environ- ments, as well as the cultural transformations of how we now define learning in the virtual. While some have welcomed the educational challenges of digital culture and emphasized its possibilities for individual emancipation and social transformation in the new information age, others accuse digital culture of absorbing its recipients in an all-pervasive virtual world. Unlike most accounts of the educational and cultural consequences of digital culture, *Learning the Virtual Life* engages both theory and forms of practice, presenting discussions to key issues involved with the integration of digital culture and education in the public sphere.

In Chapter 1, "Digital Literacy and the Spaces of Academic Discourse," Peta Mitchell engages David Bartholomae's argument that, in their writ- ten assessment, university students are required to "invent the university" by learning "our language," but this is also a language that is fundamentally bound up with the spatial politics of the academy. She points out that for Bourdieu, writing in 1965, the most salient example of this spatial politics affecting (and effecting) academic discourse is the face-to-face teacher–student relationship, which synecdochically represents the spatial order of the uni- versity: "the space of the teaching relationship imposes its law of distance so strongly [...] because it captures and expresses so much of what the university, as an institution, stands for." The chapter examines whether student–teacher use of e-learning software and social networking sites as educational tools might disrupt this sense of academic distance in students' written communication. It asks whether, in the shift to digital literacy in academia, students are beginning to invent a different university through an academic discourse that inscribes a different spatial politics.

In Chapter 2, "New Epistemologies? Rethinking Ways of Knowing in a Digital Culture," Jennifer Jenson and Suzanne de Castell argue that since its initiation into the public sphere, education has been precariously balanced between fulfilling a role of historical cultural transmission, that is of educating a society into its past ways, forms and value systems, and forging a path as a precipitator of new ideas, scientific inventions, knowledgeable domains and current social and cultural debates. Epistemology and pedagogy are at the centre of this divide: what is it we want people to know, how can we best convey what it is we want people to know, and how will we know if they know it? For example, Jenson and de Castell illustrate how these questions are crassly answered by mass standardized testing, and a "no child left behind" policy that has done little else. What still remains are questions about what and how we know, and what values that knowledge is afforded under these new media conditions.

In Chapter 3, "Update Your Status: Identity and Learning in Viral Youth Networks," Michael Hoechsmann argues that, increasingly, young people are wearing their status on their sleeves, and updating their status on Facebook and through IM and cell networks. Positioning one's identity in real time through material, semiotic means is a central preoccupation of many youth today. This still includes clothing and music choices, but it now involves as well multimodal and textual practices online and on cell phones. It's hard to get some identity traction growing up in a world of viral communication and a fast culture and economy, so it makes sense to leave real time traces of one's in-flux identity along the way. Hoechsmann analyzes how viral networks are complementing and even displacing youth subcultures as vital nodes of youth identity, and viral communication has come to the fore as a pedagogical vehicle for identity texts. He distinguishes between, on the one hand, viral networks such as IM, Facebook, MySpace, Twitter and cell phone texting, and on the other, viral communication such as socializing or hanging out. The former are spaces for the expression of status and identity, whether just-in-time (i.e., updating your status on Twitter) or static (i.e., Facebook profile page); the latter are forms of engagement practiced by young people online. Creating a profile page at Facebook or MySpace and populating it with friends is one way to perform your status and identity. Updating your status in real time, whether on Facebook, Twitter or cell phone text messages appears at first glance more enigmatic, but it is a demonstration of agency in an alienating and fast changing world. Hoechsmann draws on research data from several large-scale projects undertaken in recent years.

In Chapter 4, "Technoliteracy at the Sustainability Crossroads: Posing Ecopedagogical Problems for Digital Literacy Frameworks," Richard Kahn states that to think about digital literacy necessarily involves foundational decisions about the nature of the "technological literacy" in which the digital is grounded. Recently, a literature attempting to chart emancipatory digital technoliteracies has emerged over the last decade. But these discussions are rarely if ever based in normative demands for sustainability. The chapter begins with a brief examination of the meanings that "technology" and "literacy" have received in recent literature in order to gain insight into what sort of knowledge and skills "technoliteracy" hails therein. Kahn then summarizes the broad trajectories of development in hegemonic programs of contemporary technoliteracy, from their arguable origins as a form of digital "computer literacy" in the *A Nation at Risk* report of 1983 up to the present call for integration of technology across the curriculum and the standards-based approach of the *No Child Left Behind Act of 2001* and 2004's *US National Educational Technology Plan*. In contradistinction, Kahn reveals how this approach has been tacitly challenged at the global institutional level through the sustainable development framework of United Nations' Project 2000+, and theorizes how this might link up with a democratic ecopedagogy project of re-visioning education for sustainability though multiple literacies. Finally, in closing, the chapter addresses what it will mean to reconstruct "technoliteracy" broadly in this manner and concludes with a call for an ecopedagogy that can inform and be informed by the counterhegemonic idea of culturally relevant "multiple technoliteracies."

In Chapter 5, "Learning Environment and Digital Literacy. A Mismatch or a Possibility from Finnish Teachers' and Students' Perspectives," Liisa Ilomäki, Peppi Taalas, and Minna Lakkala argue that digital skills are regarded as basic cultural skills that should be provided for students through formal schooling, like reading and writing. Unfortunately, several studies indicate that the use of information and communication technologies (ICTs) in schools only seldom benefits from the possibilities and potential of new technologies, and, moreover, only seldom does it support young learners in achieving necessary digital skills that also foster their academic skills. The aim of the chapter is to discuss the characteristics of a learning environment that supports the development of students' digital competence and literacy, utilises the students' digital skills from their informal settings, and offers multifaceted support for the regular school knowledge practices. Results from three studies concerning ICT skills, use and competence both in formal and informal educational settings are used as examples of the connection between learning and teaching activities and the digital competence they promote. The first study (Second Information Technology in Education Study, SITES) is an international comparison on the use of information and communication technology at schools; the second study (Towards Future Literacy Pedagogies, ToLP) examines the literacy practices of Finnish 9th graders and teachers in school and out-of-school contexts; and the third study investigates, through observations, the characteristics of learning practices in several technology-intensive classrooms in selected Finnish primary and secondary schools. Based on the studies along with relevant literature, suggestions and outlines are made for new kind of teaching practices that integrate informal and formal learning to advance students' digital competence and improve academic oriented digital skills.

In Chapter 6, "What Haunts the Narcissus-Narcosis: Media Education and the Social Life of Digital Technologies," Stuart R. Poyntz argues that within the field of media literacy, the development of global media cultures alongside the evolution of digital technologies has brought to the fore a whole set of pressing issues having to do with the nature of young people's mediated experiences. These include: the rise of global media conglomerates and the ongoing commercialization of youth cultures; the development of interactive media and newly configured relations of production and consumption; ongoing debates about the digital divide; concerns about the technologizing of schools and the role of ICTs in the development of more democratic pedagogical cultures; and debates about the new configurations of childhood and the extent to which anything like a digital generation has evolved. Underlying these discussions, there is also a more basic question central to media education and communication and media studies more generally: how is it that the social life of technology is to be understood? In this chapter, while not resolving this question, Poyntz draws on Jacques Derrida's work on spectrality and Marshall McLuhan's work on acoustic space to unpack the relationship between the social life of digital technologies and the meaning of critical agency in the field of media literacy. Derrida's work on the spectral is helpful in this regard because with this concept he is able to foreground an emancipatory promise at the heart of all mediated practices. Through this, he calls attention to the fundamental role of the enunciative moment as this pertains to student involvement in media education. At the same time, Derrida cannot address how the aforementioned emancipatory promise operates through the unique materialities of digital technologies. To help compensate for this shortcoming, Kahn turns to McLuhan's work on acoustic space. McLuhan's writing about electronic and digital media could be seen as "old news." Yet, Kahn shows how McLuhan's descriptions of new media environments continue to be valuable, particularly for delineating the specific conditions that nurture critical agency in an age of digital culture.

In Chapter 7, "Wikilearning as Radical Equality," Juha Suoranta and Tere Vadén characterize wikilearning—co-operative online learning—as a form of collaborative, collective and democratic learning using digital technologies; this form of learning is especially suitable in the hands of social movements and other activists as they "learn in struggle." Wikilearners build online communities of learning (e.g., Wikipedia, Wikiversity, and smaller sites based on wiki software and other so-called social media) in which they share their learning and help each other to learn perhaps without even realizing it. Ideally anyone can join these rhizomatic communities and contribute without top-down guidance or leadership. In developing the idea of wikilearning, Suoranta and Vadén refer to French philosopher Jacques Rancière's notions on teaching and studying without authorities as a foundation of radical equality. It is our contention that wikilearning consists of several qualities necessary for the creation of and full participation in a more humane and just society.

In Chapter 8, "Learner Voice and Lived Culture in Digital Media Production by Younger Learners: Implications for Pedagogy and Future Research," John Potter discusses three recent ethnographic research projects carried out in formal educational settings which engaged with digital cultures and pedagogy. In the first case study, fieldwork was carried out in two schools among children taking part in video projects on themes of self-representation and identity. The findings in this study suggested that this new media literacy practice can be metaphorically conceived as a form of "curatorship" in the organisation of digital media assets and that this connects to an important set of dispositions and skills in lived culture. In the second case study, video and audio recording under the control of younger learners was used to explore the differences between children's experience of new media technology at school and at home. The findings in this study suggested that the desire to engage with the "learner voice" approach was representative of a wider need to see experience of popular culture reflected and acknowledged within pedagogy. In the third case study, self-authored animation was the vehicle for an exploration of the ways in which pedagogy can engage with wider popular culture in an agentive and productive sense and have an impact on learner development in what is constructed as the "formal curriculum". The discussion of these case studies leads to a set of proposals for further research which connects pedagogy with a productive engagement with digital cultures and which is cognisant of the changing dispositions and skill sets of younger learners.

In Chapter 9, "Wikipedia Is the New Public Literacy: A Case Study in the Field of Philosophy," John Willinsky examines how new forms of "public literacy" work with more traditional forms by considering how Wikipedians are citing the open-access and peer-reviewed *Stanford Encyclopedia of Philosophy* (SEP) to strengthen and enrich English language Wikipedia articles both within and outside of traditional philosophy topics. A high proportion of the SEP's entries are being cited by Wikipedians, both in writing and discussing articles—with some of them providing pivotal points in the learning that goes into the articles—and the majority of those citations were used by Wikipedia readers over a two-week period. Finally, as a further indication of how Wikipedians are responding to questions of verification and reliability, the SEP links in Wikipedia are compared to the links from a a range of other academic resources, both open and closed, indicating how the SEP represents part of the larger public and educational benefit of open access to research and scholarship.

In Chapter 10, "The Future of Learning and the Virtual Life of Knowledge," Robert Luke and Peter Pericles Trifonas ask, "What does it mean to 'Learn the Virtual life'? What does it mean to learn how to live online, or within online spaces? How is the transition from traditional modes of learning to those mediated by new technologies affecting the way(s) in which learning is constructed?" These questions are fundamental to the future of engaging the ground of our own knowledge and what it means to know because new technologies and digital media have created the possibility for place-independent learning and for the evolution of new pedagogies. Within this conception of learning to learn the virtual life, the predominant issues centre on information and media literacy, online learning, the nature of virtual space, and a kind of archaeology or history about the evolution of online media themselves.

In Chapter 11, "'Tomorrow We Go Bowling': Covert Intimacy and Homosocial Play in the *Grand Theft Auto IV* Series," Marc Ouellette describes how the interactions among the male characters in the controversial but extremely popular video game, *Grand Theft Auto IV (GTA 4)*, and its *The Ballad of Gay Tony* expansion pack, effectively provide a ritualized series of explorations of homosocial bonding within the context of otherwise traditional forms of masculinity. Indeed, the situation of the routines within familiar paradigms may ultimately be a key factor in the undoing of the incumbent masculine privilege, especially since befriending and defending openly gay characters figures in the central stories and operations of the game. The main character, Niko Bellic, regularly behaves in a manner consistent with hegemonic masculinity: he resorts to violence, he resists conversation, he reduces women to objects and he relies on Machiavellian logic. Rather than offering a linear narrative which becomes a celebration of the hypermasculine, *GTA 4* regularly exposes the contradictions and the ambivalence of hegemonic masculinities and even of its own audience and genre. Although the game's kernel story remains true to the formula of following a thug's progression from bit player to master criminal, in this iteration Niko's success depends upon regularly socializing with the other male characters in the game. Depending on one's perspective, *GTA 4* not only confronts players with a surprising perspective on masculine relations but also provides a place for exploring and for negotiating—i.e., for playing—the homosocial. Indeed, the play of the game and of the homosocial cannot be easily separated into the purely ludic or the purely narratological realms that seem to demarcate the critical imperatives incumbent in game studies. Therefore, the game demands an approach which integrates rather than delineates the available readings to show how the game's ergodic dimension occasions and even encourages the homosocial. That *GTA 4* belongs to a game franchise assailed for its overall content makes the negotiations of masculine behaviours more extraordinary since this genre traditionally relies on hypermasculine modes, often to the exclusion and even detriment of women and minorities.

In Chapter 12, "From Greek School to Greek's Cool: Using Weblogs in a Greek Heritage Language Program," Themistoklis Aravossitas outlines how online education is used in a Heritage Language Education in Toronto, Ontario. The Heritage Language Program is considered a cornerstone of Canada's multiculturalism policy. Aravossitas details what has been done in the program to preserve the linguistic and cultural capital of the Greek communities with limited or no support of educational authorities. The chapter is an autobiographical inquiry of an internationally educated teacher who is involved as an instructor, a parent, a student and an administrator in a Greek language credit program of the Greek Community of Toronto. It details the commitment to understanding the needs of the new generation of Heritage Language learners by presenting aspects of a case of an applied bottom-up reform attempt which is based on critical and transformative pedagogy sensitivities and brings heritage language education to the epicentre of community activity and educational change in the 21st century.

In Chapter 13, "The Digital Game as a Learning Space," Peter Pericles Trifonas looks at the characteristics of the digital game and how it constitutes a strategic research site for studying the cultural transformations of learning through play. Digital games exemplify the cultural transformations in perception and participation of learning through play that are characteristic of learning through virtual learning environments. Studied as converging forms of narrative and representation compared with literature or television, for example, digital games reveal the convergence of diverse modes of literacy required by the player and evident in the production of the digital game environment. The chapter presents an opening into the following questions: What do cultural transformations consist of as moments of learning for players engaged in the virtual environment of the digital game? What aspects of learning are foregrounded during digital game play and how? How are these moments of learning synthesized in relation to the converging forms of literacy required and exemplified by the virtual learning environments of digital games?

1

DIGITAL LITERACY AND THE SPACES OF ACADEMIC DISCOURSE

Peta Mitchell

In this chapter, I wish to argue that digital literacy poses a particular challenge to the research-led university. Although these universities are often at the forefront of introducing digital literacy initiatives—such as e-learning platforms, technological infrastructure, and digital repositories—these applications of digital literacy tend to be more instrumental or functional than critical or creative. As Robert Samuels argues in his 2007 essay "The New Literacy Agenda for Higher Education: Composition, Computers, and Academic Labor at Us Research Universities," there is a "potential conflict" in the push for universities to "embrace simultaneously both functional and critical models of [digital] literacy" in that "the government wants these institutions to affirm a modern rhetoric of technological progress and cost-effectiveness at the same time that these universities provide a critical venue to explore the positive and negative aspects of the postmodern information economy" (p. 107). This leaves universities at an impasse: how do they "at the same time utilize new information technologies and remain critical of these same technologies?" (p. 108).

Certainly, this clash of cultures between the instrumental/functional and the critical/analytical is at the heart of debates over the uses of digital literacy in higher education. However, this simple equation of political forces with instrumentality and the corresponding equation of the university with a tradition of reflective thought that brings criticism to bear on instrumentality elide the fact that this conflict is more deeply rooted within the academy. I wish to argue that, in fact, much of the resistance to critical uses of digital literacy comes from within the institution of the university itself. That is, the university is bound up in a scriptural economy that prioritises the printed word and that reinforces its power by way of a normative, political, and spatialised academic discourse. It is this print-based scriptural economy—in which this essay must acknowledge its own complicity—that a critical approach to digital literacy threatens to disrupt or lay bare.

I do not wish to imply that creative or critical applications of digital literacy will bring about a de-politicised or non-hierarchical academy. Rather, I propose that examining the ways in which the tensions between digital literacy and (traditional) academic literacy are played out within the institution of the university exposes, to some degree, a relative lack of critical self-awareness in the research and teaching practices of the contemporary research university. It reveals a university caught between competing desires to critique and to perpetuate traditional notions of research and pedagogy in higher education.

The Scriptural Economy of the University

In his 1974 work *The Practice of Everyday Life*, Michel de Certeau outlines the birth of writing and the development of a "scriptural economy" in the West. Driven by the need for Western culture to record its history, literacy (or writing) displaced orality as the dominant mode of communication. Writing carried with it a certain legitimising power and a "mythical value" that it achieved by opposing itself to orality (p. 133). Orality, in turn came to be "defined by (or as) that from which a 'legitimate' practice—whether in science, politics, or the classroom, etc.—must differentiate itself" (p. 134). The scriptural economy privileges the construction of texts, texts that record the inscription of the trace upon the proper space of the blank page. Confronted with the blank page, Certeau writes, "every child is already put in the position of the industrialist, the urban planner, or the Cartesian philosopher—the position of having to manage a space that is his own and distinct from all others and in which he can exercise his own will" (p. 134). And yet the writer's will is not entirely free; rather, it is held in check by the bourgeois power inherent in the scriptural economy, which reinforces the dominance of writing. For Certeau, writing, or rather literacy, now "functions as the law of an educational system organized by the dominant class, which can make language (whether rhetorical or mathematical) its instrument of production" (p. 139).

The institution of the university is an almost perfect example of the workings of Certeau's scriptural economy. Orality remains important within the university, but only insofar as it supports and subsequently makes way for literacy. For instance, in the scriptural economy of the university, an academic is required to treat the orality of the conference paper as an intermediate stage in the production of legitimate research (i.e., the "published" conference paper, or the conference paper transformed into the written book chapter or journal article). Similarly, the academic's apprentices—their students—are taught that orality (in the form of presentations, classroom discussion, etc.) is largely formative rather than summative. The assessment of students' academic literacy is bound up with the scriptural economy of the institution and is rarely questioned: the final exam or the final essay remains the default mode for measuring whether a student has sufficiently mastered academic discourse and has become a part of the university's discourse community.

Underlying the university, then, is a scriptural economy that reinforces the primacy of the written word. Moreover, this scriptural economy has generated a normative discourse through which academic credibility and authority are constructed. This might be an obvious and unremarkable statement to those within the discourse community; however, as composition scholars such as David Bartholomae, Patricia Bizzell, Cheryl Geisler, and Donna Le Court have demonstrated, for students, who are largely still being taught in an apprenticeship model of academic teaching and learning, the underlying assumptions of academic discourse are far from "natural" or "obvious." Further, in students' attempts to become a part of the academic discourse community, the spatial and textual politics of academic discourse become pronounced.

The Spatial and Textual Politics of Academic Discourse

> Academic language is a dead language [ ] and is no one's mother tongue.
>
> *(Bourdieu and Passeron, 1994/1965, p. 8)*

Academic discourse is fundamentally bound up with the spatial politics of the academy. For Bourdieu and Passeron, writing in 1965, the most salient example of this spatial politics affecting (and effecting) academic discourse is the face-to-face teacher–student relationship. This relationship synecdochically represents the spatial order of the university: as Bourdieu and Passeron argue, "the space of the teaching relationship imposes its law of distance so strongly [...] because it captures and expresses so much of what the university, as an institution, stands for" (pp. 12–13).

Nowhere are the spatial politics of academic discourse more evident than in the still predominant genre of student academic writing: the essay. In his seminal essay of 1985, Bartholomae argued that, in their written assessment, university students are required to "invent the university" by learning "our language," and that in this process they must "appropriate (or be appropriated by)" academic discourse (pp. 135, 139). In appropriating academic discourse, the student writer must imaginatively step across the student–teacher divide in order to write to and from a privileged position within the discourse. That is, the writer must imagine herself to be "equal to or more powerful than those she would address"—her teachers (p. 140). In this model of student writing as academic apprenticeship, the basic student writer's appropriation of academic discourse may well take the form of crude mimicry until she is sufficiently ensconced within the discourse (p. 162). As such, basic student writers can only act out a privileged speaking position, always aware of the distance that continues to exist between themselves and their addressees, and that their appropriation of discourse is also one that threatens to appropriate them. Bourdieu and Passeron (1994/1965) skeptical about the possibility for students to overcome the distancing effects of academic discourse and the university as institution, for, he argues

> the most influential factors underlying and perpetuating linguistic misunderstanding are embedded in the very nature of the institution itself. Everything in the present organization of university teaching—from the physical form and layout of the lecture theatre to the examinations regime and its criteria, from the assignments leading up to the exams to the organization of the *curriculum*—favours the reciprocal distancing of teacher and student.
>
> *(p. 10)*

It is here, though, "in the writer's divided relationship with academic discourse," that Donna Le Court says, "we get the clearest picture of a discourse seeking to act upon those who would speak its language, 'hailing' those who would write 'as if' they controlled the discourse itself to identify with its subject positions" (2004, p. 41). In this sense, academic discourse "possesses a power of its own" that the student writer cannot fully control. Although the student writer is able to exert their power by employing the language of academic discourse, "that power is granted through the discourse rather than the writer's agency" (p. 41).

We can see the development of the scriptural economy of the university in the history of its dominant genre. From its more speculative, free-form roots in Montaigne's *Essais*, the critical essay became, as Gregory L. Jackson argues in his 1997 essay "Literary Theory and the Essay," the "material sign of authority within the academy" (p. 490). The essay became, according to Theodor Adorno, "the critical form *par excellence*," one that establishes its own authority and "settles itself into texts, as though they were simply there and had authority" (1984, pp. 165, 167). Jackson argues that not enough attention has been paid to the genre of the essay: "[b]y failing to address the essay as a material component of academic life," he maintains, "scholars of the essay have failed to account for the genre's role in shaping institutional priorities" (p. 492). According to Jackson, the development of the modern critical essay was linked to the 18th-century development of the bourgeois public sphere, which "was accompanied by an increase in leisure time, a boom in print culture, the birth of literary and philosophical societies, and the legislation of civic institutions, such as libraries and museums" (p. 488). In the late 19th century, as the university underwent a process of "departmentalisation" in which "classical education" gave way to the modern disciplines, the essay became the embodiment of academic legitimacy. As the essay dispersed into "highly specialized subgenres," it moved further away from its "democratic roots" (p. 490). Moreover, the "struggle for academic legitimation" played out in the genre of the essay "and the inter-departmental skirmishes over disciplinary boundaries brought with them an increase in specialized, professional scholarly journals," as well as the "abstract conceptual languages" of academic discourse that, Jackson argues, would "culminate in contemporary literary theory" (p. 490). While academic discourse became increasingly narrow and normative, its authority was increasingly shored up by print publication in specialist journals and scholarly monographs. Thus, we see the interrelationship of the genre of the essay, academic discourse, and print publishing regimes giving rise to the scriptural economy of the university. In academic research, the genre of the essay contributed to the prestige of print publication; in academic teaching, the genre of the essay became analogous with academic literacy.

Academic Literacy/Digital Literacy

Although academic literacy underlies all higher education pedagogy that goes beyond a purely vocational intent, given the scriptural nature of the academic institution, it is largely the province of "composition," "writing," or "rhetoric" academics to teach its principals—to teach students how to enter into the academic discourse community by writing effective academic essays. Given this, it is unsurprising that the vast majority of published research on academic literacy is generated by composition scholars. The same cannot be said, to the same degree, of academic research on digital literacy, which might be generated from any number of disciplines, including education, sociology, cultural studies, library science, literature, and so forth. And yet, when we look at some of the established working definitions of digital literacy, they begin to look rather like a technological support to functionalist notions of academic literacy—notions composition scholars are often at pains to disrupt.

For instance, in her article on social networking sites and the composition classroom, Stephanie Vie looks back to Lester Faigley's 1997 speculation at a composition conference that soon academics "will be teaching an increasingly fluid, multi-media literacy" that will likely displace the essay from "center stage," and that this "will not mean the end of our discipline" (Faigley, p. 41, quoted in Vie, 2008, p. 12). However, as Vie argues, existing definitions of digital literacy, such as the definition of technological literacy proposed by the Association of College and Research Libraries (ACRL) in 2000 as "a set of abilities requiring individuals to 'recognize when information is needed and have the ability to locate, evaluate, and use effectively the needed information'" is "still strongly grounded in the genre of the written essay" (p. 13). Ilana Snyder and Mastin Prinsloo (2007) similarly note the instrumentalism at the core of prevailing definitions of digital literacy: the recurring uses of the words "effectively" and "correctly" in a 2004 definition by Leu et al., they argue, "assume a universality and generality of function and practice which is not appropriate or helpful for understanding the differentiated, situated and enculturated ways in which digital practices happen" (p. 173).

More telling is Jan Steyaert's often-cited distinction of the three core skills that make up digital literacy. In a chapter for a social work anthology published in 2007, Jackie Rafferty and Steyaert identify these core skills as instrumental skills, structural skills, and strategic skills. Instrumental skills include skills such using word-processing or other forms of software, sending e-mail, and even simply being able to use a computer keyboard and mouse. Structural skills include being able to insert hyperlinks, to search for information online, and to assess information found online. Finally, strategic skills include proactive searching and critical analysis of online information (pp. 169–70). While, they argue, these strategic skills are becoming "more critical" in the information age, they are not "essentially digital," and are, in fact, "very similar for non-digital media" (p. 170). Interestingly, all three skills refer only to the *use* of digital media or digital texts, and not to the production of them. Not even "strategic" skills encompass using digital literacy in a creative or counter-discursive way. In these instrumentalist definitions, digital literacy serves only to reinforce traditional academic literacy and the scriptural economy of the university.

Even two very recent books generated by the discipline of cultural studies (a discipline that, throughout its history, has done much to subvert normative modes of academic discourse) and related to digital literacy do little to examine the relationships between digital literacy and academic literacy. In his 2009 book, *The Uses of Digital Literacy*, John Hartley maintains that "we need to extend the notion of 'media literacy' beyond the defensive notion of 'critical reading' and 'media literacy' as taught in schools, towards what ought to be called 'digital literacy'—a form of hands-on productive expression, taught by and within the milieu in which it is deployed, using multi-media platform devices to 'write' as well as 'read' electronic media" (p. 21). Hartley's call is an important one, for he is asking us to take seriously the idea of digital literacy as creative rather than as simply functional or instrumental. "This is," he says, "not just a shift in the lexicon but a transformation of practice" (p. 37). But a transformation in whose practice? Hartley is asking for a shift in *teaching*, but does his *research* practise what it preaches? The answer can only be "no." Hartley, as a representative of the Creative Industries school of cultural studies, is interested in mapping and creating a space for creative forms of digital literacy, such as digital storytelling etc., but he does not appear interested in how digital literacy might problematise the scriptural call to authority and legitimacy his own research makes. Hartley has chosen to publish a print monograph on others' uses of digital literacy. Moreover, he has chosen not to question how this choice might or might not partake in the exclusionary print practices he sees being unsettled by the democratising aspects of digital literacy, aspects he sees the creative industries—the "generative engine of emergent knowledge"—as being in the best place to nurture (p. 69).

This resistance by researchers to question their own complicity in the scriptural economy while promoting digital literacy is also evident in debates about open access, a movement that similarly threatens the hegemony of print publishing in notions of academic literacy. Gary Hall's 2008 book *Digitize This Book! The Politics of New Media, or Why We Need Open Access Now* appears, on the surface, to throw down the gauntlet. Hall calls for the digitisation of all research, while noting that "electronic publications do not have the same aura of authority as professionally produced paper text" (p. 58). Open-access journals, he continues,

> have responded to this challenge to their authority by imitating their paper counterparts: in their "page" layout; their publication of material in the form of "essays" or "papers" written in a linear, sequential form; their size and length; their reliance on international editorial boards of established academics who have already proven themselves in the "paper" world; and most especially in their peer-reviewing and certification processes. They have done so in order to try to reassure the university about something that is still relatively new by demonstrating that they are providing recognizable forms of quality control and editorial legitimacy within this new medium.
>
> *(p. 58)*

Hall is, to give him his due, a strong and active advocate of open-access research: he has published a significant amount of his research in open-access forums, and he is founding co-editor of an open-access journal. But how are we expected to interpret Hall's call to action to "digitize this book!"? Hall has not simply digitized his research, presented it in such a way as to mimic a printed book (thereby attempting to gain some of the prestige of the book), and offered it to the general public in an open-access repository. Hall's book *is* a book, published by the University of Minnesota Press, with a copyright notice that forestalls any attempt to reproduce the text electronically or otherwise. So Hall's imperative call to "digitize this book!" is a call to *someone else* to break the circuit of the scriptural economy, and, in the process, to breach copyright. Geoffrey Rockwell (2009), in his blog review of Hall's book, noted the book's copyright notice and the seeming lack of a digitised copy. In a follow-up post, Rockwell noted that Hall had responded, saying that "[h]e is trying to get the publisher to allow a digital copy to be posted online, but in the meantime pointed out online versions of what became chapters in the book."

Of course, my own research is not exempt from these same politics of academic discourse—this very book chapter is reliant upon the same nexus of academic literacy and print publication that it seeks to interrogate. The problem, as I see it, is not so much that academics discuss or promote digital literacy and open-access publishing in print or in a form and a language that invokes traditional academic discourse. Rather, it is that many academics writing on digital literacy do not take this opportunity to question the ways in which their published research draws authority from a scriptural economy that side-lines the very initiatives they are promoting. In other words, I would argue that we have not heeded enough Cynthia Selfe's decade-old injunction to move beyond the "problem of the polemic" in the debate over digital literacy. In *Technology and Literacy in the Twenty-First Century*, Selfe (1999) suggests that the tendency towards simple binaries in the digital literacy debate works to " distract us from the more complicated project of identifying the related social dynamics that underlie the technology–literacy link." "Even worse," she continues, "such a representation gives us an excuse for avoiding our responsibility to address the effects of this formation" (p. 37). If academic research on digital literacy does not take into account in a self-conscious way the complex interaction between academic and digital literacy and the possibility for counter-discursive dialogue that this interaction might afford, digital literacy will remain anterior to the university. It will remain an instrumentalised site of teaching and a polemicised object of research.

In her 1994 book *Academic Literacy and the Nature of Expertise*, Cheryl Geisler makes the following telling observation:

> [A]s long as research on expertise is written as the account of what other people do, the account will be a false account. Real reform can only be accomplished through an attempt to understand how our own practices of reading, writing, and knowing operate [...] thereby creating and re-creating the great divide. Only by engaging with this problem of reflection, seeking explanations that ring bells with our own experience, with what we ourselves do, will we be getting closer to the truth—and getting closer to change.
>
> *(p. 94)*

Geisler's point is about academic literacy in general, but it is particularly relevant, I would argue, to thinking about digital literacy in the university. Despite radical shifts in the role of the university over the past fifty years, in their research and teaching, academics continue to be bound by and to reinforce the traditional scriptural economy of the institution. Academics largely continue to accept the prestige of print publication (even if they do not personally agree with it) and to teach an apprenticeship model of academic literacy. This model of academic literacy is, in turn, predicated on the primacy of print and the student's appropriation of a normative academic discourse that elides its own spatial politics. Academics such as Hall and Hartley, even while they implicitly call into question the scriptural economy of the university (and, in Hartley's case, while they explicitly call into question purely functional applications of digital literacy), treat the digital in a purely functional way. That is, to borrow again from Geisler, until digital literacy is not just something academics write about and publish in print as an "account of what other people do," a critical digital literacy will not be possible; it will simply reinforce the status quo.

Towards A Critical Digital Literacy

As individuals and as educators, we have a responsibility to understand the power of purposeful discourse—particularly in public digital spaces—and the ways it can either be used for democratic, socially responsible ends, or used to marginalize and colonize. [...] [A]ny writing technologies have altered and, at times, streamlined the writing process. Only a few writing technologies, however, have had truly dramatic social impact. The printing press is one; the networked computer is another. The convergence of digital tools is yet another that we will witness unfolding in the coming years. It is crucial that we are equipped to chronicle, to research, and to interrogate these technologies for the ways in which they alter the landscape of our pedagogy, our approaches to research, and our conceptions of how individuals write and publish together.

(DigiRhet.org, 2006, p. 241)

Meaning depends on the platform. [...] When the printing press appeared, the centuries before that became illegible to us, and we called them 'the Dark Ages'. A whole new sensation of meaning came to us with the advent of Renaissance, with people like Montaigne, Erasmus, Rabelais ... The Reformation heralded the liberty of thought, something unimaginable in a tradition grounded on the transfer of knowledge that was not based on the printed word. Today, a new platform appears, and thus a new meaning will appear too. [...] With this change of platform, everything is going to change: knowledge, meaning, the human mind, just as when the printing press was introduced.

(Serres, 1997)[1]

If we can accept that, as Bizzell states, "academic discourse *constitutes* the academic community" (1992, p. 113), one of the most interesting questions we can ask of digital literacy is not how it might simply support the existing print-based scriptural economy of academic literacy, but how it might allow us to reevaluate academic literacy. What, then, might a critical approach to digital literacy in the university look like? At the level of research, I would argue, we need to get beyond talking "about" digital literacy and instead begin to speak "to" it. We need to avoid eliding our own discursive participation in the dominant mode of academic literacy as we produce research on digital literacy. Bracketing out our participation in the scriptural economy of the university must necessarily lead to research that treats digital literacy as an object of study anterior to our own practice and our own modes of research production. Bringing academic literacy into dialogue with digital literacy would enable us to see more clearly the ways in which academic literacy is evolving, even as a result of its instrumental uses of digital technologies. In turn, this would allow us talk about the dominant form of academic literacy as a discursive formation, as a normative, but not inevitable, construction that was itself born from an earlier technologisation—in Walter Ong's (1992) words, from the "technologisation of the word."

At the level of teaching, this more nuanced appreciation of the arbitrariness of academic discourse would enable us to rethink how we introduce students to the academic discourse community, and it might lead us to use digital technologies in more reflective ways in order to encourage our students to critically engage with academic literacy and with literacy more broadly. Incorporating writing in networked digital environments into our teaching alongside traditional written modes of assessment (the essay and the exam) might be one way of bringing digital literacy into a more complicated dialogue with academic literacy.

To conclude this chapter, I wish to look briefly at some of the ways in which sites for networked digital writing in the university, such as blogs, wikis, and social networking sites, might open up different spaces in our pedagogy for academic discourse to "speak to" the prevailing order of academic literacy in interesting ways. For the purposes of this chapter, I must set aside a number of salient questions about access to technology, about the material conditions and material spaces of writing and writing instruction (see Reynolds, 1998), and about the pragmatic aspects of digital literacy. More telling is Jan Steyaert's often-cited distinction of the three core skills that make up digital literacy: instrumental skills, structural skills, and strategic skills (2000). Steyaert further elaborates on these digital literacy skills in a chapter he co-wrote with Jackie Rafferty for a for a social work anthology published in 2007. Instrumental skills, Rafferty and Steyaert explain, include skills such using word-processing or other forms of software, sending e-mail, and even simply being able to use a computer keyboard and mouse, These are important issues that have very real effects on writing and that serve to temper some of the more liberatory discourse that circulates around digital writing. I am also setting aside the multimedia aspects of digital literacy to focus mainly on writing. What these locations of networked digital writing do offer in response to traditional academic literacy is a different sense of discursive space—a different sense of the possible audiences for academic writing and a different sense of the distance between writer and reader, student and teacher.

Blogs and wikis disturb the solitude and interiority of the essay, the traditional instantiation of academic literacy. Where wikis foreground communities of writing through communal writing, blogs tend to retain the essay's singular authorial voice and its construction of a singular subjectivity. Blogs do, however, offer the possibility of public writing in a communal space and the possibility of ongoing public dialogue. As Melissa Gregg noted in her

2006 article on blogging as "conversational scholarship," academics who blog exist in a grey area "between disciplinary insularism and public intellectual practice," a space that the university as institution is decidedly uncomfortable with. Gregg argues:

> The issue [for universities] seems to be with the technology itself: the simultaneously anonymous and public nature of blogging as well as the instant feedback the software make possible. Indeed, the virulence that typifies many blog debates, and which is often the cause for their scorn, arises from a lack of common ground and/or vocabulary. Blogs reveal in a very overt way how regularly writing fails to communicate intention. They also indicate how much distance a tertiary education can put between people trying to engage in a conversation.
>
> *(p. 153)*

If the university is uncomfortable with academics blogging, why is it that blogs are increasingly being used as pedagogical tools in higher education? One response to this question is that they are, perhaps, being used in relatively narrow ways—that is, as digital versions of the private reflective journal. In 2004, Jeremy B. Williams and Joanne Jacobs noted the "dearth of scholarly journal articles" on pedagogical uses of blogs outside "teacher training and other professions where the use of reflective journals as a learning tool is accepted custom and practice, and where, as a consequence, there is an increased likelihood of a favourable disposition to blogs in the first place" (p. 236). Another response is that there is a disjunct between what is valued pedagogically and what is valued as research within the university. In a pedagogical sense, using blogs and wikis to open up dialogue amongst a network of peers and the public more broadly is desirable in that they model the kind of public writing many students will perform in careers outside the university. According to Diane Penrod, "[i]t is the 'public' characteristic of online writing that infuses the words with meaning and elevates them to a communicative act. To write publicly means that student writers make their words available to all in the course or in cyberspace, not just for the exclusive private classroom relationship built on paper between student writer and instructor or the semi-public partnership peer groups evoke" (2005, p. 3). And yet, as Gregg demonstrates, it is the same possibilities of public discourse and dialogue that makes the university profoundly uneasy about academic blogging.

Gregg's article is an ideal example of research that brings digital literacy into sustained dialogue with academic literacy. By extension, the opportunity exists for pedagogical applications of blogs to be less instrumental and more self-aware. To take part in a dialogue about academic and digital literacy, blogs in teaching need to encourage more than individual self-reflection, they need to encourage reflection on the public and communal aspects of networked digital writing and the place of that writing within academic discourse. This would also have the effect of establishing a common critical objective for academic teaching and research in digital literacy.

As well as opening academic writing up to new publics and audiences, networked digital writing also opens up new spaces for writing and different spatial politics of writing. Since the publication of Jay David Bolter's proclamatory book *Writing Space: The Computer, Hypertext, and the History of Writing* in 1991, it has become commonplace to characterise networked digital writing (such as hypertext, blogs, wikis, MOOs, etc.) as fundamentally spatial and spatializing. For instance, as the authors of a 2004 article on teaching digital rhetoric maintain, "[n]etworked devices create a new kind of writing space, and this space changes not only writing processes, but also communication dynamics between writers and readers, and between writers and the devices themselves" (DigiRhet.org, 2006, p. 234). I do not wish to suggest, as was frequently implied in much early writing on the hypertext phenomenon during the early 1990s, that the spaces of networked digital writing are essentially liberatory; however, I do wish to suggest that these spaces can to some degree expose the often overlooked spatial politics of traditional academic literacy. For instance, in her 2008 article on the ways in which social networking sites, such as Facebook, might be brought into the composition classroom, Stephanie Vie argues that these sites have the ability to

> topple traditional classroom hierarchies of power in unpredictable ways. While such spaces certainly offer varied ways for participants to broaden their literacy skills through their involvement in media-rich environments, social networking sites also pose a potential threat to the established order of things in academia, particularly the classroom. If we are standing at a moment of possibility wherein the old rules are open to change and relationships are forced into negotiation, then online social networking sites may be one of the major forces in a convergence culture that force us to look at the deepening divide between students and instructors—not only in terms of the skills and abilities that preclude a digital divide but also the participatory democracy encapsulated in each classroom.
>
> *(p. 19)*

This view is supported by Mazer, Murphy, and Simonda, who in 2007 published a study concluding that teacher self-disclosure on Facebook can lead to a more positive student–teacher relationship. Pedagogical uses of online social networking sites as writing sites, therefore, tend to some degree to collapse the distance between student and teacher that is discursively so much a part of traditional academic literacy as it is embodied in the research essay. We cannot, of course, pretend that this democratising tendency results in a pure democratic writing undifferentiated by pedagogical power relations. Moreover, we cannot simply assume that this democratising tendency is fundamentally desirable to students, for as Bourdieu and Passeron (1994/1965) explain,

> Distancing gives as much protection to the student as the professor. Entrenched in the magistral chair from which he holds forth, the professor is enclosed by it. If he addresses no one in particular, neither can he blame anyone personally. Without collective sanctions, a responsibility which is diffuse turns into no one's responsibility. The student, too, remains deeply attached to the traditional teaching relationship and to the sites and instruments which distinguish it. His search for 'reconciliation' with a remote professor only rarely involves a wish to reduce the obligatory distance which separates them.
>
> *(pp. 18–19)*

Rather, as I have argued, what the different audiences and spaces digital literacy can give us is a more critical understanding of traditional academic literacy, the scriptural economy of the university, and the ways in which they may or may not be changing. Above all, thinking critically about digital literacy in our research and teaching may allow us and our students to begin to reinvent the university through an academic discourse that inscribes a different spatial politics.

Note

1 I have quoted Patrice Riemens's English-language translation of Serres's article, which is published on the nettime.org mailing list. http://www.nettime.org/Lists-Archives/nettime-l-9810/msg00137.html

Works Cited

Adorno, Theodor W. "The Essay as Form." *New German Critique* 32 (1984): 151–71.

Bartholomae, David. "Inventing the University." *When a Writer Can't Write: Studies in Writer's Block and Other Composing-Process Problems.* Ed. Mike Rose. New York: Guilford, 1985. 134–65.

Bizzell, Patricia. *Academic Discourse and Critical Consciousness.* Pittsburgh: U of Pittsburgh P, 1992.

Bolter, Jay David. *Writing Space: The Computer, Hypertext, and the History of Writing.* Hillsdale, NJ: Erlbaum, 1991.

Bourdieu, Pierre and Jean-Claude Passeron. "Language and Relationship to Language in the Teaching Situation." *Academic Discourse: Linguistic Misunderstanding and Professorial Power,* by Pierre Bourdieu, Jean-Claude Passeron, and Monique de Saint Martin. Trans. of *Rapport pédagogique et communication* (Richard Teese, Trans.) 1965. Cambridge: Polity, 1994. 1–34.

Certeau, Michel de. *The Practice of Everyday Life.* Trans. of *Arts de faire* (Steven Rendall, Trans.). Berkeley: U of California P, 1984.

DigiRhet.org. "Teaching Digital Rhetoric: Community, Critical Engagement, and Application." *Pedagogy* 6.2 (2006): 231–59.

Faigley, Lester. "Literacy after the Revolution." *College Composition and Communication* 48.1 (1997): 30–43.

Geisler, Cheryl. *Academic Literacy and the Nature of Expertise: Reading, Writing, and Knowing in Academic Philosophy*. Hillsdale, NJ: Erlbaum, 1994.

Gregg, Melissa. "Blogging as Conversational Scholarship." *Continuum* 20.2 (2006): 147–60.

Hall, Gary. *Digitize This Book! The Politics of New Media, or Why We Need Open Access Now*. Minneapolis: U of Minnesota P, 2008.

Hartley, John. *The Uses of Digital Literacy*. St Lucia: U of Queensland P, 2009.

Jackson, Gregory S. "Literary Theory and the Essay." *Encyclopedia of the Essay*. Ed. Tracy Chevalier. London: Fitzroy Dearborn, 1997. 487–93.

Le Court, Donna. *Identity Matters: Schooling the Student Body in Academic Discourse*. Albany: State U of New York P, 2004.

Leu, Donald J., Jr. Charles K. Kinzer, Julie L. Coiro, and Dana W. Cammack. "Toward a Theory of New Literacies Emerging from the Internet and Other Information and Communication Technologies." *Theoretical Models and Processes of Reading*. 5th ed. Ed. Robert B. Ruddell and Norman Unrau. Newark, DE: International Reading Association, 2004. 1568–1611.

Mazer, Joseph P., Richard E. Murphy, and Cheri J. Simonds. "I'll See You on 'Facebook': The Effects of Computer-Mediated Teacher Self-Disclosure on Student Motivation, Affective Learning, and Classroom Climate." *Communication Education* 56.1 (2007): 1–17.

Ong, Walter. *Orality and Literacy: The Technologizing of the Word*. London: Methuen, 1982.

Penrod, Diane. *Composition in Convergence: The Impact of New Media on Writing Assessment*. Mahwah, NJ: Erlbaum, 2005.

Rafferty, Jackie, and Jan Steyaert. "Social Work in a Digital Society." *Social Work: A Companion to Learning*. Ed. Mark Lymbery and Karen Postle. London: Sage, 2007. 165–75.

Reynolds, Nedra. "Composition's Imagined Geographies: The Politics of Space in the Frontier, City, and Cyberspace." *College Composition and Communication* 50.1 (1998): 12–35.

Rockwell, Geoffrey. "Gary Hall: Digitize This Book." 8 March 2009, http://www.philosophi. ca/theoreti/?p=2391

Samuels, Robert. "The New Literacy Agenda for Higher Education: Composition, Computers, and Academic Labor at Us Research Universities." *Brave New Classrooms: Democratic Education and The Internet*. Eds. Joe Lockard and Mark Pegrum. New York: Peter Lang, 2007. 105–23.

Selfe, Cynthia. *Technology and Literacy in the Twenty-First Century: The Importance of Paying Attention*. Carbondale: Southern Illinois UP, 1999.

Serres, Michel. "La Rédemption Du Savoir." *Revue Quart Monde* 163 (1997), http://www.edition-squartmonde.org/rqm/document.php?id=386

Snyder, Ilana, and Mastin Prinsloo. "Young People's Engagement with Digital Literacies in Marginal Contexts in a Globalised World." *Language and Education* 21.3 (2007): 171–79.

Vie, Stephanie. "Digital Divide 2.0: 'Generation M' and Online Social Networking Sites in the Composition Classroom." *Computers and Composition* 25 (2008): 9–23.

Williams, Jeremy B., and Joanne Jacobs. "Exploring the Use of Blogs as Learning Spaces in the Higher Education Sector." *Australasian Journal of Educational Technology* 20.2 (2004): 232–47.

2

NEW EPISTEMOLOGIES?

Rethinking Ways of Knowing in a Digital Culture

Jennifer Jenson and Suzanne de Castell

Introduction: "What has become of knowledge ...?"

As Jean Francois Lyotard (1984) anticipated, changes in the status of knowledge, that is what is of and has value, accompany the social, cultural and economic shifts of a post-industrial world. Knowledge under "conditions of computerization" has "exchange value." That is:

> The relationships of the suppliers and users of knowledge to the knowledge they supply and use is now tending, and will increasingly tend, to assume the form already taken by the relationship of commodity producers and consumers to the commodities they produce and consume—that is, the form of value. Knowledge is and will be produced in order to be sold, it is and will be consumed in order to be valorised in a new production: in both cases, the goal is exchange. Knowledge ceases to be an end in itself, it loses its "use-value."
>
> *(Lyotard 1984, p. 112)*

This shift in the relative value of knowledge should be seen as a fundamental, foundational change. New questions now need to be asked, not just about what knowledge is "worth" but about what counts as knowledge, what it means to "know" and how someone comes to know. The semi-globalized culture of the internet, with its public forms of display, its grassroots production capabilities, and its potential worldwide audience is an ideal site for exploring these kinds of questions, with a view to better understanding these new knowledge conditions.

In the literate past, knowledge was encoded in primarily textual form. David Olson remarked long ago on the ease with which we mistake linguistic fluency for cognitive competence, noting that "we often see as intellectual accomplish-ment what is in fact merely mastery of a particular form of language" (Olson 1977, 267). The authority given to text in both intellectual and school work, and its potential hazards, has been around since Plato's critique of writing as substitute for memory and understanding, and Wittgenstein's much later warn-ing about how language had "gone on a holiday," and about the "bewitchment" of the intellect by language. Today, education still suffers this same bewitch-ment, despite radically altered media conditions, and post-literate practices. This shift was not unanticipated: Marshall McLuhan, whose own work across media modeled a reflexive appreciation of and responsible engagement with theoretical studies of media forms and functions, tried to wake us up from what he described as "the habits of rigid perspective induced by three centuries of print hypnosis" (McLuhan 1955, n.p.). Now, many years later, these argu-ments seem especially salient for education, whose currency is the representa-tion, transmission and development of knowledge and understanding. Today's diverse forms of mediation effect transformations of what knowledge is, what knowledge is of most worth, what are legitimate processes of coming to know, and who can legitimately assume the identity of knower (Lankshear & Kno-bel 2003). Once we see what differences can be made to knowledge, know-ing, and knowers by the forms on which and the tools through which human understandings are mediated, we confront a new kind of imperative: that of "rhetorical responsibility," that is to say, responsibility for the ways and means we deploy to achieve our communicative purposes. We hope by looking more closely at new forms of reflexivity that inflect these spaces—the digital mixed-media environments of MySpace, *Second Life*, and Wikipedia—to become bet-ter aware of those which inflect our existing places and practices, but to which we have become inured by habit. We do see value for an educationally inter-ested study of these spaces as a way to understand emergent ideas which assist us in revising and rethinking what school knowledge may best become, and to understand more clearly why it makes best sense to refuse and rethink forms of educational evaluation, which persist in the face of and in often-uncomfortable relations to online spaces in which much of comparable cultural significance is arguably learned and exchanged. In this paper, we will focus on three current forms of mass-representation through digital media—MySpace, *Second Life,* and Wikipedia—in an attempt to show what forms of knowledge are encoded there, what counts as "knowledge" and what knowledge is of and has value in those online communities. Because these are representational forms, and because they are very much connected to lay-production, similar to the ways in which early print culture massively over-produced in local settings, we will also look at the relationship between production and consumption in these very public settings as well. Our purposes for examining each of these online "communities" is three-fold: in the case of MySpace we will look particularly at the ways in which the "self" is represented in and through the affordances of the "space" (text, images, videos, and the general website "template") and the way users appropriate that space. In *Second Life* we will also look at representations of the "self" as avatar, and look particularly to how the users construct and maintain a virtual world, a kind of "community." In this vein, Wikipedia will be examined not only as a community which has a "knowledge-building" mandate, but also what forms and kind of knowledge are represented there. While MySpace and *Second Life* serve as examples of what knowledge constitutes in relation to self and virtual world, Wikipedia is a unique example of a community of knowledge producers who remain virtually anonymous and whose knowledge is often-times deeply flawed. Despite its inconsistencies and a resident public acknowledgement of its short-comings as an accurate source of factual information, Wikipedia represents what could be considered to be a fully post-modern view of knowledge: it does not rely on modernist notions of what is "true," instead it is a kind of rhizomatic entity, which does not and need not distinguish among its various parts (see, for example, http://arstechnica.com/old/content/2006/08/7396.ars and http://slashdot.org/articles/06/08/02/1747238.shtml). Gilles Deleuze and Felix Guattari use the figure of the rhizome to describe a kind of non-hierarchical network:

> A rhizome as a subterranean stem is absolutely different from roots and radicles. Bulbs and tubers are rhizomes. Plants with roots or radicles may be rhizomorphic in other respects altogether. Burrows are too, in all their functions of shelter, supply, movement, evasion, and breakout. The rhizome itself assumes very diverse forms, from ramified surface extension in all directions to concretion into bulbs and tubers ... The rhizome includes the best and the worst: potato and couchgrass, or the weed.
>
> *(1987, pp. 6–7)*

In each of these spaces, the production of self, "second self" and information encourage a hybridity not only of form, but of connectivity, making each of these sites pulsate with democratizing possibility.

Lost in Space: Vacuity, Cognition and Capacity in MySpace

MySpace, for those out there who do not read print or online media, do not watch television news, or do not have a host of friends who are already participating, is perhaps the first major "global" online social networking website in which people purportedly come "together," add friends to their friends list, block others, try to find long lost loved ones and basically construct for themselves an online presence which others (who "know" or do not "know") can comment on and attempt to build fleeting and/or meaningful relations with. In many circles, the pressure to join is insurmountable, as recently, a graduate student I am working with confessed that he had finally broken down (at his girl friend's persistent behest) and joined MySpace, the only trouble being, that he did not really want anyone who knew him (beyond his girlfriend) to be able to find him, thus undermining one of the primary goals of the space—social networking—to find others and to be found. MySpace and its major successor, Facebook, have been in the public eye long enough that they have a kind of meta-commentary surrounding them that the global media has taken up: a voyeuristic fascination with what will those crazy "Facebookers" do next.[1] Not so long ago, those juicy participants have delivered: in Toronto, students in a high school were arrested at a public protest after they had been forced to removed slanderous comments on teachers from their MySpace blogs, and outside of London, England, a young woman who held a MySpace party (inviting her 350+ "friends") was arrested following her party in which over 20,000 pounds worth of damage was done to her parents home (including holes in walls, vomit in all corners of the house, and smashing of furniture), and even more recently, an MLA candidate was forced to withdraw his bid in British Columbia when "inappropriate pictures" pictures were posted to his Facebook account. In this space, the "self" is represented within a kind of template driven system of information exchange—likes, dislikes, friends, videos, music, pictures—which is, for those people who actively participate, frequently changing. Those listed as "friends" can expand and contract, new pictures are added, new words to a blog, new missives from "friends" are received and publicly viewed, and so on. The inherently rhizomatic possibilities of the technology mean that someone can post their own pictures of friends, and then "tag" those pictures to other Facebook or MySpace participants, thereby creating, producing and maintaining their "social" network.

Tila Tequila is a particularly good example of MySpace "success." In December 2006, she was featured by *Time Magazine* as a "big hit" on MySpace where she has more than 1.5 million "friends" listed, and receives up to 5,000 requests a day to be added as friends (Grossman 2006). Tila Tequila is one of the most "successful" examples of the production, or perhaps more accurately, the viral re-production, of self on MySpace: she moved from Playboy pornographic photography to raunchy recording artist to a "legitimate" online celebrity and now has her own television program. A large part of her "success" was simply her self-production: a thin, attractive Asian woman who dances in her underwear, sings and rolls around looking "sexy." The difference between her "self production" and everyone else's on the Internet, is that "There's a million hot naked chicks on the Internet…. There's a difference between those girls and me. Those chicks don't talk back to you" (Grossman 2006). Interestingly, she moved away from the social media possibilities of MySpace, directing fans and those simply curious to her own website where she is not confined by the MySpace templates, is more able to produce her own "look and feel" and in that way is much more able to re/produce herself and her content as she sees fit. Michael Hirschorn (2007) posits that social media sites like MySpace will be left behind in the future as users begin to grapple with questions of ownership:

"MySpace may sell the idea of itself as being without boundaries, but in fact the digital mayhem lives within a tightly controlled environment. MySpace does not let users network meaningfully with people outside its walls, and it does not let them import some functionality that promotes or drives revenue to other corporations" (p. 138). This is clearly the case now for Tila, whose own website "Tila's Hot Spot" (http://www.tilashotspot.com) is the location of content related to her and up-to-date information on her activities and public appearances.

On a more serious side, the MySpace population responded nearly immediately to the shootings at Virginia Tech. One prominent blog on the day after the shootings (first click accessible off blog portion of site, and ranked number 3, behind "why I have the best f*ing blog on MySpace") details a young woman's day as she learned of the shootings; there is some attempt at sense-making in her account: "I'm not sure why such great things, such as the Twin Towers and Virginia Tech have to be tarnished by pointless violence. I also lived in New York City on September 11, 2001. What I felt then is similar to what I feel now. I feel grief; I feel personally insulted; I feel shocked; I feel confused and detached." What is interesting is there is little uptake, beyond prayers and one longer commentary on how schools should be "safe places" of the woman's trying to come to terms with a near-violence experience: it is as if what is compelling is just the distance, and little else—no outrage, no demands place on anyone, including the government to better regulate guns, and no culpability placed on any shoulders—these things simply "happen." (This is *not* to single out this young woman: the press did little else, and her account is simply evocative of the kinds of discourse the slayings received: very little about guns or violence, and much made of the "South Korean" who was very much a United States *citizen*.)

So what does count as "knowing" on a social networking site like MySpace? Knowing seems to amount to a kind of obsessive account keeping: of friends, of favorites, of likes and dislikes, and of most clicked on kookiest, strangest, prettiest, ugliest, and so on people. Knowing in this context includes close friend and acquaintances, people who have signed up to be your friend, knowing about other people's friends and acquaintances, lurking, seeking out others, and lists of things. It also seems to include a kind of endless, paradoxically *self*-interested, reaching out into other people's business, a kind of publicity for one's own sake, conjoining high profile events with a kind of everyday autoethnography, put out there, for consumption by mostly unknown others. MySpace straddles and problematizes (somewhat) the traditional line between production and consumption—on MySpace you are both producing and consuming—and it thrives on the blurring of the distinction. For example, a user produces (or re-uses, precisely in the ways Lyotard forshadowed, their own material—images, text, video, music—and uploads it to their MySpace, template driven "space" which they customize within that organizational space. It is here marital and sexual status are indicated, likes and dislikes and a kind of "web ring" of friends is created. MySpace users produces their own relations, inventories and classification systems, and meantime they are consumed by friends/relations and other MySpace users, lurkers and general surfers' not the least MySpace producers themselves. Knowing here is knowing'about, a kind of short form synech-dotal simulacrum.

The important point here, though, is that the "self," as it is represented and as it is "known," is always in flux, meaning on any given day, either a user makes changes to their MySpace self *or* what is represented there is out-of-date—an inevitability now structurally always already pre-empted by social networking's latest and always just in time incarnation, Twitter. MySpace is a particular kind of social networking: one where people might strategically and selectively represent their "real self" in partial form, and while it is, in effect, "public," it is not the "self" that many people would willingly choose to show their employer. In 2006, the *New York Times,* for example, reported that more and more companies were checking Facebook and MySpace profiles of potential employees. This caused a rippled outrage among users of such sites, and generated much discussion about privacy, social media sites and the rights and responsibilities of users of those sites.

For our purposes, what is significant is the blurring of public/private: these sites are inherently public, to be pursued by anyone, with greater access granted to those with an account, which anyone can obtain. The "violation" of people's perceived boundaries seems to be that employers are not *meant* to have access to the self that occupies a community of users whose intent and purposes are both inside and outside an office or place of business. There are many stories to enumerate of people being fired for their MySpace or Facebook practices—a young journalist fired for posting what he claimed to be a tongue-in-cheek "kill list," 27 American Automobile Association workers fired for harassing comments, an employee of a professional football team for critiquing his team's decisions, or the young Montana deputy fired for explicit sexual chatting while on duty. What is at stake here then is not simply self-representation, but the permeabilities and permutations of self through these rhizomatic networks, through the literal social constructive work of the users enabled by the technology. In educational terms, this is active "constructivist" self-formation which is neither trivial nor should it be simply dismissed. It is noticeably ironic that a medium driven by an entrepreneurial orientation to self-expression and social communication should now be the site for a re-invocation of individual/"privacy rights" and new domains of "the personal."

Second Life: Producing "Other" in an Online Virtual World

Second Life (SL) is a "free" online virtual world (multi-player, 3-D) where "adults" (you must claim to be over 18 years of age to join, otherwise you are directed to *Teen Second Life*) ostensibly go to "hang out" with others in this online space. When you first enter the world, you create an avatar (male or female) that you name and which looks much like the enduring plastic of a Barbie and Ken doll. The player then navigates the world of SL with/as the avatar, purchasing clothes and adding accessories, hanging out in bars and clubs, gambling, going to malls, conducting experiments in avatar sex, and so on. SL is the graphics- and network-enhanced chat room of old, with one important caveat: *Second Life* is economically driven. So while it might be seen to be a Web 2.0 version of a chat room, it very much relies on virtual and world exchange. In order to have cool clothes, and interesting (and anatomical) attachments as well as land or other objects, your character must purchase them using the currency of SL, "Linden dollars" which you can either earn through trading goods, or the "old-fashioned" way through sexual trade, by buying and selling in world real estate or by converting "real world" dollars to Linden cash. According to *The Guardian*, daily *Second Life* economic trade is as much as $265,000 U.S. dollars, making it one of the more active, "virtual" economies online (Sweeny, 2007b), and, of course, this economy, like its real world equivalents, has since greatly inflated. In addition, large companies are actively advertising and "selling" in SL—IBM, Toyota, Starwood Hotels and Resorts, General Motors, and Sony, among many others.

What drives this economy? Its users, of course, entrepreneurial people like Anshe Chung (SL name) who is a virtual property tycoon in the world, and recently claimed to be its first millionaire (Irvine 2007). Goods and services, in fact, trade a whole lot in SL: in one month three virtual malls sold for over $150,000 U.S. Sex also sells in SL: currently the largest growing economic area, according to one commentator, is in genital design that you must equip your avatar with and purchase in order to have sex (Hyde 2007). For some, it seems there is excitement to be had in watching two avatars engage in sexual exchange. As one reviewer commented:

> the creatively minded don't seem to be running the show these days. With all the media attention that Second Life has been getting, its population has skyrocketed (as I write, there are more than 36,000 players online). Hardly anybody you meet has been in the game for more than a couple of months. And the new player who wanders around talking to dolls, asking about the world's most popular places, will find the same things over and over again: clothes for sale, and the opportunity to witness awkward doll sex with a girl named Larry.
>
> *(Tossel 2007)*

Beyond the chance to build the Great Wall of China or own a car for as little as $1U.S. or watch two avatars you don't know engage in cartoon sex, what is so compelling about this virtual world? What is drawing users to it and, for a number much smaller than the 5 million plus registered on the site, what keeps them in that world? Unlike MySpace and Facebook, SL offers a chance for self-representation that is not quite so literal,[2] or at least not as dependent on representing oneself: choosing, outfitting and equipping an avatar means that, at least for some, they are released from the burden of a self that might not be able to afford an expensive suit or wear size zero clothing or have funky pink hair or simply be able. But how liberating is it to be able to represent oneself as an avatar that looks like it belongs in a nightclub? And how compelling is it to receive free pizza handed out by a campaign lackey (Hyde 2007)? Despite its global success and its burgeoning economy, the backbone of SL is still text-driven chat: do we see a significant shift in its popularity now its technology enables voice? Will people want to imbue their avatars with the timbre and tone of their own voice or will users shy away from the anonymity afforded by simply typing?

Education is a different matter. There continues to be a lot of press on SL as a potential "educational" site: courses have been held in the virtual world by New York University and Harvard, and INSEAD (a leading business school in Singapore and France) has created a virtual campus to bring together students from all over the world who will pay real money to enroll in virtual courses there (Walker 2007). But what kind of "courses" are these? SL's affordances, beyond building, buying and organizing parties and sexual encounters, do allow for audio, video and other kinds of encounters, including educational ones. Interestingly enough, many of these are synchronous, meaning that they are one time events held in SL and are not "captured" or "recorded" to be replayed. Writing on the potentialities and limitations of online learning, Peter Taylor argued some time ago that a shift in the educational environment, in his case to what is now widely accepted as online education, amounts to far more than a changed content delivery system, and should result both in a overhaul of pedagogy as well as curriculum. In SL, the curriculum will likely always already be located outside the world (unless the world itself is incorporated in some meaningful relation) and the kind of pedagogy that is afforded by the space is one that has been extremely difficult to "get right" as users are required (most often) to type in order to interact. A recent academic presentation on educational uses (AERA 2009) reporting the disappointingly low participation of SL conferees in a "vitual fireside chat" typifies the mismatches that result when the distinctive affordances and constraints of teaching and learning in virtual environments are not taken substantively into account. Not to mention the inherent inequities present and produced by such an online space: bandwidth, prior familiarity with 3-D and 3-D game environments, typing ability, linguistic competence and participatory comfort (Macleod 2008).

All of that aside, perhaps the most compelling educational possibility for SL is its hardwired "virtual world" that could be seen to support a community of practitioners who are co-producing their environment (through the constructive possibilities in SL—building homes, islands, shopping malls, etc.) and their interactions as well as co-authoring and co-constructing what is considered to be legitimate participation or not. For example, in March of 2007 it was reported that Italians gathered in SL to protest an Italian minister's setting up an office because it would "change the rules" and "It doesn't seem right to make this a photocopy of real life, we get enough politics there already" (Kington 2007). And in April 2007, in support of Earth Day, the SL worlds of Ibizia, Japan, and the Netherlands were "flooded" in an effort to draw attention to the potential effects of global warming and to incite discourse on the topic within the SL community. Interestingly, the intent of this move, at least according to the UK director of interactive communications, Giles Rhys Jones, was to try to get people to act not only within SL but also in their own lives. He states: "Not only that, [*Second Life*] is created, owned and maintained by its citizens. They have the power to change things for the better. We are hoping that this sense of empowerment will be reflected when Second Life citizens move from the virtual to the real world" (Sweney 2007a). Might SL be a community where people really do feel like they have the power to change things? And if so, is it at all remotely possible that this will "transfer," as Jones hopes, to the "real world?" Of course, this remains to be seen, but if history helps at all in the prediction, the likelihood is that agency of this kind will not simply "transfer." What is intriguing, however, is the notion that the communities within SL might well view themselves as having the means to incite change through protest, through "simulations" and through general and ongoing participation, and that is very different than a world that has been actively idle in the face of intense environmental change (see, for example, the "Tea Party" protests over tax increases http://sl-newspaper-pnn.blogspot.com/2009/04/tea-party-protest-in-second-life.html and the IBM staff protest http://www.theinquirer.net/inquirer/news/095/1019095/ibm-staff-plan-second-life-protest).

Whether many of the educational uses to which SL has been put have yet exploited its affordances and whether there is a critical dimension to be explored beyond its oft-cited economic infrastructure remain to be seen, however. Many of the criticisms raised to its environments have in effect condemned the application as a whole for the limitations of the templates it provides. Those who visit SL as consumers will inhabit a very different and surely less engaged and engaging life than as producers in this domain. Apart from its economic disincentives (an island is prohibitively expensive for most),[3] there is the educationally interesting requirement that one become an active producer of code to ensure that the so-called simulated Great Wall of China doesn't allow students to put their hands through it, your avatar needn't look like Barbie in butt-less chaps, and the Imperial meeting hall doesn't look remarkably like a contemporary shopping mall.

Perhaps this helps to explain why people would want to actually stay in this environment more than have the countless journalists and reviewers who have declared it tedious and uninhabitable: that while in the real world, you cannot force people to contend with what a tsunami is like in the hopes they will somehow change their environmental practices, a coder in SL can actually harness that which has gone, for mere mortals, incredibly and dizzyingly out of our own control—as humans that is. As posthumans, we get a second life, but it is one which acquiescently schooled consumers are less likely to enjoy than restive and creative producers.

Something Wikied This Way Comes

If schools and universities are pivotal, centrally located brokers in and of the contemporary knowledge economy, in a time of remediation of cultural knowledge, it should be instructive to examine everyday practices of knowledge-focused communications: what now constitutes *education's* media of exchange? Wikipedia, for one thing, "The biggest multilingual free-content encyclopedia on the Internet. Over two million articles and still growing" (http://www. wikipedia.org). Wikipedia, the online encyclopedia that anyone can edit, with 3,752,200 articles in English, is the crux of the problem here. Its representation of knowledge challenges and threatens to destabilize conceptions and practices of knowledge long privileged by the academy. Many people have already noted that as Google has become for all practical purposes operationally synonymous with research, so Wikipedia has become operationally synonymous with knowledge. It has also come to signify, for some critics, a worrying educational foe: what Plato might have called an epistemic rule of the ignorant, a Gallup poll epistemology against which right-thinking professional and public intellectuals alike need to be vigilant, responsible, and suspicious.

Notwithstanding any and all of this, its use is, arguably, nowadays pervasive across both public school and university, and if an educator does not explicitly prohibit its evidential or citational use, what one student presentation after another will include is more or less of what they learned from Wikipedia, whether that be about bran flakes or brain surgery. In education, objections to students' increasing uses of Wikipedia as the contemporary voice of epistemic authority is a source of great concern to their teachers and instructors. It is important to pay attention to the grounds of these objections, however, to see the specific forms which this awkward transitioning into contemporary media takes across particular cases. In the case of Wikipedia, we see a kind of legitimation crisis. The epistemic basis of its claims to knowledge is seen as unstable, unreliable, possibly completely invalid, and this is of course because Wikipedia is radically 'open:' anyone can contribute content, and there are few safeguards, tests, or other processes for warranting the truth of the claims made there. Interestingly, this appears to be a problem primarily for education; we hear little concern from the many using Wikipedia outside the contexts and purposes of educational institutions, perhaps because they don't contend with the same high-stakes legitimation game. For ordinary users, there are no tests which require warrantable validity claims to be made: people use Wikipedia to get an initial idea about something, and seem content enough to treat such information as a starting point, and a possibly quite fallible one at that.[4]

So What Is Wrong with This?

In a posting to the Habermas list at Yahoogroups, "Re: Habermas at Wikipedia: Definitely under constructed," group moderator Gary Davis suggested that

> Discussing how to best improve that article [http://en.wikipedia.org/wiki/Jürgen_Habermas] would be an excellent topic for this forum.

And he goes on to specify a number of areas that list members could consider contributing to (including the entry of his own) and asks:

> What other articles at Wikipedia form the "spirit" of public understanding of Habermas? What is the Habermasian round at Wikipedia? Let's get a comprehensive list and make improvement of the Habermasian legacy at Wikipedia a project.

The posting that follows is from a self-described "beginner" in Habermasian studies who has "taken a peek" at the Wikipedia entry on Habermas, and he identifies a number of foundational areas in which it is incorrect or misleading, for example noting a confusing (mis)representation of strategic action as an attempt to achieve understanding which has failed, as if strategic action were parasitic upon, and not a distinct kind of enterprise from, communicative action oriented to reaching an understanding. Fairly sophisticated stuff for a beginner.

Whether or not this particular Habermas list actually contributes to this revision of Wikipedia on Habermas (although the list moderator has already done so), the point is that an online community of readers of Habermas is being encouraged to create content and are able to do so.

This is a dramatic shift in the post-literate mediascape, and it calls for a corresponding shift in post-literate pedagogy which understands and respects production as a necessary and enduring condition of knowledge-transmission, formation and transformation. Wikipedia's radically democratized, digitally re-mediated epistemic conceptions and practices make continuous revision and reviseability simply an inherent and ongoing condition of "knowledge." Given those necessarily 'under construction' conditions, why would (and how could) anyone intelligibly encourage knowledge-telling and fact-stating as paradigmatic classroom performances? It's not Wikipedia's fallibility which is the problem here, but an engrained disposition to represent knowledge as explicit and testable statements of fact.

Historical documentation of cultural transitions in the validity basis of knowledge claims demonstrates how changes in communicational media, in the forms that knowledge claims took, in effect, drove changes in what knowledge could be *trusted*, how, and why. In societies organized around mythological and religious authorities, that is societies in which cultural knowledge was not yet differentiated into separate epistemic spheres, and systematized within these separate spheres, gods and other deities grounded appeals to truth and were guarantors of truthfulness. One swore an oath in the name of one's god, who, being almighty, could mightily smite down she who uttered a falsehood, broke a promise, deceived another. In the ancient world, the challenges to traditional religion and the repudiation of traditional gods brought with it a major cultural crisis: what could be believed if there were no gods to secure promises and punish those who broke them, or who stole from others, or uttered falsehoods or misled other people?

How does a secular preliterate culture deal with this same set of issues? By investing authority not with an almighty god, but with the speaker: "My word is my bond," "A man is as good as his word." As we know, when a man swore an oath, he might draw his own blood or make a bodily mark as warrant for the truth of his word, or he might raise one palm to testify to the truth: an oath-taking practice of placing one's other hand on one's genitals while speaking, to guarantee and authorize the claim in a highly personal *manner*. Epistemic validity was as good, but only as good, as its expositor. In the oral past, a statement was only as reliable as the person who uttered it and its credibility a function of its speaker's own, contradicting in practical terms the old philosophical dictum that "it's what is said, not who said it that matters." Because in practice, it has always been very much who speaks that matters.

Literacy, Ivan Illich reminds us, "separated a man from his word," and early legitimation practices were designed to re-forge that embodied connection by material means, by media, in the words of Marshall McLuhan, as "extensions of man."

As literacy both supplemented and supplanted oral transmission, it gave birth to a new attentional economy involving physical immobility, fixity of gaze, and meanings stabilized in a text "authored" by the actual person who "penned" it.

We know that it took a great deal of time before people would respect and trust communications conveyed in writing, as these came to be done less through personal representation/delegation and increasingly more by means of documents authorized by sealing in wax. Initially, early documents written in ink on vellum were reportedly dismissed as marks on a sheepskin having neither power nor legitimacy. For a long time, seals of authenticity were used to testify to the authority of a text, tying it to its origins and standing, itself, as testimony to the truth of what it enunciated. Branding does this, or some of this, today.

With the spread of print literacy, it would be the publisher upon whose reputation rested the responsibility of ensuring that the text printed was the authorized version, that is the version declared to be the complete and correct one by its author.

With its increasing institutional and official uses, the value of a personal warrant of legitimacy, an author's own authorization of print-based knowledge was superceded by the importance of its institutional authorization. When, for example, public schools began to use purpose-built textbooks to represent the "authoritative version" of the official prescribed curriculum, institutional authorization carried greater legitimacy than any declaration of accuracy by authors.

Undoubtedly, public schooling helped in large measure to make acceptance of and use of literate tools and methods, and with it, literate epistemologies separating speakers and their words (and worlds), ubiquitous. Pervasively, whatever is, is written; everything which is thinkable can be written. That there is "nothing beyond the text" has long been operationally true in education, in which textbook knowledge becomes synonymous with that which cannot be questioned, that which is above criticism and, conversely, that whose mastery is the route to success as a learner.

A Cultural Shift: Knowledge Production

Wikipedia has taken the place of the encyclopedia, and, later on, of Encarta in the cultural history of one-stop-shopping for knowledge. But whereas these earlier knowledge-repositories were authorized as having been informed and in fact written by accredited experts in their respective fields and norms of knowledge, Wikipedia, prided as being the most democratic and truly public knowledge bank ever created, is always and inevitably under construction, and that by a completely *un* authorized multitude of volunteers. In terms of location, if encyclopedias were available at the public school and the public library, and Encarta brought knowledge access as well into the home, Wikipedia makes its knowledge banks available anywhere and everywhere, at all times, in all places, across locations, across languages, and even in a basic English version. Wikipedia pages are some of the very few in which the majority appear in a language other than English. What Wikipedia offers, far from seeming an impediment to education, is a re-mediation of its foundational epistemic means: an incredibly useful space to pursue producer-like understandings of culturally significant and locally informed and responsive knowledge, under construction, just as *we say* in education, but have this far failed entirely to carry out, that we see knowledge from a *constructivist standpoint*. A production pedagogy takes it for granted that knowledge is locally and humanly produced, and although it necessarily relinquishes strong claims to universality, it makes a lot more educationally defensible the value of Wikipedia's epistemic affordances than does their prohibition. Rather than forbid students use Wikipedia, might we not far more productively engage with its content including perhaps especially its absences, and take seriously whatever flaws or questions may be found in its entries? This would require a much more profound study of the subject matter at issue than we are currently promoting, as well as in insider's critical inquiry into the possible complications, complexities and contra-factuals of the particular knowledge-representation under discussion. A lot more would have to be learned this way than through the received practices of knowledge-telling and testing which currently drive public educational policies and practices. Arguably, the refusal to engage with Wikipedia content on the part of many teachers and professors may signify a more general and worrying refusal to engage with student-produced work (see TurnItIn at https://www.turnitin.com/static/index.php). The chief question here might instead more profitably be not how to prevent the use of Wikipedia to support teaching and learning, but how do we best and most powerfully engage our students—not as in the past as receptive consumers of textually conveyed ideas—but as thoughtful producers in a global participatory community of scholars that we might yet produce by working on the human knowledge project openly, actively and freely together.

Conclusion/s

What we see across the preceding three cases is education's understandably clunky attempts to negotiate the new terms of a digitally re-mediated "attentional economy" (de Castell & Jenson 2004), and its equally understandable attempts to do so by implementing and enforcing received practices of creating and exchanging knowledge often scarcely recognizable as such. What we predict initially at least is an intensification in the levels and kinds of coercion which, until a deeper understanding of the digital reconfiguring of knowledge is arrived at, must and will be exercised by educational, familial and related cultural authorities in *personal* website surveillance and censorship, in regulation and prohibition of kinds of online *social* interaction and participation, and a materialist refiguring of ideas as *property*, resulting in intensified plagiarism charges, copyright enforcement and intellectual ownership legislation and prosecution. This is a time in which economic values—not epistemic ones—regulate knowledge and its public access and use. And yet, remarkably enough, this temporary pathology, symptomatic of media in transition, might yet be treatable to the extent that education is capable of taking seriously, and seriously taking, the measure of these new forms and practices: that knowledge is productive participation in communities of practice, that it can look nothing like what we have grown accustomed to, and that it is always and necessarily under construction and has always been so, even though we have been blinded for too long to that condition by literate culture's textually induced myopia. To steal from Pope, the proper study of education is education: only when we are prepared to learn reflexively about the ways in which the traditional textual preferences of modernist education have constructed knowledge and knowing, teaching and learning, truth and uncertainty, will we be in a position to educate ourselves about what education might yet become were it able to reverse its value basis from an alienated consumption of credentials to an intellectual engagement in the production of knowledge with understanding. Until then, we continue as we have been, absurdly, ostrich-like, championing epistemic illusions that we ourselves have conjured and which offer no suitable means to the advancement of educational ends under postmodern, postliterate conditions.

Notes

1 Here we focus our argument on MySpace rather than Facebook, however, we would argue that they are for the purposes of what we are claiming here, virtually interchangeable. The reason we have steered clear of Facebook here is simply because we chose to focus our attention on two "points in time"—the Virginia Tech killings and Tila Tequila. There are, of course, similar examples to be found using Facebook, but at the time of those two events (2007), MySpace users outnumbered Facebook users. The opposite is now the case.

2 This is not to say the MySpace and Facebook users all rely on literal self-representation, there is a lot of playfulness in many peoples' self-accounting, and there are endless reports of people constructing false identities and falsely representing themselves. But the premise of those social networking spaces is to construct a network and community of people who might not "know" you, but who at least can make some claims about their connection to you, however trivial.

3 The *Second Life* website offers three types of islands, or "private regions." These include Full Regions, which support the most activity, Homestead Regions, for "quiet residential" or "light commercial" use, and Openspace Regions, for scenery. The latter two are only offered to those that already own a full region. A price quotation for a Full Region is US$1,000 for 65,536 square meters (about 16 acres). Monthly land fees for maintenance are US$295. There is a discount for verified educational and non-profit organizations who use the regions for their work at US$700 for the full region and US$147.50 for maintenance fees (http://second life.com/land/privatepricing.php; accessed 19 April 2009).

4 Wikipedia has, in fact, had ongoing problems with editing and legitimation. It allows readers to "flag" problematic, erratic, or incorrect content/claims and as recently as January 2009 was contemplating having a group of editors approve all content before it is posted (Johnson 2009). The wiki "model" is also being used to house more and more specialized content, some examples including Recipes Wiki, Star Wars Wiki (Wookieepedia) and many more.

References

AERA (2009). Interactive symposium: "World of warcraft, *Second Life* and other virtual environments for K-12 education and beyond." American Educational Research Association Annual Conference, San Diego, California.

de Castell, S., & Jenson, J. (2004). Paying attention to attention: New economies for learning. *Educational Theory, 54*(4), 381–97.

Deleuze, G., & Guattari, F. (1987). *A thousand plateus: Capitalism and schizophrenia.* Minneapolis: University of Minnesota Press.

Grossman, L. (2006, December 16). Tila Tequila. *Time Magazine.* http://www.time.com/time/magazine/article/0,9171,1570728,00.html. Accessed 22 April 2007.

Hirschorn, M. (2007, April). The Web 2.0 bubble. *The Atlantic, 299*(3), 134–38.

Hyde, M. (2007, April 14). New technology, new lows for political discourse. *The Guardian Online.* http://www.guardian.co.uk/comment/story/0,,2057057,00.html. Accessed 14 April 2009.

Irvine, D. (2007, March 12). Virtual worlds, real money. *CNN.Com International.* http://edition.cnn.com/2007/TECH/science/03/12/fs.virtualmoney/index.html. Accessed 24 April 2008.

Johnson, B. (2009, January 29). Wikipedia editors may approve all changes. *The Guardian Online.* http://www.guardian.co.uk/technology/2009/jan/27/wikipedia-may-approve-all-changes. Accesed 13 April 2009.

Kington, T. (2007, March 5). Minister upsets Italians. *The Guardian Online.* http://www.guardian.co.uk/international/story/0,,2026443,00.html. Accessed 24 April 2008.

Lankshear, C., & Knobel, M. (2003). New literacies: Changing knowledge and classroom learning. Buckingham, UK: Open University Press.

Lyotard, J-F. (1984). *The postmodern condition: A report on knowledge.* Minneapolis, University of Minnesota Press.

Macleod, D. (2008, November 18). *Second Life:* Is this the future of the academic conference? *The Guardian.* http://www.guardian.co.uk/education/mortarboard/2008/nov/11/highereducation-secondlife. Accessed 13 April 2009.

McLuhan, M. (1955). New media as political forms. Online at: http://gingkopress.com/02-mcl/z_new-media-as-political-forms.html. Last accessed October 17, 2011.

Olson, D. R. (1977). From utterance to text: The bias of language in speech and writing. *Harvard Educational Review, 47*(3), 257–81.

Sweeny, M. (2007a, January 16). Social networking fees predicted. *The Guardian* online. http://media.guardian.co.uk/newmedia/story/0,,1991085,00.html. Accessed 22 April 2008.

Sweeny, M. (2007b, April 5). Virtual floods in *Second Life. The Guardian online.* http://media.guardian.co.uk/newmedia/story/0,,2050845,00.html. Accessed 24 April 2009.

Taylor, P. G. (1996). Pedagogical challenges of open learning: Looking to borderline issues. In E. McWilliam & P. G. Taylor (Eds.), *Pedagogy, technology and the body* (pp. 59–77). New York, Peter Lang.

Tossel, I. (2007, April 5). Playing with dolls. *The Globe and Mail.* http://www.theglobeandmail.com/news/technology/article751692.ece Last accessed October 17, 2011.

Walker, P. (2007, April 10). The first virtual business school campus. CNN.Com International. http://edition.cnn.com/2007/BUSINESS/04/02/execed.virtual/index.html. Accessed 24 April 2009.

3

UPDATE YOUR STATUS

Identity and Learning in Viral Youth Networks

Michael Hoechsmann

It is no longer news that a whole lot of young people are spending a heck of a lot of time and energy "prosuming" social media on the Web 2.0. Not just producers, nor just consumers, the prosumers (Toffler, 1980) both make media and consume media. It is evident from the frenzy of activity in the Web 2.0 domains that a seismic shift in the means and modes of communication is taking place, but the pace of change is so quick that even recent statistics on participation may lag behind actual practice. The Young Canadians in A Wired World study (Media Awareness Network, 2005) reported that 30% of kids in Grades 6–7 had their own website and that 12% of them regularly write and post a blog. The numbers of young people hosting a website in Grades 10–11 was down to 26% but the rate of blogging was up to 18%. This is a significant participation rate and given that the study was conducted before the biggest gains in traffic to MySpace, YouTube and Facebook had occurred, these numbers are quite high. The study claims that 94% of kids have Internet access, and that by Grade 11, 51% of them had their own Internet connected computer, separate from the rest of the household. In the United States, the numbers are similar, yet the findings distinct. For example, the Kaiser Family Foundation found in 2005 that more than half of online teens in that country had created content for the Internet (including creating a blog or personal web page, or sharing artwork, photos, stories or videos online). It was estimated that 87% of U.S. teens were using the Internet, and half of those were online daily (Kaiser Family Foundation, 2005).

In these fast times, citing statistics from over a half decade ago may appear quaint, anachronistic and "so yesterday" as to be a pointless exercise. The point of this chapter, however, is to question the whole notion of assessing youth media practices through a quantitative lens, and to ask, what are youth primarily doing when online? What is the nature of online participatory culture in this age of interactive media? While it is undeniable that some exceptional youth put sustained effort in to creating sophisticated blogs, elaborate websites and complex videos, the majority of young people spend their online time creating and sharing identity texts in highly constrained, commercial environments. Increasingly, young people are wearing their status on their cyber skins, and updating their status on Facebook and through IM and cell networks. Sharing the minutiae of everyday life with various virtual and real life friends may appear at first glance superficial, but for many young users of viral networks, keeping tabs on friends' coming and goings and reporting on their own current actions and feelings is a lingua franca of contemporary youth culture and a way of performing an identity self in real time. The reality is that even while inhabiting the new participatory media, most young people are not creating media in anything like the traditional sense of the word. If anything, their engagement with the new media mixes key aspects of previous forms of youth culture such as the telephone, the street corner and the television. As Hobbs and Jensen argue, youth online practices are different from those of adults and closely emulate what young people have been doing all along:

> Some scholars and educators don't yet fully realize that young people's online media use is entertainment-centered. Adults are using the Internet for email, to get medical information, and to buy things. Young people are using the Internet to interact socially, to play games, and to watch video on their computers and their mobile devices—the two other "screens" in American life.
>
> *(2009: 6)*

In this chapter, I will argue that the primary online activity of young people can be encapsulated by the 4-Cs of youth media practices: Consciousness, Communication, Community and Consumption. We will return to the 4-Cs in the latter portion of this chapter.

Growing Up Online

Kids will be kids. Or don't trust anyone over 30 years old. Whichever way you slice it, generational differences will exist to some extent in the public imaginary. These days we talk about Gen Net, digital natives, Millennials, and the shape shifting digital portfolio generation. For the sake of this chapter, however, we will dispense with the whole notion that those young people inhabiting our classrooms and shuffling along our streets are any different from ourselves. Rather, we will assume for the time being that these young folks are just like us (except, for the most part, they are not reading this piece, so we can stick to the us and them narrative for the time being). If we accept that these young people are just like us, then what is it in the material conditions of life that have changed to transform *the experience of growing up*? Here we should be quick to recognize changes in the social, economic and political conditions of our world. But, for the purposes of this chapter, the focus is solely on the new media technologies used for the purpose of communication, creative expression and consumption. If young people today are no different from those of us guiding them along their life pathways—whether as educators, parents or community leaders—then what is it that they are doing that we were doing in our day only differently?

While new digital divides are increasingly apparent, a great number of young people—middle- and upper-class kids with modems and those of lower economic status who get involved in youth media organizations or media education in school—have the capacity today to create and share media. That is an extraordinary development, and cannot be minimized. Power is a scarce resource for young people and if we consider social, political, economic and cultural arenas of power, then we must recognize the potential that laptop and camera toting young people have an extraordinary advantage over previous generations of a comparable demographic. While some corporations are making a fortune producing and selling the new relatively low-cost hardware and software for the new hyper media generation, the reality is that the costs of production and distribution have dropped so low that millions of young people can join the new virtual studio, some becoming instant celebrities and most others just having the potentially feel good moment of being a part of the hyper media world.

Young people are among the many who have begun to inhabit the Web and to populate it with visual, audio, print and multimodal texts. We are still in relatively uncharted waters, multiple cartographers of the new medias and new literacies notwithstanding. For this reason, it warrants caution to not get caught up in the allure of new platforms and new contexts of cultural production, but to look at how youth are articulating themselves in the liminal spaces between and around texts. Richard Lanham's *Economics of Attention* (2006) is useful here, because it is precisely a sense of deficit in the attention economy that fuels the imaginary of youth anomie and the generative, albeit fictional space recorded in the Generation X literature at the end of the last century (Hoechsmann, 1996). Youth anomie as imaginary construct feeds both ways; it is at once proof or evidence both of adult indifference and youth slackerdom. Outside of a real appreciation for youth cultural production, generations of adults misinterpret youth intentions and practices, while youth sense indifference and inattention to their needs and desires. It is a vicious circle, as real as the set of symbolic exchanges that occur in the circuits of consumption. There, the opposite happens. Adults, or more specifically marketers, spend great resources and time trying to understand youth. While Lanham helps us to identify the new conditions of scarcity—not of information, but of attention—it is attention that youth have been clamouring for throughout the years, both at a biographical level as young people growing up and at a generational, sociological level as a social demographic. In this regard, this generation is no different from previous ones, though it has access to communication resources previously unheard of.

In the mass media era, centralized media production entities, whether corporate or governmental, would send messages to a mass audience. Media messaging was highly controlled and only afforded to a small portion of the population who would produce for the masses. With advances in interactive media and technology, first the Web 1.0 of the World Wide Web and e-mail and now the Web 2.0 of social networking and user-driven content generation, communication is becoming increasingly participatory and viral. While the mass media continue to exert their dominion over the public imaginary, spaces have emerged for random messages from regular folks to gain the attention of a mass audience. For the most part, however, the new participatory media operate on a horizontal axis as peer-to-peer communication among friends and their social networks. Viral communication and networks operate through point to point contact between technological nodes, the latter being the technologies or platforms used to communicate. The notion of viral communication derives from the concept of point to point contact, an actual one to one transmission that quickly multiplies exponentially as more people become involved in communicating a given message or idea. An originary message or idea is referred to as a meme, a viral knowledge cluster that seeks out other minds to propagate itself further (Lankshear and Knobel, 2003). This concept enables us to conceptualize a type of face-to-face communication that has been around for millennia but that has now been given a technological delivery system and a high speed, worldwide distribution network. Thus, viral communication is not historically new, in fact it is the everyday form of communication associated with our oral past and present, those forms and modes that have lingered through the period Tom Pettitt (2007) refers to as the Gutenberg Parenthesis, that period of history characterized by one-way information flow from book publishers and modern mass media of all sorts. Whereas formerly memes could only pass to and from people in several degrees of separation from one another, now total strangers can learn directly from one another. Thus, ideas can proliferate across space and time at a speed and scale formerly unimaginable. And whereas in an era of mass media, a small number of powerful corporations controlled the air waves, in this interactive media environment, virtually anyone—the virtual every one— can at least try to transmit their ideas to a broad audience and as ideas come into contact with other, new knowledge can form.

In this context of participatory media, social networking sites such as MySpace, YouTube, Facebook, and many other lesser-known sites have come of age. Regardless of its past in community activism, the term social networking has become the adopted and adapted term that describes websites where people typically post a personal profile with the goal of sharing it with others. MySpace and Facebook are basically virtual online scrapbooks, and YouTube is an online sharing site for streaming video, either home produced or media industry produced clips, old and new. There is a tremendous range of other social networking sites, some of which mobilize affinity groups and some of which enable cultural practices. Affinity groups might take the form of specific demographics (African American people, wealthy people, etc.) or people with shared interests (fan sites). Cultural practices sites center around shared activities (hobby sites, activism sites, profession sites). A common denominator across social networking sites is a sense of connecting with others, sometimes with flirtatious intentions, but in a broad sense for increasing a virtual sense of community. The virtual relationship is very real to the participants despite the mediation of distance and technology. While there are privacy settings on v-log and blog sites that can limit who will be able to view or read a posting, this just means the poster is selecting to narrowcast to a limited audience.

And many people can participate, even some who are differently abled and others without economic privilege. The learning curve involved for participation is modest. As learning economies, rather than structured learning environments, social networking sites function through emulation and peer-to-peer support. There are no manuals to read, nor classes to attend. Pedagogy is just-in-time and task oriented. Rather than the reciprocal relations of the real world, learning is networked, involving multiple learners with varying levels of expertise at multiple nodes, united by shared interests and goals. For young people growing up with this technology, the lure of social networking is irresistible. On the one hand, there is the real and perceived need of performing one's self to others. It is hard to get some identity traction growing up in a world of viral communication and a fast culture and economy, so it makes sense to leave real time traces of one's in-flux–identity along the way. But, more significantly, social networking is a way of staying in touch with peers, of knowing what is going on in the off-line, real world of everyday life. Ultimately, participatory media enable youth to perform identity, to communicate with one another, to form and maintain peer groups, and to consume entertainment media, usually mainstream material shared by friends, but also sometimes DIY media produced by peers. For the most part, youth online are just hanging on, chatting with peers and checking out curious tidbits of media selected and shared by friends. In this sense, they are no different from previous generations. In sum, youth online media practices can be encapsulated by the 4-Cs: Consciousness, Communication, Community, and Consumption.

Consciously Communicating and Consuming Community

1. Consciousness

Identity formation is at the heart of young people's biographical trajectory of growing up. A consciousness of self in relation to others, and of cultural and subcultural belonging, is intertwined with early experiences of communication in online environments. Performing and positioning one's identity in real time through material, semiotic means is a central preoccupation of many youth today. The process of identity performance on the part of young people still includes residual cultural practices associated with fashion and pop music, but it now involves as well multimodal and textual practices online and on cell phones. Online social networks are complementing and even displacing youth subcultures as vital nodes of youth identity, and viral communication has come to the fore as a pedagogical vehicle for identity texts. To get some scale of the level of involvement of young people in online social networking, consider that one-sixth of Internet users worldwide connected to Facebook. com, the world's fourth most visited site, in May of 2009. According to Alexa Internet (n.d.), the largest demographic on Facebook is the 18–24 year age group (http://www.alexa.com/siteinfo/facebook.com#), but it is important to note that Alexa Internet does not include the under 18-year-old population in its demographic profile. Like other popular social networking sites, Facebook allows users to create on online profile, basically a home page that draws on the user-friendly functionality of a Web 2.0 interface. The upshot of sites like Facebook is that creating one's own Web portal is no longer the province of the techies. Anyone with Internet access can participate and register their identity in the virtual world. Two of the key functions on Facebook are the news feed and the status updates where one can access brief updates on what one's "friends" are doing and thinking. Here, in real time, people can update their status, a double entendre for sharing information and showing off. The identity performances enable the writer to represent themselves in place and time ("I communicate, therefore I am") and allows the reader to imagine a sense of belonging to a virtual community. The importance of these sites to contemporary youth is enormous. As danah boyd found out in her ethnographic work on kids who use Friendster and MySpace, the rewards of participation stand in contrast to the terror of non-participation. Said one 18-year-old interviewee: "If you are not on MySpace, you don't exist" (2007, p. 1).

As well as serving as a vehicle for identity display, online spaces allow for the expression of alternative selves. The virtual worlds of video games, for example, provide a space for a re-staging and performance of self that allows for identity play. By creating avatars and participating in virtual environments, youth are able to disinhibit their minds and displace their physical bodies in favour of simulative, performative virtual selves. In creating an avatar for the social network virtual world, Second Life, for example, a person can try on a different identity, be it something as profound as switching gender or race, or as simple as changing their manner of dress. The reactions to this new self from other Second Life netizens allows the person to experience their identity differently. As well, simulations created by educators and other Second Lifers allow users to experience different cultures and historical period, as well as distinct physical environments.

As more and more educators recognize the potential of virtual environments for educational "play," this role playing and virtual experiencing will become a greater component of New Literacies. More significantly, however, a broad understanding of the centrality of online identity performance by young people will help educators to better comprehend youth online behavior.

2. Communication

Today's "tethered" teens (Turkle, 2008) are constantly in contact with their peers, using new media to get connected and stay in touch. The primary means of communication are Instant Messaging, narrowcasting to peers over social network sites such as Cyworld (Asia), Sonico (Latin America) and Facebook (North America), and texting over cell phones. It is important to recognize that socializing with friends is nothing new or extraordinary, but rather an essential part of transitioning into adulthood. In previous decades, street corners, bedrooms and family phones were the nexus of youth communication, but young people today have an abundance of communicational capacities, both stationary (in home, school, library and Internet cafes) and mobile (cell phones), as well as greater restrictions in their everyday lives. Internet ethnographer danah boyd argues that young people are in constant negotiation between public, private and controlled space, particularly in an era when hanging out on streets is considered more hazardous and when teen lives are increasingly regulated by activities and obligations:

> Adults with authority control the home, the school, and most activity spaces … To [teenagers], private space is youth space and it is primarily found at the interstices of controlled space … By going virtual, digital technologies allow youth to (re)create private and public youth space while physically in controlled spaces. IM serves as a private space while [social networking sites] provide a public component. Online, youth can build the environments that support youth socialization.
>
> *(boyd, 2006)*

Adults may worry about what youth are doing on the Internet, but, for the most part, young people are sitting within earshot of parents and other adults while communicating with their peers. Youth are hanging out, gossiping, shooting the breeze and coordinating offline meetings and events. They are sharing media, some homemade (particularly photos shot of one another) and some from the vast array of amateur and professional material online (particularly music related).

Kaveri Subrahmanyam and Patricia Greenfield (2008) conducted an audit of existing research studies on adolescent communication and found that much of the activity of teens online is centered on reinforcing "existing relationships, both friendships and romantic relationships, and to check out the potential of new entrants into their offline world" (p. 120). The notion that young people primarily use the Internet to communicate with their offline friends flies in the face of much of the early hype about the perils of the Internet predator. Among other findings, Subrahmanyam and Greenfield dispute the stereotype of vulnerable adolescents who unwittingly leave themselves vulnerable to strangers. For most part, youth do use the privacy settings available online, and many text communications are followed up by a phone call.

Of course, there are hazards online, such as electronic bullying and interactions with troublesome strangers, but these are perils also found in the offline world and they must be weighed against the benefits to seeking out others online. As Subrahmanyam and Greenfield state, "research has found that interactions with strangers may also help alleviate the negative effects of social rejection in the physical world" (p. 140). In particular, they point out that young people with illnesses or stigmatisms can find support online, and youth with questions they might be uncomfortable to ask a friend, family member or teacher, may find advice on Internet forums. Ultimately, however, the primary youth activity online is hanging out with one's extended peer group and for the most part keeping adults at bay.

3. Community

Social networking involves developing networks and community-building (usually by collecting friends and joining groups). The process of developing virtual community has been much advanced by the advent of online social networking. Each user in social network sites builds their own network and no two networks are identical, each always representing the character and idiosyncrasies of its producer. These peer-centered virtual communities lie at the heart of Internet activity, functioning as communicational and identity hubs for young people. In relation to the latter, who you know is increasingly public and status can be attained by securing certain "friends" to your network. While we would argue that these peer-centered communities are the most prevalent form of networking online, there is a vast set of more specialized networks to which youth belong. Other important forms of online community are affinity groups, usually organized around shared interests. These may involve advocacy (i.e., YAHAnet.org), creativity (MySpace.com was created as a site for musicians), fantasy (fanfiction sites such as harrypotterfanfiction.com), game-playing (multi-player online video games such as Sony's Everquest), conventional politics (i.e., Obama's Facebook page), or self-help and group therapy (i.e., Weight Watchers' Health Discovery site). Community can be built in a slow and stable manner, or, in the manner of the "flash mob," can develop and recede quickly.

Belonging to an online affinity group can take the form of a hobby or correspond to a social or personal need, yet the line between the two can blur. If an overweight person chooses to use the Health Discovery site to reach out to others with the same predicament, it seems apparent that this fulfills a social and personal need. Yet if that same person plays Everquest and writes fiction at harrypotterfanfiction.com, this apparent hobby might also be a remedy for social isolation. It is possible that the very same person visits YAHAnet.org to feel socially involved, maintains a page at MySpace to stay plugged in to the music community, and visited the Obama Facebook page regularly during the presidential election of 2008 to express political views.

Involvement in virtual communities can provide a sense of connectedness for people living in societies where older forms of community have eroded, for instance the side of the U.S. Robert Putnam documents in his impactful article, "Bowling Alone" (1995). Where many technologies—such as the automobile, the mp3 player and sunglasses—provoke social isolation, social networking platforms create community, albeit communities of physically atomized individuals sitting alone in front of personal computers. Peer-centered communities that allow young people to recreate private youth space with their offline friends while physically present in adult controlled space arguably enhance social relationships. Online affinity groups that enable contact with people of shared interests and/or circumstances can fulfill personal and social needs. Hobby sites that connect people with shared passions provide stimulus and motivation to perform certain actions, whether creating art for social change, writing fan fiction or playing complex games. Whatever the outcome, community building online appears to perform valuable functions, and it appears that people are hungrily availing themselves of the opportunities to make connections online. As well as boasting the involvement of on one-sixth of the world's Internet users, Facebook has an average user viewing time of 25 minutes. Thus, this "sticky" site draws people in, and keeps them online for a substantial amount of time in Internet terms. Many users are multitasking while on Facebook, but nonetheless they are sticking around for interactions with their online "friends." Just as in real life, some peer communities are seen to be a bad influence on their participants, such as Vampirefreaks.com where Kimveer Gill posted his malevolent intentions before entering a Canadian college with guns blazing (Hoechsmann & Low, 2008). There is also speculation that terrorists such as those involved in Al Qaeda use social networking to their advantage, but this begets the question, is it the technology or the real-world motivations that causes online organizing? If these technological applications did not exist, would vampire freaks and terrorists find another way to communicate? Online communities have developed quickly and grown exponentially. They are clearly among the most important forms of interaction online.

4. Consumption

For the most part, the new media environments inhabited by youth are virtually unregulated domains run by private enterprise. Many sites visited by youth advertise products for purchase, and the gadgets and service packages people need to access online and cell communication are commodities and for-profit services. Despite the fact that, once online, much activity is free of charge, there is no free lunch in new media environments. Sefton-Green, Nixon and Erstad (2009) describe how in the 1990s personal computers made their initial entrance into the mainstream through the home market as part of a broad marketing strategy targeted at parents to help their kids "'get ahead' and to 'keep up' with the information and communication requirements of contemporary society" (p. 111). With an average shelf life of three years before hardware and software becomes outdated, computers and their accessories are ideal commodities for producers and merchants. That the new online functionalities require a stable broadband connection which is also a mercantilized "service" adds greater value to home computing from a commercial perspective. The ongoing proliferation of mobile media—also discrete commodities that require pricey service contracts—enables some to get into the new digital markets for the first time, as is the case particularly in the developing world, and offers others a secondary product/service to link to the primary communicational hub while on the go. In many middle- and upper-class households in the global North, there is a minimum of three, but often more digital nodes (discrete computers and mobile media). Each of these apparatuses requires some forms of updating from time to time, whether in hardware renewal, software upgrades, or service contract renewals. But that is only the tip of the iceberg, as the role of digital media in the buying and selling of goods and services proliferates. The digital marketplaces of E-Bay and Craig's List were in 21st and 23rd place respectively on the list of most visited sites worldwide in May 2009 (http://www.alexa. com/topsites/global;1). These sites are Web 2.0 interfaces for regular folks to sell goods to one another, but corporate sites are ratcheting up their online sales as well. The site Amazon.com that sells books, music, toys and accessories sat in 34th place in May 2009, and many millions of commercial sites are available to sell anything from underwear to heavy machinery.

Straightforward commerce is only one aspect of consumption online, and perhaps of less consequence for young people than the pervasive marketing and cross marketing of product on web domains. Not only is the digital equivalent of traditional advertising ubiquitous online, many corporations have created web properties with games or other add-ons to draw young people into immersive advertising experiences, where form and content blurs into one promotional rub. David Buckingham cautions that for young people "commercial influences ... are often invisible to the user" (2007, p. 83). In Israel, the children's website Webkinz.com ranked 37th nationally in May 2009. Children who have purchased a Webkinz plush pet doll have a unique access code that allows them to play on the site. As children grow into teens, they are drawn to social networking sites, but they continue to flock to purely commercially driven sites such as MTV.com which ranked 169th in the United States in May of 2009. On social networking sites, youth are targeted with demographic specific advertising. One of the many great innovations of Google, the world's #1 website, is intuitive advertising, a Web 3.0 innovation which responds to the user's online profile, the sites they visit, and the clicks they make on individual sites. Thus, part of the social networking experience, and web trolling in general, is to view ads chosen just for you. In general, on the Internet you have to pay to play, whether in direct purchase of goods online, or by being added into the demographic sold back to corporate sponsors. Here too, young people today differ little from previous generations who are still being relentlessly courted by advertisers, albeit more subtly.

Despite the rhetoric of change that permeates the early discourses of youth online media practices, the reality is as much as things change, they also stay the same. In sober after thought, many techno optimists would acknowledge that peoples and cultures cannot make radical change so quickly. These are still the early moments of a broad technological revolution that is impacting how we communicate and produce and share knowledge. We are adapting our cultural practices in exciting new directions and the potentials of digital literacies are vast and in flux. The notion that youth have changed, however, that there is a new and culturally distinct generation of media makers among us, is an overwrought claim. Young people are living in interesting times of uncertainty and doubt. Those not excluded by the digital divide have access to exciting new communication tools at a young age. Time will only tell how many of them will use the new tools to their full, sophisticated potential and which ones will draw broad public attention through extraordinary creativity and/or quirks of fate. The rest will just keep on consuming media and communicating with friends.

References

Alexa Internet. (n.d.). Statistics drawn from site, www.alexa.com, May 15, 2009.

boyd, danah. (2006). "Identity Production in a Networked Culture: Why Youth Heart MySpace." Paper presented at the American Association for the Advancement of Science, St. Louis, MO. February 19.

boyd, danah. (2007). "Why Youth (Heart) Social Network Sites: The Role of Networked Publics in Teenage Social Life." *MacArthur Foundation Series on Digital Learning – Youth, Identity, and Digital Media Volume* (Ed. David Buckingham). Cambridge, MA: MIT Press, pp. 1–26.

Buckingham, D. (2007). "Defining Digital Literacy." *Nordic Journal of Digital Literacy.* Special Issue, pp. 78–91.

Hobbs, R., and Jensen, A. (2009). "The Past, Present, and Future of Media Literacy." *Journal of Media Literacy Education* 1, pp. 1–11.

Hoechsmann, M. (1996). "I am White, Male, and Middle Class in a Global Era: Marketing (to) Generation X." In M. Pomerance and J. Sakeris (Eds.) *Pictures of a Generation on Hold.* Toronto: Media Studies Working Group, pp. 85–96.

Hoechsmann, M., and Low, B. (2008). *Reading Youth Writing: "New" Literacies, Cultural Studies and Education.* New York: Peter Lang.

Kaiser Family Foundation. (2005). "Generation M: Media in the Lives of 8–18 Year-olds." Retrieved on March 7, 2009, from http://www.kff.org/entmedia/entmedia030905pkg.cfm.

Lanham, R. (2006). *The Economics of Attention.* Chicago IL: University of Chicago Press.

Lankshear, C., and Knobel, M. (2003). *New Literacies: Changing Knowledge and Classroom Practice.* Buckingham, UK: Open University Press.

Media Awareness Network. (2005). "Young Canadians in a Wired World." Retrieved March 7, 2009, from http://www.media-awareness.ca/english/research/ycww/index.cfm.

Pettitt, T. (2007). "Before the Gutenberg Parenthesis: Elizabethan-American Compatibilities." *Media in Transition 5* Conference. MIT, April 27.

Putnam, R. (1995). "Bowling Alone." *Journal of Democracy* 6:1, pp. 65–78.

Sefton-Green, J., Nixon, H., and Erstad, O. (2009) "Reviewing Approaches and Perspectives on 'Digital Literacy.'" *Pedagogies: An International Journal* 4, pp. 107–125.

Subrahmanyam, K., and Greenfield, P. (2008) "Online Communication and Adolescent Relationships." *The Future of Children* 18.1, pp. 119–146.

Toffler, A. (1980). *The Third Wave.* New York: Bantam Books.

Turkle, S. (2008). "Always-On/Always-On-You: The Tethered Self." In J. Katz (Ed.) *Handbook of Mobile Communications Studies.* Cambridge, MA: MIT Press, pp. 121–138.

4

TECHNOLITERACY AT THE SUSTAINABILITY CROSSROADS

Posing Ecopedagogical Problems for Digital Literacy Frameworks

Richard Kahn

The great advance of electrical science in the last generation was closely associated, as effect and as cause, with the application of electric agencies to means of communication, transportation, lighting of cities and houses, and more economical production of goods. These are social ends, moreover, and if they are too closely associated with notions of private profit, it is not because of anything in them, but because they have been deflected to private uses: a fact which puts upon the school the responsibility of restoring their connection in the mind of the coming generation, with public scientific and social interests.

(Dewey, 1916, p. 117)

Introduction

The ongoing debate about the nature and benefits of technoliteracy is without a doubt one of the most hotly contested topics in education today. Alongside their related analyses and recommendations, the last two decades have seen a variety of state and corporate stakeholders, academic disciplinary factions, cultural interests, and social organizations ranging from the local to the global weigh in with competing definitions of *technological literacy*. Whereas utopian notions such as Marshall McLuhan's "global village" (1964), H. G. Wells's "world brain" (1938), and Teilhard de Chardin's "noosphere" (1965) imagined the positive emergence of a planetary techno-ecology,[1] the contemporary situation is perhaps better characterized as the highly complex and sociopolitically stratified global culture of media spectacle[2] and the ever-developing megatechnics of a worldwide digital information (Castells, 1996) cum technocapitalist infotainment society (Kellner, 2003a, pp. 11–15). In other words, while contemporary information-communication technologies (ICTs) offer plenty of examples and reasons to believe that they can further the proliferation of sustainability values, even as they develop the organization of pro-ecological resistance movements to an unprecedented degree (see Kahn and Kellner, 2006, 2005), the ecological threats posed by a digitized global media ecology—whose real political and cultural economies are shielded from popular understanding and deliberation—are even more greatly manifest.

But *there are both* the possibilities to use technology to promote and develop ecoliteracy widely as well as the opportunity to critique present day technopoly (Postman, 1992) as being gravely ecologically damaging. Hence, those interested in ecopedagogy for sustainability must begin to ask critical questions about the types of knowledge that may be entailed by contemporary programs of technoliteracy, what sorts of practices might most greatly inform or be informed by them, as well as what institutional formations technoliteracy can best serve and be served by in kind. Further, it should be noted that despite the many divergent and conflicting views about technoliteracy that presently exist, it is only relatively recently that existing debates have begun to be challenged and informed by oppositional movements based on race, class, gender, anti-imperialism, and the ecological well-being of all. As these varying movements begin to ask their own questions about the ever-dovetailing realms of technology and the digital facilitation of a globalized culture, political realm, and economy, we may well yet see technoliteracy at once become more multiple in one sense, even as it becomes more and more singularly important for all in another.[3]

Much has been written that describes the history of the concept of "technological literacy"[4] and, as noted, a literature attempting to chart emancipatory technoliteracies has begun to emerge over the last decade.[5] In this chapter, I do not seek to reinvent the wheel of all this research or to reproduce yet another account of the same. Yet, considering that significant variance exists in the published definitions of technoliteracy, it will prove productive to begin with a survey of the meanings of the terms *technology* and *literacy* in order to more precisely conclude what sort of knowledge and skills "technoliteracy" might hail.

From this, I will summarize the broad trajectories of development in hegemonic programs of contemporary technoliteracy, beginning with their arguable origins as "computer literacy" in the United States *A Nation at Risk* report of 1983, through the Clinton years and the economic boom of ICTs in the 1990s, up to the more recent call for integration of technology across the curriculum and the standards-based approach of the No Child Left Behind Act of 2001 and 2004's U.S. National Educational Technology Plan. Agreeing with Stephen Petrina (2000), that the dominant trend in the United States on these matters over the last few decades has been toward the construction of a neutralized version of technoliteracy, which bolsters a neoliberal politics of ideological "competitive supremacy," I will show how this has been tacitly challenged at the international institutional level through the sustainable development vision of the United Nations' Project 2000+.

In following, I will then analyze how these contestations link up with an ecopedagogical demand for educational praxis that is at once oppositional, radically democratic, and committed to sustainability. Here it seems that we must seek a reconstruction of education such that it accords with a project of multiple literacies, and I argue for a dialectical critical theory of technology that overcomes one-sided technophobic or technophilic responses and which demands technology's own ongoing reconstruction in favor of appropriate and liberatory forms. Finally, in closing, I think about what it will mean to reconstruct *technoliteracies*, and I propose that a major goal will be to involve people in large-scale resistance movements in the transformation of mainstream understandings, policies, and practices of technoliteracy through the politicization of the hegemonic norms that currently pervade social terrains.

Technology, Literacy, Technoliteracy: Definitions

Technological literacy is a term of little meaning and many meanings.
(Todd, 1991, p. 10)

Upon first consideration, seeking a suitable definition of *technology* itself appears to be overly technical. Surely, in discussions concerning technology, it is rare indeed that people need to pause so as to ask for a clarification of the term. In a given context, if it is suggested that technology is either causing problems or alleviating them, people generally know what sort of thing is due for blame or praise.

Yet, the popular meaning of *technology* is problematically insufficient in at least two ways. First, it narrowly equivocates technological artifacts with "high-tech," such as those scientific machines used in medical and biotechnology, modern industrial apparatuses, and digital components like computers, ICTs, and other electronic media. This reductive view fails to recognize, for instance, that indigenous artifacts are themselves technologies in their own right, as well as other cultural objects that may once have represented the leading-edge of technological inventiveness during previous historical eras, such as books, hand tools, or even clothing. Second, popular conceptions of technology today make the additional error of construing technology as being merely object-oriented, identifying it as only the sort of machined products that arise through industry. In fact, from the first, technology has always meant far more; and this is reflected in recent definitions of technology as "a seamless web or network combining artifacts, people, organizations, cultural meanings and knowledge" (Wajcman, 2004, p. 106) or that which "comprises the entire system of people and organizations, knowledge, processes, and devices that go into creating and operating technological artifacts, as well as the artifacts themselves" (Pearson and Young, 2002).

These broader definitions of technology are supported by the important insights of John Dewey. For Dewey, technology is central to humanity and girds human inquiry in its totality (Hickman, 2001). In his view, technology is evidenced in all manner of creative experience and problem-solving. It should extend beyond the sciences proper, as it encompasses not only the arts and humanities, but the professions, and the practices of our everyday lives. In this account, technology is inherently political and historical, and in Dewey's philosophy it is strongly tethered to notions of democracy and education, which are considered technologies that intend social progress and greater freedom for the future.

Dewey's view is hardly naïve, but it is unabashedly optimistic and hopeful that it is within the nature of humanity that people may be sufficiently educated so as to be able to understand the problems which they face and, thusly, that people can experimentally produce and deploy a wide range of technologies so as to solve those problems accordingly. While I agree strongly with the spirit of Dewey, I also recognize that the present age is potentially beset by the unprecedented problem of globalized technological oppressions in many forms (both social and environmental).

To this end, I additionally seek to highlight the insights of radical social critic and technology theorist Ivan Illich. Specifically, Illich's notion of "tools" mirrors the broad humanistic understanding of technology outlined so far, while it additionally distinguishes "rationally designed devices, be they artifacts or rules, codes or operators ... from other things such as food or implements, which in a given culture are not deemed to be subject to rationalization" (1973, p. 22). Consequently, Illich polemicizes for "tools for conviviality," which are appropriate technologies mindfully rationed to work within the balances of both cultural and natural limits. In my view, technology so defined will prove useful for a twenty-first-century technoliteracy challenged to meet the demands of a sustainable and ecumenical world.

One of the great insights of Marshall McLuhan (1964) is that new media produce new environments in which people live and navigate. For instance, electricity produced entirely new urban and living spaces as well as new sciences that contributed to the development of contemporary physics and made new technologies, including the Internet. For McLuhan, a new technology of communication creates a new environment and he has theories of the progression of stages of society and culture depending on dominant media, moving from oral culture through print culture and electronic media. New media for McLuhan require emergent literacies and I would argue that he provides an important rationale for reconstructing education and developing the multiple technoliteracies I am discussing in this chapter in order to properly perceive, navigate, and act in an environment predicated upon the rapid evolution of industrial technology.

"Literacy" is another concept, often used by educators and policy makers, but in a variety of ways and for a broad array of purposes. In its initial form, basic literacy equated to vocational proficiency with language and numbers such that individuals could function at work and in society. Thus, even at the start of the twentieth century, literacy largely meant the ability to write one's name and decode popular print-based texts, with the additional goal of written self-expression only emerging over the following decades. Street (1984) identifies these attributes as typical of an autonomous model of literacy that is politically rightist in that it is primarily economistic, individualistic, and is driven by a deficit theory of learning. On the other hand, Street characterizes ideological models of literacy as prefiguring positive notions of collective empowerment, social context, the encoding and decoding of nonprint-based and print-based texts, as well as a progressive commitment to critical thinking-oriented skills.

In my conception, literacy is not a singular set of abilities but is multiple and comprises gaining competencies involved in effectively using socially constructed forms of communication and representation. Learning literacies requires attaining competencies in practices and in contexts that are governed by rules and conventions and I see literacies as being necessarily socially constructed in educational and cultural practices involving various institutional discourses and pedagogies. Against the autonomous view that posits literacy as static, I see literacies as continuously evolving and shifting in response to social and cultural changes, as well as the interests of the elites who control hegemonic institutions. Further, it is a crucial part of the literacy process that people come to understand hegemonic codes as "hegemonic." Thus, my conception of literacy follows Freire and Macedo (1987) in conceiving literacy as tethered to issues of power. As they note, literacy is a cultural politics that "promotes democratic and emancipatory change" (p. viii), and it should be interpreted widely as the ability to engage in a variety of forms of problem-posing and dialectical analyses of self and society.

Based on these definitions of technology and literacy, it should be obvious that, holistically conceived, literacies are themselves technologies of a sort—meta-inquiry processes that serve to facilitate and regulate technological systems. In this respect, to speak of *technoliteracies* may seem inherently tautological. On the other hand, however, it also helps to highlight the constructed and potentially reconstructive nature of literacies, as well as the educative, social, and political nature of technologies. Further, more than ever, we need philosophical reflection on the ends and purposes of education and on what we are doing and trying to achieve in our educational practices and institutions. Such would be a technoliteracy in its deepest sense.

Less philosophically, I see the types of contemporary technoliteracies that can support ecopedagogy for sustainability as involved with the need to comprehend and make oppositional use of proliferating high-technologies, and the political economy that drives them, toward furthering radically democratic understandings of and sustainable transformations of our lifeworlds. In a historical moment that is inexorably undergoing processes of corporate globalization and technological production, it is not possible to advocate a policy of clean hands and purity, in which people simply shield themselves from new technologies and their transnational proliferation.[6] Instead, technoliteracies must be deployed and promoted that allow for popular interventions into the ongoing (often antidemocratic) economic and technological revolutions taking place, thereby potentially deflecting these forces for progressive ends like social justice and ecological well-being.

In this, technoliteracies encompass the computer, information, critical media, and multimedia literacies presently theorized under the concept "multiliteracies" (Cope and Kalantzis, 2000; Luke, 2000, 1997; Rassool, 1999; New London Group, 1996). But whereas multiliteracies theory often remains focused upon digital technologies, with an implicit thrust toward providing new media job skills for the Internet age, here I would seek to explicitly highlight the social, cultural, and ecological appropriateness of contemporary technologies and provide a critique of the emergent media economy as technocapitalist (see Best and Kellner, 2001; Kellner, 1989), while also acknowledging their emancipatory potentials. Thus, in this chapter I seek to draw upon the language of "multiple literacies" (Lonsdale and McCurry, 2004; Kellner, 2000) to augment a critical ecological theory of multiple technoliteracies as I will later expound.

Functional and Market-Based Technoliteracy: United States Models

> From being a Nation at Risk we might now be more accurately described as a Nation on the Move. As these encouraging trends develop and expand over the next decade, facilitated and supported by our ongoing investment in educational technology … we may be well on our way to a new golden age in American education.
>
> *(U.S. Department of Education, 2004, p. 1)*

The very fledging Internet, then known as the ARPANET due to its development as a research project of U.S. Defense Advanced Research Projects Agency (DARPA), was still a year away when the *Phi Delta Kappan* published the following utopian call for a computer-centric technoliteracy:

> Just as books freed serious students from the tyranny of overly simple methods of oral recitation, so computers can free students from the drudgery of doing exactly similar tasks unadjusted and untailored to their individual needs. As in the case of other parts of our society, our new and wondrous technology is there for beneficial use. It is our problem to learn how to use it well.
>
> *(Suppes, 1968, p. 423)*

However, it was mainly not until *A Nation at Risk* (1983) that literacy in computers was popularly cited as particularly crucial for education.

The report resurrected a critique of U.S. schools made during the Cold War era that sufficient emphases (specifically in science and technology) were lacking in curriculum for students to compete in the global marketplace of the future, as it prognosticated the coming of a high-tech "information age." Occurring in the midst of the first great boom of personal computers (PCs), *A Nation at Risk* recommended primarily for the creation of a half-year class in computer science that would:

> equip graduates to: (a) understand the computer as an information, computation, and communication device; (b) use the computer in the study of the other Basics and for personal and work-related purposes; and (c) understand the world of computers, electronics, and related technologies.
>
> *(National Commission on Excellence in Education, 1983)*

While *A Nation at Risk* declared that experts were then unable to classify "technological literacy" in unambiguous terms, the document clearly argues for such literacy to be understood in more functional understandings of computer (Aronowitz, 1985; Apple, 1992) and information (Plotnick, 1999) literacy. Technology, such as the computer, was to be seen for the novel skill sets it afforded and professional discourse began to hype the "new vocationalism" in which the needs of industry were identified as educational priorities (Grubb, 1996). Surveying this development, Petrina (2000) concludes, "By the mid-1980s in the US, technology education and technological literacy had been defined through the capitalist interests of private corporations and the state" (p. 183) and Howard Besser (1993) underscores the degree to which this period was foundational in constructing education as a marketplace.

The 1990s saw the salience and, to some degree, the consequences of such reasoning as the World Wide Web came into being and the burgeoning Internet created an electronic frontier "Dot-Com" economic boom via its commercialization amid a range of personal computing hardware and software. In the age of Microsoft and America Online, computer and information skills were indeed increasingly highly necessary. Al Gore's "data highway" of the 1970s had grown in order of magnitude to become the "information superhighway" of the Clinton presidency and the plan for a "Global Information Infrastructure" was being promoted as "a metaphor for democracy itself" (Gore, 1994). Meanwhile, hi-tech social and technological transformation took hold globally under the speculative profiteering fueled by the "new economy" (Kelly, 1998).

By the decade's end, technological literacy was clearly a challenge that could be ignored only at one's peril. Yet, in keeping with the logic of the 1980s, such literacy was again narrowly conceived in largely functional terms as "meaning computer skills and the ability to use computers and other technology to improve learning, productivity, and performance" (U.S. Department of Education, 1996). Specifically, the Department of Education located the challenge as training for the future, which should take place in schools, thereby taking the host of issues raised by the information revolution out of the public sphere proper and reducing them to standardized technical and vocational competencies for which children and youth should be trained. Further, technological literacy, conceived as "the new basic" (U.S. Department of Education, 1996) skill, became the buzz word that signified a policy program for saturating schools with computer technology as well as training for teachers and students both. Thereby, it not only guaranteed a marketplace for American ICT companies to sell their technology, but it created entirely new spheres for the extension of professional development, as teachers and administrators began to be held accountable for properly infusing computer technology into curricula.

Come the time of the Bush administration's second term, the U.S. National Education Technology Plan quoted approvingly from a high schooler who remarked, "we have technology in our blood" (U.S. Department of Education, 2004, p. 4), and the effects of two decades of debate and policy on technoliteracy was thus hailed as both a resounding technocratic success and a continuing pressure upon educational institutions to innovate up to the standards of the times.[7] Interestingly, however, the plan itself moved away from the language of technological literacy and returned to the more specific term *computer literacy* (p. 13). Still, in its overarching gesture to the No Child Left Behind Act of 2001, which had called for technology to be infused across the curriculum and for every student to be "technologically literate by the time the student finishes the eighth grade, regardless of the student's race, ethnicity, gender, family income, geographic location, or disability" (U.S. Congress, 2001), the United States demonstrated its ongoing commitment to delimit "technological literacy" in the functional and economistic terms of computer-based competencies.[8]

Technoliteracy for Sustainable Development: United Nations Models

> Who benefits, who loses? Who pays? What are the social, environmental, personal, or other consequences of following, or not following, a particular course of action? What alternative courses of action are available? These questions are not always, and perhaps only rarely, going to yield agreed answers, but addressing them is arguably fundamental to any educational program that claims to advance technological literacy for all.
>
> *(Jenkins, 1997)*

A brief examination of the United Nations' Project 2000+: Scientific and Technological Literacy for All will illuminate how technoliteracy is being conceived of at the international level. In 1993, UNESCO and eleven major international agencies launched Project 2000+ in order to prepare citizens worldwide to understand, deliberate on, and implement strategies in their everyday lives concerning "a variety of societal problems that deal with issues such as population, health, nutrition and environment, as well as sustainable development at local, national, and international levels" (Holbrook, Mukherjee, and Varma, 2000, p. 1). The project's mission underscores the degree to which the United Nations conceives of technological literacy as a social and community-building practice, as opposed to an individual economic aptitude. Further, in contradistinction to the functional computer literacy movements found in the United States context, the United Nations' goal of "scientific and technological literacy" (STL) for all should be seen as connected to affective-order precedents such as the "public understanding of science" (Royal Society, 1985) and "science-technology-society" (Power, 1987) movements that should be considered positive forerunners of the kind of ecopedagogy movement that is required today.

Though directly inspired by the social development focus of 1990s World Declaration on Education, Project 2000+ also draws in large part from the Rio Declaration on Environment and Development agreed upon at the 1992 Earth Summit (UNESCO, 1999). While the Rio Declaration itself contains ample language focused upon the economic and other developmental rights enjoyed by states, such notions of development were articulated as inseparable from the equally important goals of "environmental protection" and the conservation, protection, and restoration of "the health and integrity of the Earth's ecosystem" (United Nations, 1992). Sustainable development, to reiterate, is defined by the U.N. as "development that meets the needs of the present without compromising the ability of future generations to meet their own needs" (Brundtland, 1987), and this cannot be properly separated from radical critiques of capitalism, militarism, and other constants of our present life that structure future threats and inequality into the social system. Yet, neither can sustainable development in this formulation be separated from the ability of people everywhere to gain access and understanding of the information that can help to promote sustainability.

UNESCO does not make ICTs a centerpiece of STL projects, however. Of course, a major reason that UNESCO downplays an emphasis upon computer-related digital technology in its approach to technoliteracy is because the great majority of the illiterate populations it seeks to serve are to be found in the relatively poor and unmodernized regions of Latin America, Africa, and Asia, where an ICT focus would have less relevance at present. A more comprehensive reason, however, is that the United Nations has specifically adopted a nonfunctional commitment to literacy, conceiving of it as multiple literacies "which are diverse, have many dimensions, and are learned in different ways" (Lonsdale and McCurry, 2004, p. 5). STL, then, calls for understandings and deployments of appropriate technology—the simplest and most sustainable technological means that can meet a given end—as part of a commitment to literacy for social justice and human dignity.[9] This is far different than in the United States, where technoliteracy has generally been reduced to a program of skills and fluency in ICTs.

Still, it would be incorrect to conclude that the United Nations is anti-computer. In fact, the institution is strongly committed to utilizing ICTs as part of its literacy and development campaigns worldwide (Wagner and Kozma, 2003; Jegede, 2002) whenever appropriate. But as it is also conscious of the ability of new technologies to exacerbate divides between rich and poor, male and female, and North and South, the United Nations promotes "understanding of the nature of, and need for, scientific and technological literacy in relation to local culture and values" (UNESCO, 1999) and believes that scientific and technological literacy is best exhibited when it is embedded in prevailing traditions and cultures and meets people's real needs (Rassool, 1999). Consequently, while the United Nations finds that technoliteracy is a universal goal of mounting importance due to global technological transformation, STL programs require that various individuals, cultural groups, and states will formulate the questions through which they gain literacy differently and for diverse reasons (Holbrook, Mukherjee, and Varma, 2000).

Expanding Technoliteracy: Toward Critical Multiple Literacies

> Technical and scientific training need not be inimical to humanistic education as long as science and technology in the revolutionary society are at the service of permanent liberation, of humanization.
>
> *(Freire, 1972, p. 157)*

As this chapter has thus far demonstrated, technoliteracy should be seen as a site of struggle, as a contested terrain used by the left, right, and center of different nations to promote their own interests, and so those interested in social and ecological justice should look to define and institute their own oppositional forms. Dominant corporate and state powers, as well as reactionary and rightist groups, have been making serious use of digital and other high-technologies to educate and advance their agendas. In the political battles of the future, then, educators (along with citizens everywhere) will need to devise ways to produce and use these technologies to realize a critical oppositional ecopedagogy that serves the interests of the oppressed, as they aim at the democratic and sustainable reconstruction of technology, education, and society itself. Therefore, in addition to more traditional literacies such as the print literacies of reading and writing,[10] as well as other nondigital new literacies (Lankshear and Knobel, 2000), I want to argue that robustly critical forms of media, computer, and multimedia literacies need to be developed as digital subsets of a larger project of multiple technoliteracies (encompassing nondigital and digital modes) that furthers the ethical reconstruction of technology, literacy, and society in an era of technological revolution.

Critical Media Literacies

With the emergence of a global media culture, technoliteracy is arguably more important than ever, as media essentially are technologies. Recently, cultural studies and critical pedagogy have begun to teach us to recognize the ubiquity of media culture in contemporary society, the growing trends toward multicultural education, and the need for a media literacy that addresses the issue of multicultural and social difference (Hammer and Kellner, 2001; Kellner, 1998). Additionally, there is an expanding recognition that media representations help construct our images and understanding of the world and that education must meet the dual challenges of teaching media literacy in a multicultural society and of sensitizing students and publics to the inequities and injustices of a society based on gender, race, and class inequalities and discrimination (Kellner, 1995). Also, critical studies have pointed out the role of mainstream media in exacerbating or diminishing these inequalities, as well as the ways that media education and the production of alternative media can help create a healthy multiculturalism of diversity and strengthened democracy. While significant gains have been made, continual technological change means that those involved in theorizing and practicing media literacy confront some of the most serious difficulties and problems that face us as educators and citizens today.

It should be noted that media culture is itself a form of pedagogy that teaches proper and improper behavior, gender roles, values, and knowledge of the world (Macedo and Steinberg, 2007). Yet, people are often not aware that they are being educated and constructed by media culture, as its pedagogy is frequently invisible and subliminal. This situation calls for critical approaches that make us aware of how media construct meanings, influence and educate audiences, and impose their messages and values. A media-literate person, then, is skillful in analyzing media codes and conventions, able to criticize stereotypes, values, and ideologies, and competent to interpret the multiple meanings and messages generated by media texts. Thus, media literacy helps people to use media intelligently, to discriminate and evaluate media content, to critically dissect media forms, and to investigate media effects and uses.

Traditional literacy approaches attempted to "inoculate" people against the effects of media addiction and manipulation by cultivating high cultured book literacy and by denigrating dominant forms of media and computer culture (see Postman 1992, 1985). In contrast, the media literacy movement attempts to teach students to read, analyze, and decode media texts, in a fashion parallel to the advancement of print literacy. Critical media literacy, as outlined here, goes further still in its call for the analysis of media culture as technologies of social production and struggle, thereby teaching students to be critical of media representations and discourses, as it stresses the importance of learning to use media technologies as modes of self-expression and social activism wherever appropriate (Kellner, 1995).

Developing critical media literacy and pedagogy also involves perceiving how media like film or video can also be used positively to teach a wide range of topics, like multicultural understanding and education. If, for example, multicultural education is to champion genuine diversity and expand the curriculum, it is important both for groups excluded from mainstream education to learn about their own heritage and for dominant groups to explore the experiences and voices of minority and excluded groups. Thus, media literacy can promote a more multicultural technoliteracy, conceived as understanding and engaging the heterogeneity of cultures and subcultures that constitute an increasingly global and multicultural world (Courts, 1998; Weil, 1998).

Critical media literacy not only teaches students to learn from media, to resist media manipulation, and to use media materials in constructive ways, but it is also concerned with developing skills that will help create good citizens and make them more motivated and competent participants in social life. Critical media literacy can be connected with the project of radical democracy as it is concerned to develop technologies that will enhance political mobilization and cultural participation. In this respect, critical media literacy takes a comprehensive approach that teaches critical attitudes and provides experimental use of media as technologies of social communication and change (Hammer, 1995). The technologies of communication are becoming more and more accessible to young people and ordinary citizens, and can be used to promote education, democratic self-expression, and sustainability. Technologies that could help produce the end of participatory democracy (if not life on Earth as we know it), that often transform meaningful politics into media spectacles concerned only with a battle of images and which turn spectators into cultural zombies, could also be used to help invigorate critical debate and participation within the public sphere (Giroux, 2006; Kellner and Share, 2005) and augment the struggle against ecologically catastrophic political orders.

Critical Computer Literacies

To fully understand life in a high-tech and global corporate society, people should cultivate new forms of computer literacy that involve functional knowledge of how computers are assembled and how hardware and software may be built or repaired. But critical computer literacy must also go beyond standard technical notions. In this respect, critical computer literacy involves learning how to use computer technologies to do research and gather information, to perceive computer culture as a contested terrain containing texts, spectacles, games, and interactive multimedia, as well as to interrogate the political economy, cultural bias, and environmental effects of computer-related technologies (Park and Pellow, 2004; Grossman, 2004; Plepys, 2002; Heinonen, Jokinen, and Kaivo-oja, 2001; Bowers, 2000).

The emergent cybercultures can be seen as a discursive and political location in which students, teachers, and citizens can all intervene, engaging in discussion groups and collaborative research projects, creating websites, producing culture jamming multimedia for cultural dissemination, and cultivating novel modes of social interaction and learning that can increase community in an often isolating world. Computers can thereby enable people to actively participate in the production of culture, ranging from dialogue and debate on social and ecological issues to the creation and expression of their own sustainability organizations or movements. Thus, computers and the Internet can provide opportunities for multiple voices beyond the monolingual mass media, alternative online and offline communities, and enhanced political activism (Kahn and Kellner, 2005). However, to fully take part in this counterculture requires multiple forms of technoliteracy.

For not only are accelerated skills of print literacy necessary, which are often restricted to the growing elite of students who are privileged to attend adequate and superior public and private schools, but a critical information literacy is demanded as well. Such literacy would require learning how to distinguish between good and what Burbules and Callister (2000) identify as misinformation, malinformation, messed-up information, and mostly useless information. In this sense, information literacy is closely connected with education itself, with learning where information is archived and how it relates to the production of knowledge or critical understanding. Thus, profound questions about the relationship between power and knowledge are raised concerning the definitions of high and low-status knowledge, who gets to produce and valorize various modes of information, whose ideas get circulated and discussed, and whose in turn are co-opted, marginalized, or otherwise silenced altogether.

Critical Multimedia Literacies

With an ever-developing multimedia cyberculture, beyond popular spectacular film and television culture, visual literacy takes on increased importance. On the whole, computer screens are more graphic, multisensory, and interactive than conventional print fields, something that disconcerted many scholars not born of the computer generation when they were first confronted with the new environments. Icons, windows, peripherals, and the various clicking, linking, and constant interaction involved in computer-mediated hypertext dictate new competencies and a dramatic expansion of what traditionally counts as literacy.

Visuality is obviously crucial, compelling users to perceptively scrutinize visual fields, perceive and interact with icons and graphics, and use technical devices like a mouse or touchpad to access the desired material and field. But tactility is also important, as individuals must learn navigational skills of how to proceed from one field and screen to another, how to negotiate hypertexts and links, and how to move from one program to another if one operates, as most now do, in a window-based computer environment. Further, as voice and sound enter multimedia culture, literacies of the ear, speech, and especially *performance* (e.g., think of the YouTube, Second Life, and Twitter-fication of the Internet) also become part of the aesthetics and pedagogies of an expanded technoliteracy that should allow for multiple methods of learning.

Contemporary multimedia environments therefore necessitate a diversity of multisemiotic and multimodal interactions that involve interfacing with word and print material, images, graphics, as well as audio and video material (Hammer and Kellner, 2009, 2001). As technological convergence develops apace, individuals will need to combine the skills of critical media literacy with traditional print literacy and innovative forms of multiple literacies to access, navigate, and critically participate in multimediated reality.[11] Reading and interpreting print was the appropriate mode of literacy for an age in which the primary source of information was books and tabloids, while critical multimedia literacy entails reading and interpreting a plethora of discourse, images, spectacle, narratives, and the forms and genres of global media culture. Thus, technoliteracy in this conception involves the ability to respond effectively to modes of multimedia communication that include print, speech, visuality, tactility, sound, and performance within a hybrid field that combines these forms, all of which incorporate skills of interpretation and critique, agency and resistance.

Reconstructing Technoliteracy

> We are, indeed, designers of our social futures.
>
> *(New London Group, 1996, p. 36)*

Adequately meeting the challenge issued by the concept of technoliteracy raises questions about the design and reconstruction of technology itself. As Feenberg has long argued (1999, 1995, 1991), democratizing technology often requires its reconstruction and revisioning by individuals and, in an ecological age, this also means seriously taking up the challenges of whether humanity intends to create sustainable designs or not (Orr, 2002). "Hackers" have redesigned digital technological systems, notably starting the largely anticapitalist Open Source and Free Software movements, and indeed much of the Internet itself has been the result of individuals contributing collective knowledge and making improvements that aid various educational, political, and cultural projects. Of course, there are corporate and technical constraints to such participation in that mainstream programs and machines seek to impose their rules and abilities upon users, but part of re-visioning technoliteracy requires the very perception and transformation of those programming limits. Technoliteracy must help teach people to become more ethical producers, even more so than consumers, and thus it can help to redesign and reconstruct technology toward making it more applicable to people's needs and not just their manufactured desires.

Crucially, alternative technoliteracies must become reflective and critical, aware of the educational, social, and political assumptions involved in the restructuring of education, technology, and society currently under way. In response to the excessive hype around new media in education, it is important to maintain a critical dimension and to actively reflect upon the nature and effects of emergent technologies and the pedagogies developed to implement and utilize them. Many academic and consumer advocates of new technologies, however, eschew critique for a more purely affirmative agenda.

For instance, after an excellent discussion of emergent modes of literacy and the need to rethink education Kress (1997) argues that we must move from critique to design, beyond a negative deconstruction to more positive construction of high technology. But rather than following such modern logic of either/or, critical ecopedagogues should pursue the logic of both/and, perceiving design and critique, deconstruction and reconstruction, as collaborative and mutually supplementary rather than as antithetical choices. Certainly, we need to design alternative modes of ecopedagogy and sustainability curricula for the future, as well as to provide appropriate tools for more democratic social and cultural relations in support of a planetary community, but we need also to criticize misuse, inappropriate use, over-inflated claims, as well as exclusions and oppressions involved in the introduction of ICTs into formal education and everyday life around the world. Moreover, the critical dimension is more necessary than ever as we attempt to develop contemporary approaches to technoliteracy, and to design more emancipatory, sustainable, and democratizing technologies in the context of transnational capitalism (Giroux, 2006; Suoranta and Vaden, forthcoming). In this respect, we must be critically vigilant, always striving to practice critique and self-criticism, putting in question our assumptions, discourses, and practices about contemporary technologies, as we seek to develop multiple technoliteracies and an ecopedagogy of resistance.

In other words, people should be helped to advance the multiple technoliteracies that will allow them to understand, critique, and transform the oppressive social and cultural conditions in which they live, as they become ecoliterate, ethical, and transformative subjects as opposed to objects of technological domination and manipulation. This requires producing multiple oppositional literacies for robust critical thinking, transformative reflection, and enhancing people's capacity to engage in the production of social discourse, cultural artifacts, and political action amid a (largely corporate) technological revolution. Further, as informed and engaged subjects arise through social interactions with others, a further demand for convivial tools must come to be a part of the kinds of technoliteracy that a radical reconstruction of education now seeks to cultivate.

It cannot be stressed enough: the project of reconstructing technoliteracy must take different forms in different contexts. In almost every cultural and social situation, however, a literacy of critique should be enhanced so that citizens can name the technological and ecological system, describe and grasp the technological changes occurring as defining features of the new global order, and learn to experimentally engage in critical and oppositional practices in the interests of democratization, ecological sustainability, and progressive transformation. As part of a truly multicultural order, we need to encourage the growth and flourishing of numerous standpoints (Harding, 2004) on technoliteracy, looking out for and legitimizing counter-hegemonic needs, values, and understandings. Such would be to propound multiple technoliteracies "from below" as opposed to the largely functional, economistic, and technocratic digital technoliteracy "from above" that is favored by many industries and states. Thereby, projects for multiple technoliteracies can allow reconstructive opportunities for a better world to be forged out of the present age of unfolding technological and ecological crisis.

Notes

1   These types of ideas are far from obsolete, and there has been a continued development of them within the environmental community itself (for a leading example see the Planetwork project at: http://www.planetwork.net/background.html). For the latest articulation of how a planetary technological edifice can generate a new level of planetary literacy, see Olson and Rejeski (2007).

2   On the concept of "media spectacle" see Kellner (2005, 2003a) that builds upon Guy Debord's notion of the "society of the spectacle," which describes a media and consumer society organized around the production and consumption of images, commodities, and staged events. "Media spectacle" defines those phenomena of media technoculture that embody contemporary society's basic values, serve to initiate individuals into its way of life, and dramatize its controversies and struggles, as well as its modes of conflict resolution.

3   The idea that different forms of knowledge (e.g., different types of questions which in turn beget different answers) are produced as an oppressed group begins to achieve a collective identity vis-à-vis the social, cultural, and political issues of the day is a central insight of the critical theory known as *feminist standpoint theory* (Harding, 2004). It can be argued that this idea girds critical theory in general, and a radical formulation can be seen in Marcuse (1965), as well as in the works of Marx and Engels as Harding points out.

4   For instance, see Petrina (2000); Selfe (1999); Jenkins (1997); Waetjen (1993); Lewis and Gagel (1992); Dyrenfurth (1991); Todd (1991); Hayden (1989).

5   See Kellner (2004, 2003c, 1998); Lankshear and Snyder (2000); Petrina (2000); Luke (1997); Bromley and Apple, (1998); Tuathail and McCormack (1999); Burbules and Callister (1996); McLaren, Hammer, Sholle, and Reilly (1995).

6   Yet, stressing the social and cultural specificity of technologies, neither am I calling for the universal adoption of high technologies, nor do I link them essentially to progress as necessary stages of development. On the other hand, I urge caution against technophobic attitudes, as I favor a dialectical view of technology and society.

7   A definition of *technocracy* is offered by Kovel (1983, p. 9) as being the social order where "the logic of the machine settles into the spirit of the master. There it dresses itself up as 'value-free' technical reasoning."

8 In 2002, the International Technology Education Association issued its *Standards for Techno-logical Literacy: Content for the Study of Technology*, which intends to be definitive for the field. To be fair, at least eight of its twenty standards evoke the possibility of affective compo-nents that move beyond the functional, market-based approaches chronicled here. However, as Petrina (2000, p. 186) notes, the Director of the Technology for All Americans project involved in creating the standards declared that they were "the vital link to enhance Amer-ica's global competitiveness in the future" and so their vocational and economic concerns must be considered central.

9 In an educational context, one interested in earlier versions of STL might look to the 1960s work of figures such as Ivan Illich and Paulo Freire (see Kahn and Kellner, 2008), who offered a critique of modern developmental strategies in the Third World and called for appropriate and democratic technological change in its place.

10 I resist that technoliteracy outmodes print literacy. Indeed, in the emergent information-communication technology environment, traditional print literacy takes on increasing importance in the computer-mediated cyberworld as people need to critically scrutinize tremendous amounts of information, putting increasing emphasis on developing reading and writing abilities. Theories of secondary illiteracy, in which new media modes contribute to the complete or partial loss of existing print literacy skills due to lack of practice, demon-strates that new technologies cannot be counted upon to deliver print literacy of their own accord.

11 To critically participate in such a reality does not mean serving as its booster or even acqui-escing to its adoption in one's life. The point here is that even someone living nondigitally in relative simplicity participates increasingly in a society and world that are moving in contrary directions. My supposition here is that the refusal represented by someone having gone back to the land is augmented by her/his being knowledgeable about what is being rejected and why. This transforms place from a life formed through naive inhabitation to one based in "decolonization and reinhabitation" (Gruenewald, 2003) of the planetary commons.

References

Apple, M. (1992). Is New Technology Part of the Solution or Part of the Problem in Education? In J. Beynon and Hughie Mackay (Eds.), *Technological Literacy and the Curriculum*, pp. 105–124. London: Falmer Press.

Aronowitz, S. (1985). Why Should Johnny Read? *Village Voice Literary Supplement*, May, Vol. 13.

Besser, H. (1993). Education as Marketplace. In R. Muffoletto & N. Knupfer (Eds.), *Computers in Education: Social, Historical, and Political Perspectives*, pp. 37–60. Cresskill, NJ: Hampton Press.

Best, S. and Kellner, D. (2001).*The Postmodern Adventure: Science, Technology, and Cultural Studies at the Third Millennium.* New York and London: Guilford Press and Routledge.

Bowers, C. A. (2000). *Let Them Eat Data: How Computers Affect Education, Cultural Diversity, and the Prospects of Ecological Sustainability.* Athens: University of Georgia Press.

Bromley, H. and Apple, M. (Eds.). (1998). *Education/Technology/Power: Educational Computing as Social Practice.* Albany: State University of New York Press.

Brundtland, G. H. (1987). *Our Common Future: Report of the World Commission on Environment and Development.* Oxford: Oxford University Press.

Burbules, N. and Callister, T. (1996) Knowledge at the Crossroads. *Educational Theory*, 46(1): 23–34.

———. (2000). *Watch IT: The Risks and Promises of Information Technology.* Boulder, CO: Westview Press.

Castells, M. (1996). *The Information Age: Economy, Society and Culture. Vol. 1. The Rise of the Network Society.* Cambridge: MA: Blackwell.

Cope, B. and Kalantzis, M. (Eds.). (2000). *Multiliteracies: Literacy Learning and the Design of Social Futures.* New York: Routledge.

Courts, P. (1998). *Multicultural Literacies: Dialect, Discourses, and Diversity.* New York: Peter Lang.

Dewey, J. (1916). *Democracy and Education: An Introduction to the Philosophy of Education.* Carbondale: Southern Illinois University Press.

Dyrenfurth, M. J. (1991). Technological Literacy Synthesized. In M. J. Dyrenfurth and M. R. Kozak (Eds.), *Technological literacy*, pp. 138–186. Peoria, IL: Glencoe, McGraw-Hill.

Feenberg, A. (1991). *Critical Theory of Technology.* New York: Oxford University Press.

———. (1995). *Alternative Modernity.* Berkeley: University of California Press.

———. (1999). *Questioning Technology.* New York: Routledge.

Freire, P. (1972). *Pedagogy of the Oppressed.* New York: Herder & Herder.

Freire, P. and Macedo, D. (1987). *Literacy: Reading the Word and the World.* Westport, CT: Bergin & Garvey.

Giroux, H. (2006). *Beyond the Spectacle of Terrorism: Global Uncertainty and the Challenge of the New Media.* Boulder, CO: Paradigm.

Gore, A. (1994). Remarks Prepared for Delivery. Speech at the International Telecommunications Union (Buenos Aires, Argentina). Available at: www.itu.int/itudoc/itu-d/wtdc/wtdc1994/speech/gore_ww2.doc.

Grossman, E. (2004). High-tech Wasteland, *Orion*, July/August. Available at: http://www.orion-online.org/pages/om/04-4om/Grossman.html.

Grubb, W.N. (1996). The New Vocationalism—What It Is, What It Could Be. *Phi Delta Kappan*, 77(8): 535–546.

Gruenewald, D. (2003). The Best of Both Worlds: A Critical Pedagogy of Place. *Educational Researcher,* 32(4): 3–12.

Hammer, R. (1995) Strategies for Media Literacy. In P. McLaren, R. Hammer, D. Sholle, and S. Reilly (Eds.), *Rethinking Media Literacy: A Critical Pedagogy of Representation*, pp. 225–235. New York: Peter Lang.

Hammer, R. and Kellner, D. (2001). Multimedia Pedagogy and Multicultural Education for the New Millennium. *Current Issues in Education*, 4(2). Available at: http://cie.ed.asu.edu/volume4/number2/.

Harding, S. (Ed.). (2004). *The Feminist Standpoint Theory Reader: Intellectual and Political Controversies.* New York: Routledge.

Hayden, M. (1989). What is Technological Literacy? Bulletin of Science. *Technology and Society*, 119: 220–233.

Heinonen, S., Jokinen, P., and Kaivo-oja, J. (2001). The Ecological Transparency of the Information Society. *Futures*, 33: 319–337.

Hickman, L. (2001). *Philosophical Tools for Technological Culture.* Bloomington: Indiana University Press.

Holbrook, J., Mukherjee, A., and Varma, V. S. (Eds.). (2000). *Scientific and Technological Literacy for All.* UNESCO and International Council of Associations for Science Education. Delhi, India: Center for Science Education and Communication.

Illich, I. (1973). *Tools for Conviviality.* New York: Harper & Row.

Jegede, O. (2002). An Integrated ICT-Support for ODL in Nigeria: the vision, the mission and the journey so far. Paper prepared for the LEARNTEC-UNESCO 2002 Global Forum on Learning Technology. Karlsruhe, Germany.

Jenkins, E. (1997). Technological Literacy: concepts and constructs, *Journal of Technology Studies*, 23(1): 2–5.

Kahn, R., and Kellner, D. (2005). Oppositional Politics and the Internet: A Critical/Reconstructive Approach. *Cultural Politics*, 1(1): 75–100.

———. (2006). "Reconstructing Technoliteracy: A Multiple Literacies Approach." In J. Dakers (Ed.), *Defining Technological Literacy: Towards an Epistemological Framework*, pp. 231–248. London: Palgrave.

———. (2008). Paulo Freire and Ivan Illich: Technology, Politics, and the Reconstruction of Education. In P. Noguera and C. Torres (Eds.), *Social Justice Education for Teachers: Paulo Freire and the Possible Dream,* pp. 13–34. Urbana: University of Illinois Press.

Kellner, D. (1989). *Critical Theory, Marxism and Modernity*. Baltimore: Johns Hopkins University Press.

———. (1995). *Media Culture: Identity and Politics Between the Modern and the Postmodern*. New York: Routledge.

———. (1998). Multiple Literacies and Critical Pedagogy in a Multicultural Society. *Educational Theory*, 48: 103–122.

———. (2000). Globalization and New Social Movements: Lessons for Critical Theory and Pedagogy. In N. Burbules and C. A. Torres (Eds.), *Globalization and Education: Critical Perspectives*. New York: Routledge.

———. (2002). Theorizing Globalization, *Sociological Theory*, 20 (3, November): 285–305.

———. (2003a). *Media Spectacle*. London: Routledge.

———. (2003b). *From 9/11 to Terror War: The Dangers of the Bush Legacy*. Lanham, MD: Rowman & Littlefield.

———. (2003c). Toward a Critical Theory of Education, *Democracy & Nature*, 9(1): 51–64.

———. (2004). Technological Transformation, Multiple Literacies, and the Re-visioning of Education. *E-Learning*, 1(1): 9–37.

———. (2005). *Media Spectacle and the Crisis of Democracy: Terrorism, War, and Election Battles*. Boulder, CO: Paradigm.

Kellner, D. and J. Share. 2005. Toward Critical Media Literacy: Core Concepts, Debates, Organizations and Policies. *Discourse: Studies in the Cultural Politics of Education*. University of Queensland, Australia: Routledge.

Kelly, K. (1998). *New Rules for the New Economy*. London: Fourth Estate.

Kovel, J. (1983). Theses on Technocracy. *Telos*, 54 (Winter): 155–161.

Kress, G. (1997). Visual and Verbal Modes of Representation in Electronically Mediated Communication: The Potentials of New Forms of Text. In I. Snyder (Ed.), *Page to Screen: Taking Literacy into the Electronic Era*, pp. 53–79. Sydney, Australia: Allen & Unwin.

Lankshear, C. and Knobel, M. (2000). Mapping Postmodern Literacies: A Preliminary Chart, *Journal of Literacy and Technology*, 1(1) (Fall). Available at: http://www.literacyandtechnology.org/v1n1/lk.html.

Lankshear, C. and Snyder, I. (2000). *Teachers and Technoliteracy: Managing Literacy, Technology and Learning in Schools*. Sydney, Australia: Allen & Unwin.

Lewis, T. and Gagel, C. (1992). Technological Literacy: A Critical Analysis. *Journal of Curriculum Studies*, 24(2): 117–138.

Lonsdale, M. and McCurry, D. (2004). *Literacy in the New Millennium*. Adelaide, Australia: NCVER.

Luke, C. (1997). *Technological Literacy*. Melbourne, Australia: National Languages & Literacy Institute. Adult Literacy Network.

———. (2000). Cyber-schooling and Technological Change: Multiliteracies for New Times. In B. Cope and M. Kalantzis (Eds.), *Multiliteracies: Literacy, Learning, and the Design of Social Futures*, pp. 69–105. South Yarra, Australia: Macmillan.

Macedo, D. and S. Steinberg (2007). *Media Literacy*. New York: Peter Lang.

Marcuse, H. (1969) [1965]. Repressive Tolerance. In R. P. Wolff, B. Moore, and H. Marcuse (Eds.), *A Critique of Pure Tolerance*. Boston: Beacon Press.

McLaren, R. Hammer, D., Sholle, and S. Reilly (1995). *Rethinking Media Literacy: A Critical Pedagogy of Representation*. New York: Peter Lang.

McLuhan, M. (1964). *Understanding Media: The Extensions of Man*. New York: Signet Books.

National Commission on Excellence in Education. (1983). *A Nation at Risk: the imperative for educational reform*. Washington, DC: US Government Printing Office.

New London Group. (1996). A Pedagogy of Multiliteracies: Designing Social Futures. *Harvard Educational Review*, 66: 60–92.

Olsen, R. and Rejeski, D. (Eds.). (2007). *Environmentalism and the Technologies of Tomorrow: Shaping the Next Industrial Revolution*. Washington, DC: Island Press.

Park, Lisa S.-H. and Pellow, D. (2004). Racial Formation, Environmental Racism, and the Emergence of Silicon Valley. *Ethnicities*, 4(3): 403–424.

Pearson, G. and Young, A. T. (2002). *Technically Speaking: Why All Americans Need to Know More About Technology*. Washington, DC: National Academies Press.

Petrina, S. (2000). The Politics of Technological Literacy. *International Journal of Technology and Design Education*, 10(2): 181–206.

Plepys, A. (2002). The Grey Side of ICT. *Environmental Impact Assessment Review*, 22: 509–523.

Plotnick, E. (1999). Information Literacy. ERIC Clearinghouse on Information and Technology, Syracuse University. ED-427777.

Postman, N. (1985). *Amusing Ourselves to Death*. New York: Viking-Penguin.

———. (1992). *Technopolis: the Surrender of Culture to Technology*. New York: Random House.

Power, C. (1987). Science and Technology Towards Informed Citizenship. *Castme Journal*, 7(3): 5–18.

Rassool, N. (1999). *Literacy for Sustainable Development in the Age of Information*. London: Multilingual Matters.

Royal Society. (1985). *The Public Understanding of Science*. London: Royal Society.

Selfe, C. (1999). *Technology and Literacy in the Twenty-First Century: The Importance of Paying Attention*. Carbondale: Southern Illinois University Press.

Street, B. (1984). *Literacy in Theory and Practice*. Cambridge: Cambridge University Press.

Suppes, P. (1968). Computer Technology and the Future of Education. *Phi Delta Kappan*, April: 420–423.

Suoranta, J. and Vaden, T. (Forthcoming). *Wikiworld*. London: Pluto Press.

Teilhard de Chardin, P. 1965. *The Phenomenon of Man*. New York: Harper and Row.

Todd, R. D. (1991). The Natures and Challenges of Technological Literacy. In M. J. Dyrenfurth and M. R. Kozak (Eds.), *Technological Literacy*, pp. 10–27. Peoria, IL: Glencoe, McGraw-Hill.

Tuathail, G. and McCormack, D. (1999). The Technoliteracy Challenge: Teaching Globalization Using the Internet. *Journal of Geography in Higher Education*, 22: 347–361.

UNESCO. (1994). *The Project 2000+ Declaration: The Way Forward*. Paris: UNESCO.

UNESCO. (1999). *Science and Technology Education: Philosophy of Project 2000+*. Paris: Association for Science Education.

United Nations. (1992). *Report of the United Nations Conference on Environment and Development*. Rio de Janeiro, Brazil: UNCED.

U.S. Congress. (2001). No Child Left Behind Act of 2001. Public Law 107-110. Washington, DC.

U.S. Department of Education. (1996). Getting America's Students Ready for the 21st Century. *Meeting the Technology Literacy Challenge, a Report to the Nation on Technology and Education*. Washington, DC: National Education Technology Plan.

U.S. Department of Education. (2004). *Toward a New Golden Age in American Education: How the Internet, the Law, and Today's Students Are Revolutionizing Expectations*. Washington, DC: National Education Technology Plan.

Waetjen, W. (1993). Technological Literacy Reconsidered. *Journal of Technology Education*, 4(2): 5–11.

Wagner, D. and Kozma, R. (2003). New Technologies for Literacy and Adult Education: A Global Perspective. Paper presented at the NCAL/OECD International Roundtable, Philadelphia. Available at: http://www.literacy.org/ICTconf/PhilaRT_wagner_kozma_final.pdf.

Wajcman, J. (2004). *Technofeminism*. Malden, MA: Polity Press.

Weil, D. (1998). *Toward a Critical Multicultural Literacy*. New York: Peter Lang.

Wells, H. G. (1938). *World Brain*. New York: Doubleday.

5

LEARNING ENVIRONMENT AND DIGITAL LITERACY

A Mismatch or a Possibility from Finnish Teachers' and Students' Perspectives

Liisa Ilomäki, Peppi Taalas, and Minna Lakkala

Introduction

Young people today live in a digitalized world, which is characterized by ubiquitous and blended technology. The mobile tools, virtual applications and traditional computers form "an information ecology," as Nardi and O'Day (1999) call it, by which they mean a system of people, practices, values and technology in a certain environment. Such an "ecosystem" technology is integrated into a wide variety of existing practices and manners, and users and tools that complement each other. In the lives of young people, the Internet has a central and multi-faceted role: it is a way to gather information and it is a tool and channel for virtual collaboration and communication through new applications of social media. It is also a space for leisure time activities, such as virtual collaborative games. Moreover, the Internet is an extensive arena for publishing, sharing and commenting on various kinds of texts, pieces of art, music and videos. Buckingham (2007) and Bryant (2007) emphasized that in this new reality, the social affordances and practices are new and exciting, not the technology itself. These new applications are not only tools that replace some earlier analogue practices; they alter the basic foundations of our existing conceptions of own cultural basis and values, attitudes and activities.

As a consequence of the digitalization of the lives of young people, their digital worlds in and outside of school are quite different. The very different use ICT in school and outside school is discussed and highlighted in several studies: free time use of media is more active, richer, more extensive and more recreational oriented than is school use (Ching, Basham, & Fang, 2005; Ilomäki & Kankaanranta, 2008; Lewin et al., 2004; Luukka et al., 2008; Pedersen et al., 2006). In school, the informal learning of digital skills is still typically neglected and the curriculum does not reflect the changes in the subject of domains. There is a need for a general revision of the curriculum, not only in some specific subject areas, as emphasized by Erstad (2010) and Hague and Williamson (2009). In the most recent policy papers, the importance of relevant digital competencies is an aim of education as well (OECD, 2010).

The aim of the chapter is to discuss the characteristics of a learning environment that supports and promotes digital competence in a wide context of uses and bridges some of the gaps of digital literacy in formal and informal educational settings. We use two Finnish studies as examples to demonstrate the connection between the learning activities and the digital competence they promote. We will also offer suggestions about new approaches to teaching practices that encourage an integration of informal and formal learning as well as improve the academic oriented digital skills; that is, digital skills that also improve academic achievement.

Digital Competence—an Evolving Concept

Digital competence is a novel term that describes technology-related competence. In recent years, several terms have been used to describe the skills and competence of using digital technologies, such as ICT skills, technology skills, information technology skills, 21st century skills, information literacy, digital literacy, and digital skills. In addition, the word competence has recently been substituted with the word skills as competence refers to a wider scope of skills and includes also beliefs, attitudes and values. The terms are often used as synonyms interchangeably; e.g., digital competence instead of digital literacy and vice versa. Sometimes the terms are more specific and narrow by nature, e.g., Internet skills, referring only to a limited area of digital technology, while some terms are expanded to include also media and literacy, e.g., media literacy skills or digital literacy. The wide variety of terms reflects the rapid development of technologies but also the different areas of interest, such as library studies or computer science (Jones-Kavalier & Flannigan, 2008). Moreover, technological changes in society and culture have a great effect on the evolution of the terminology too. It is to be expected that the content and the scope of the terms will continue to change: Ala-Mutka, Punie, and Redecker (2008) recommended in their policy-related paper that the approaches should be dynamic and regularly revised because of the evolving technologies and their use in society. The OECD (2010) in turn recommends that governments should make an effort to identify and conceptualise the required set of skills and competences that can then be incorporated into the educational standards. In response to this recommendation, there are several national projects that seek to define and explore these national standards.

There do not yet exist any general, research-based agreements on or a justification of the concepts, as van Deursen and van Dijk (2009) stated when referring to the terms and the various interpretations of Internet skills and digital skills (see also Aviram & Eshet-Alkalai, 2006; Jones-Kavalier & Flannigan, 2008). This lack of theoretical justification results to different definitions that ignore the full range of skills and focus only on some limited aspects of the phenomenon, often for practical purposes of educators and designers (Aviram & Eshet-Alkalai, 2006). In addition, *digital competence* is a policy-related concept, sometimes used in a normative way, representing goals to be achieved.

Digital literacy (or *digital literacies*) is often used as a synonym for digital competence. This concept has a longer tradition than digital competence, associated with media literacy (Erstad, 2010). The elaboration of this concept is related to both traditional literacy and to media studies. An example of such a definition is the one that Jones-Kavalier and Flannigan (2008) suggested: Digital literacy represents a person's ability to perform tasks effectively in a digital environment; *digital* means information represented in numeric form and primarily use by a computer, and *literacy* includes the ability to read and interpret media, to reproduce data and images through digital manipulation and to evaluate and apply new knowledge gained from digital environments. Aviram and Eshet-Alkalai (2006) described digital literacy as a combination of technical-procedural, cognitive and emotional-social skills. Sefton-Green, Nixon, and Erstad (2009) explained that the concept is used to describe our engagement with digital technologies as they mediate many of our social interactions; they said, however, that the literacies associated with participation in digital practices and cultures are complex. The authors regarded the concept *digital literacy* fundamentally useful but stated that it needs to be analysed far more at the intersection of formal and informal learning domains.

It is common to regard the term digital literacy as something generic and wide; for example Eshet-Alkali and Amichai-Hamburger (2004) gave a broad meaning to the term: they suggested digital literacy to consist of five major digital skills: photo-visual skills ("reading" instructions from graphical displays), reproduction skills (utilizing digital reproduction to create new, meaningful materials from existing ones), branching skills (constructing knowledge from non-linear, hypertextual navigation), information skills (evaluating the quality and validity of information), and socio-emotional skills (understanding the "rules" that prevail in cyberspace and applying this understanding in online cyberspace communication). In addition, one more skill was added to the list: real-time thinking skill (the ability to process and evaluate large volumes of information in real time (Aviram & Eshet-Alkalai, 2006). Erstad (2010) broadened digital literacy to media literacy and proposed the following aspects of media literacies as part of school-based learning: (1) basic skills, (2) media as an object of analysis, (3) knowledge building in subject-domains, (4) learning strategies, and (5) digital *bildung*/cultural competence.

Another term close to *digital competence* is *literacy skills for the twenty-first century*, sometimes called *21st-century skills*. Jenkins, Clinton, Purushotma, Robinson,

& Weigel (2006) defined these as a set of skills that enable participation in the new communities emerging within a networked society.

Digital Divide Among the Young in the Western World

Digital divide was originally used to describe the access (or the lack thereof) of different social groups to digital services and their ability to make use of various digital possibilities (see Facer, 2002; Kucukaydin & Tisdell, 2008; Norris, 2001; van Dijk & Hacker, 2003), but at present, the concept also emphasizes social and cultural circumstances and competences in using digital resources. In this present line of thinking, it is the *quality of use* that creates the gap.

Several studies demonstrate a digital divide based on economic factors also among children and young people concerning the availability of resources for their ICT use (e.g., national studies in Greece by Vekiri and Chronaki, 2008, and in the UK by ImpaCT2, 2001). Although these digital gaps are less notice-able, they exist on several levels—between countries, within a country between schools and social classes and even within school classes. Gaps can also exist among tech-savvy students as some of them may not be able to use technology to guide their lives and learning, as their skills are mostly limited to recreational uses of media. Kucukaydin and Tisdell (2008) regarded this gap as one of the indicators of the overall educational inequalities in the society; moreover, they suggested that the diffusion of IT not only adds another layer on top of existing inequalities, but it also creates inequities in itself, to which they referred to as "digital inequities.. Similarly, Erstad (2006) asked whether the digital divide is "between those who know how to operate the technology and those who do not, and between those who use the technology to gain relevant knowledge for education and those who use it for other purposes" (p. 417). Some new evidence confirms these expectations. In a study about content creation and sharing on the Internet, Hargittai and Walejko (2008) found that the frequency of creating and sharing on-line content was dependent on social background (the higher, the more activity); they called this "participation divide." There-fore, in practice the digital gap among children and young people is less based on access to technology, but on the nature of activities in using technology. For instance, playing digital games improves digital competence, but working with knowledge and content, like creating wiki-pages, participation in artistic activities or comparing information, improves also academic skills. The ability and competence of participation as digital literacy was emphasized by Hague and Williamson (2009). In their review, digitally literate students will be able to judge and choose what to participate in and how to participate in the digi-tal culture. One aim for formal education could be to decrease this type of a digital gap and to prevent new marginalizing mechanisms by improving digital competence in school and by helping all students participate in a digital culture (Erstad, 2010; Hague & Williamson, 2009; OECD, 2010).

Digital Skills in Formal Schooling

In the Nordic countries, digital skills are gradually gaining a position among the essential cultural skills, like reading and writing (Pedersen et al., 2006). Unfortunately, several studies indicate that the use of ICT in formal schooling only seldom utilizes the possibilities of new technologies, and moreover, only seldom supports young learners to achieve necessary digital skills that foster also their academic skills. Students', especially boys', ICT skills are mainly acquired in informal learning contexts, at home and with friends. However, informal learning often means insufficient or odd ways of working, and especially the information-processing skills do not necessarily improve and develop by themselves: students' searching procedures are inefficient and they need more systematic guidance to develop them (Coleman, 2005; Ruthven, Hennessy, & Deaney, 2005). As an example of missing/insufficient information skills, Kiili, Laurinen, and Marttunen (2008–2009) found that most of the upper secondary school students only seldom evaluated the credibility of information, and the evaluation of relevance was more important than the evaluation of credibility. Some students did not find relevant and correct information. Further, the Internet is often used infrequently and mainly for information search without students practicing information organization and analysis (Gibson & Oberg, 2004; Jedeskog & Nissen, 2004), with students being more often consumers than producers, working more often alone than collaboratively (Jedeskog & Nissen, 2004; Pedersen et al., 2006). Jedeskog and Nissen (2004) reported that students still worked with facts and specific skills development instead of aiming at understanding the matter at hand, e.g., through collaborative discussion. Twist and Withers (2007) claimed that the formal education system misses the opportunity to provide useful, contextual instruction which is invaluable for young people's assimilation of new technologies, and their building of digital literacy skills.

In contrast, there are some reported examples of good practices to foster digital skills in the school context. In her study, Rantala (2009) described how various digital applications were used for a school task in a way that combined the school-based subject content, student role and teacher authority with out-school digital practices, such as multitasking, mixing media and modalities and knowledge creation. Rantala suggested that to promote digital literacies in formal education, we should understand them as central school practices, and learn how to promote better school-based digital literacies. Walsh (2007) described an action research study in which the aim was to incorporate and extend the use of digital technologies from students' out-of-school repertoires of practice to school activities. He reported changes, first, in his own understanding; he (the teacher) became better acquainted with the concept of multimodality and possibilities of including texts from youth digital culture into his own teaching, and second, a shift of focus from traditional literacy instruction where students imitated literacy practices the teacher had modeled for them, to students becoming inventors/designers of new genres. Mills (2010) had collected results of learning outcomes after integrating new digital media into the official literacy curricula. The results showed that the content of literacy studies was expanded to include digital media, and this new literacy was linked more closely with the students' everyday life: to popular culture, recreational contexts, and digital art.

Many researchers seem to share the opinion that the development of digital competence is best supported by pedagogical methods that include rich and integrated use of various technical tools, and a wide range of activities that are based on complex and challenging tasks, such as students' own knowledge creation or product construction, solving multidisciplinary problems, collaborative activities (Labbo, 2006; Pruulmann-Vengerfeldt, Kalmus, & Runnel, 2008; Tierney, Bond, & Bresler, 2006), or project work (Erstad, 2010). Competencies related to technology should not be seen as too being narrow skills that are mere mechanical skills of using a specific software application. Likewise, also the methods for learning such skills require practicing them in settings where multiple technological tools are used in an integrated way in "authentic," complex tasks and for real life purposes as much as possible. Examples of such activities and tasks are rapid prototyping with realistic resources and tools (Dlodlo & Beyers, 2009); problem-solving games that give student teams complex, real-life contextualized problems asking them to systematically use various information sources to create solutions (Turcsányi-Szabó, Bedő, & Pluhár, 2006); or digital storytelling (Robin, 2008).

Finnish Examples: Digital Literacy and Pedagogical Practices

In this section, we present results from two Finnish studies concerning ICT skills, use and competence both in formal and informal educational settings. The studies are: (1) ToLP, Towards Future Literacy Pedagogies, a Finland's Academy funded project that Examined Finnish 9th graders' and teachers' literacy practices in and out-of-school contexts (2006–2009); and (2) FICTUP, Fostering ICT Usages in pedagogical Practices (2009–2010), an EU-supported project (http://fictup.inpl-nancy.fr/index.php/Main_Page) in which two Finnish teachers, among other European teachers, conducted projects using ICT together with their classes. ToLP outlines the general situation in the comprehensive schools with respect to digital and analogue literacy practices. FICTUP presents results of teachers' practices that support the improvement of digital literacy.

1. ToLP, Towards Future Literacy Pedagogies

The project dealt with literacy practices of Finnish students and mother tongue and foreign language teachers. The project aimed to explore pedagogies and teaching practices that prepare young people for the literacy challenges of a globalized, networked and culturally diverse world and to develop proposals for interventions in teaching, curriculum planning, assessment, and teacher education.

The project consisted of both quantitative and qualitative research. A large survey was conducted in spring 2006 on a representative sample of 9th-grade pupils (15-year-olds) and their language teachers. Information was collected on current literacy practices, media and text choices, teaching practices and prevailing attitudes towards literacy. The survey replies were received from about 1,700 pupils from 102 Finnish-speaking lower secondary schools and 740 mother tongue (MT) and foreign language (FL) teachers.[1] Response rates were 80 percent for the pupils and 40 percent for the teachers. The surveys of teachers and pupils were to a feasible degree identical despite the fact that the pupil survey offered more concrete phrasing in certain questions.

The questions about materials used in language classrooms took place in the second part of the survey, and the use of media in free time in the third part. These questions related to the themes, such as materials used in mother tongue and foreign language classroom, materials used in classrooms of other subjects, media used in free time, time spent daily on using various media. Both the teachers and pupils were also asked about their media and technology skills and their improvement needs. Media-related questions about attitudes and beliefs were phrased as statements that the respondents reacted to on a 4-point Likert scale. These included statements such as "The Internet is a valuable learning environment," "It is important to discuss pupils' free time media use in the classroom," and "Playing games is useful for learning languages". There were altogether 62 (for teachers) and 48 (for pupils) thematically organised attitude statements.

The results (see Luukka et al., 2008; Taalas, Tarnanen, Kauppinen, & Pöyhönen, 2008) indicated clearly that the gap between the in-school activities and out-of-school activities is wide. If we look at free time use of the new media between the students and teachers, it becomes very apparent that they, on a larger scale, represent very different approaches. For the students, the new media is the most important way of spending time. They spend a lot of time in various online communities and/or playing online games. Even if there are clear differences between the girls and boys, they still have a very strong online presence. Dedicated learning sites are not very frequently used, but many of the sites the pupils visit are in other languages than their mother tongue. This fact alone is significant for foreign language teaching. In very few occasions, however, were these sites and student activities discussed in the language classroom.

Only less than 6% of the pupils reported to not using any online resources. The teachers' free time media use is more instrumental; there is a practical purpose for most of the use. They use the Internet for finding information, taking care of certain everyday chores (banking, checking time tables, etc.) whereas the pupils' use is mainly social and relates to their hobbies. Online gaming is typical for boys mostly, more than half of the girls (60%) do not play, and the teachers play very little.

When we look at the classroom, the picture is very analogue. For 98% of the FL teachers, the study book is the primary material used and the exercise book follows at a strong second place (95%). For 93% of the MT teachers, the study book is the primary material and fiction comes second (90%). The high percentage for fiction is explained by the fact that the subject is actually "Mother tongue and literature." Newspapers are used in MT teaching (as reported by 59% teachers). In the foreign language classroom, the add-on audio and visual materials that come with the study book are frequently used by 93% of the teachers. The Finnish learning materials are usually of very high quality so these figures are not problematic per se. The challenge is to expand these study books to include more varied activities and offer more active participation for the students. The other types of materials fall clearly behind the "regular" materials and especially the various digital resources are used very sparingly in teaching. Of the MT teachers, 44% reported very infrequent use of various online learning materials, 35% used other Web pages, and 51% used games or other learning materials rarely. The situation is very similar for the foreign language teachers: 44% used various online materials seldom, and Web pages were used rarely by 47% of the teachers. The FL teachers used games and learning software a little bit more than the MT teachers as 51% reported using these resources sometimes. As many as 32% of the MT teachers reported using them rarely. The materials pupils read or write in their free time are rarely used in the classroom. In all, 36% of the MT teachers reported integrating pupils' writings into teaching sometimes, and 39% of the FL teachers never integrate pupils' writings produced in their free time. This is a notable point as the curriculum for mother tongue teaching specifically emphasises the pupils' voice and text as the point of departure for teaching.

In the Lankshear and Knobel (2006) terminology, the results indicate strongly that the school still lives in the old mindset where information exists in a printed book space and where expertise lies with recognised authorities and individuals. This old mindset is contrasted with a new mindset where information is fluid and cannot be owned, activity is within groups where expertise is established and distributed. It seems that the students' free time activities can well be placed within the new mindset as their existence in the digital worlds is not ruled and regulated by the current formal school order.

2. FICTUP, Fostering ICT Usages in Pedagogical Practices: Experienced Teachers Applying ICT in Their Classrooms

The FICTUP project aimed at transforming expert teachers' pedagogical practices with technology through written scenarios, short videos and tutoring. The project was conducted on a European level, and it had partners in several European countries. We concentrate in this chapter on the two Finnish cases in which two primary school teachers in Finland designed pedagogical scenarios and carried them out in their classrooms. In the first case, students conducted an inquiry project in teams, and in the second case, students learnt the principles of publishing through making a Web journal for their school.

Teachers were experienced with pedagogical uses of ICT, they both trained other teachers to use various applications and various pedagogical practices with ICT, and they had participated in various ICT development projects. They both had also previously collaborated with educational researchers, and they were chosen for FICTUP because of their expertise in the pedagogical uses of ICT. The cases were designed and conducted by teachers themselves, and the cases represented ordinary practices of these teachers. (Detailed written description of the classroom projects and related video clips of the teacher's guidance practices are available at http://www.fictup-project.eu/index.php/ Pedagogical_scenarios.) Some results of the study are published by Lakkala and Ilomäki (2010a, 2010b).

Case 1: Exploring Growth Factors through Inquiry

In the project, primary school students (9 to10 years of age) studied wild courtyard plants and practiced the construction of a simple experimental design related to growth factors. They carried out an inquiry project in small groups, practicing scientific skills such as formulation of research questions and hypotheses, information search, making and documenting observations, and writing and commenting scientific explanations. The duration of the educational unit was ten lessons. A Web-based collaboration system (Fronter; http://com. fronter.info/) was used for structuring the inquiry process through working spaces and written instructions created by the teacher, for collaboratively sharing and commenting on ideas and explanations, for documenting the research process and presenting the results, and for sharing information resources.

The educational objectives of the project related to learning the subject domain content (to understand the role of growth factors for wild courtyard plants) and also to improving more general skills, such as native language and writing skills, information search and categorisation of knowledge, science skills, and collaboration skills.

The inquiry process had various phases in which the students took turns in working alone (when producing research questions and commenting on others' questions and explanations), in pairs (when searching for information from literary sources) and in teams of four (when examining the courtyard plants, writing explanations to observations and presenting the outcomes). Varying tools of the Web-based collaboration system were used during the process for documenting and sharing all ideas and contributions, depending on the nature and requirements of the activity in each phase.

During the project, the following *digital skills* were fostered through student activities, organised and scaffolded by the teacher:

• *Communication and interaction practices through Web technology.* Students used a virtual brainstorming tool for generating starting questions for the research projects, and discussion forums for sharing and commenting on their scientific explanations.
• *Understanding and improving skills for collaborative knowledge production.* Each student team made a shared project documentation of their research using an editable Web document. In addition to writing texts, they also constructed a simple table about their research results in the Web document.
• *Knowledge seeking and knowledge application skills.* The students searched for relevant information from a textual, digital information source to add explanations from authoritative sources in their research document. They were also provided with a link to a video in the Web relating to their project theme.
• *Technical digital skills*: The students' learned to use the Web as an information source and various functionalities of the Web-based collaboration system. During computer sessions, the students' managed multiple working spaces in the computer (Windows desktop, browser) and in the Web-based system (instructions page, brainstorming, discussion forums, editable Web documents) and constantly moved between them. They also practiced how to work by following written instructions instead of leaning on the teacher's oral instructions.

There were various elements in the way the teacher described designing the educational unit and scaffolding student work during the process, which can be considered to have created a supportive learning environment for improving students' digital literary skills:

• *The well-structured pedagogical infrastructure* (see Lakkala, Ilomäki, & Kosonen, 2010). The teacher had structured the pedagogical processes to follow a collaborative inquiry model; this model was explained to the students in each phase by a short general guidance.
• *Engaging students in a complex and challenging task.* The teacher counted on the students to be capable of carrying out a relatively complex, overarching inquiry process that simulated inquiry practices seen in professional inquiry teams. He also gave students much responsibility in their group work.
• *The teacher's deliberate guidance.* In every working phase, the teacher gave explicit recommendations and guidelines for appropriate and effective ways of working and collaboration, and also made sure that the students worked

in a proper way. During the computer sessions, the teacher walked around the classroom and checked if any groups needed coaching in effective technological, knowledge and collaboration practices.

- *Reflecting the working process for improving students' practices.* The teacher modelled the working strategies through cumulative guidelines made available in the Web-based environment and gradually encouraged the students to follow the guidelines to guide their own learning process. He also intervened in the students' processes of self-evaluation and corrective actions in their writing and commenting practices during the online discussions when he noticed that the practices needed improvement.
- *Meaningful and challenging multimodal technical environment.* The teacher introduced the students to versatile tools and taught them concrete practices in using the different tools for different purposes and for managing the multiple working spaces.

Case 2: School Children's Web Journal

During the project, 11- to 12-year-old primary school students created stories for a virtual school magazine. The project lasted for six weeks. Students worked in school two hours each week for the project, but spent also time for the project at home, during their free time. Students worked with the Magazine Factory (www.mazinefactory.edu.fi/), a free publishing application for schools. Besides that, they used also digital Notepad, digital cameras and interactive whiteboards. This was the first time that students practiced this kind of work, but they had used various ICT applications for learning before.

The aims of the project were, first, to get acquainted with the principles of publishing a journal, creating a Web journal and practicing editorial tasks, and second, to develop skills for creating and developing digital materials through practicing writing for a story in the journal, practicing shooting with digital camera and using image processing, and pasting pictures and text in a publishing software.

The students worked in pairs or small teams which were responsible for the practical work for creating stories. They decided on the themes, wrote the stories, took digital pictures, and they also made some proposals for layouts for their stories, although the teacher was the "head editor." Moreover, they evaluated the outcomes and the working process throughout the project. The teacher's role was to organise the pedagogical setting, to give general orientation for the different steps of the process, and to guide students when needed.

During the project, the following *digital skills* were fostered through student activities, organised and scaffolded by the teacher:

- *Writing practices with technology.* Students planned and brainstormed their texts and topics, they improved and edited their stories based on feedback from other students; and they wrote for an authentic audience, which they also kept in mind throughout the process.

- *Understanding and improving skills for virtual creation.* Students were not merely users of the Internet but also content producers as they created and published stories and pictures on the Internet.
- *Improving understanding about virtual contents and journals especially.* Students worked as an "editorial team" and they planned what to publish with the help of examples in existing virtual journals.
- *Technical digital skills.* Students used Notepad for writing, moved text elements around in the journal template, used a digital camera as well as transferred pictures from the camera to a computer and pasted them in the journal template.

Essential elements for supporting the digital competence in the learning environment were the following:

- *The well-structured pedagogical infrastructure* (see Lakkala et al., 2010). The teacher had structured the pedagogical processes to follow a true process of publishing a journal; this structure was made clear to students in the beginning of each phase by a short general guidance.
- *Teacher's deliberate guidance.* The teacher guided new skills for each group when they needed them in their own process, not in a general manner for everybody. Furthermore, the teacher let the students be the active users of technology and new skills, although he was available for help and only gave oral instructions.
- *Supporting ownership.* The students were allowed to choose the topic for their story according to their own interests, which increased feelings of ownership in the work and integrated school work in the students' everyday life.
- *Reflecting the working process for improving the future outcomes.* There were explicit phases included in the working process were students' were directed to purposefully evaluate and reflect on the outcomes: to peer review the first article drafts and to be active in the final evaluation session where the final articles, group work and individual contributions were evaluated. The final evaluation process was made visible to all students by using the interactive white board for writing notes during the discussion.
- *Connecting formal school work to everyday life.* The journal aimed to be an open publication also available for the outside world beyond the school; mainly to families and friends, of course, and this was also emphasized by the teacher several times during the process. In addition, the teacher encouraged students to continue writing stories in their free time and after the school project was over. The technology that was used was everyday technology (e.g., digital camera) so the new practices acquired are useful outside school too.
- *Meaningful and challenging multimodal technical environment.* Students used several digital tools and applications; some were already familiar to the students but they also had to learn new ones as well as new technical practices (loading pictures from camera to a computer, adding texts and pictures to the

publishing environment). During the process, the tools were not used in a complicated way, although many of them were new and thus challenging for the students.

In both cases, it was essential that the *digital skills* were taught within a context and not as separate skills. This helped the students and the teacher to apply the practices for authentic activities that, in this case, were writing stories for a real audience in a "professional" way. The project was not only "a school task" but close to the students' own life.

Discussion

As *digital competence* is clearly becoming one of the core competences that all citizens, and especially young people, should learn and possess, educational institutions as well as educational researchers have to react and face up to the challenge. Our interest is, similar to that of Rantala (2009), to find out how to link the informal practices and formal school. The two reported studies indicate that, on the one hand, the gap between informal and formal learning of digital competences is wide, and on the other hand, that the formal schooling can help all students to acquire relevant digital competence in a well-designed learning environment.

Changes in Pedagogical Practices Instead of Focusing on Technology

The responsibility of formal schooling is to take care of every student's digital competence by revising pedagogical practices. Currently, this is not happening to a wide extent or as a sustainable element in the educational establishment. Counting on and leaving it to informal learning is not enough for assuring adequate competence. For digital competence to build and develop, sustainable pedagogical and curricular structures are essential, not just the technologies or how they are used. The two described classroom cases are examples of exceptionally well-planned processes in which the whole pedagogical setting is modified: the aims (focusing on general competences instead of narrow subject of domains), the organizational structures (such as multiple working hours, long-term processes, or not making strict division between home and school tasks), the responsibilities of the teacher and the students, and the variety of technological tools and applications. Pedagogical changes ought to take place in knowledge practices; that is, how students work with knowledge, do they only "use" knowledge presented on the Internet or are they also active in creating it, or how they are guided to use knowledge resources. The pedagogical and knowledge practices are as important as the use of technology for improving digital competence.

Background of the Pedagogical Changes

As previously stated, the classroom teachers involved in the projects had much experience in using technologies and had several technology and pedagogy related responsibilities and activities outside of their own school. They were exceptionally well equipped to meet the challenges of digitalization. An essential feature in the designed units was that both teachers concentrated primarily on the pedagogical processes, and technology was only used as a tool like any other.

It is apparent that these cases represent situations that only seldom present themselves in school. The first study indicated that the traditional approach is still dominant, and students' informal and formal uses of technology are not linked. There are still several obstacles to overcome before teachers, first, use the new technology fluently and, second, apply it for changing pedagogical practices. We claim that too often an individual teacher is asked to make major changes in his or her pedagogical practices without relevant help and guidance. Similarly, individual schools are usually left alone to carry out changes in the curriculum without resources and support. Fundamental changes will need to happen in the way we perceive learning, teaching, and knowing. Planning, resourcing, and supporting such change is not a task for a teacher or an individual school.

Note

1   The foreign language and mother tongue teachers are treated as two separate groups, as the curriculum plans and goals for the subjects vary considerably and that has affect on the classroom practices.

References

Ala-Mutka, K., Punie, Y., & Redecker, C. (2008). *Digital competence for lifelong learning.* Luxemburg: Office for Official Publications of the European Communities. Retrieved August 20, 2010, from http://ftp.jrc.es/EURdoc/JRC48708.TN.pdf

Aviram, R., & Eshet-Alkalai, Y. (2006). Towards a theory of digital literacy: Three scenarios for the next steps. *European Journal of Open Distance E-Learning,* I. Retrieved January 13, 2011, from http://www.eurodl.org/materials/contrib/2006/Aharon_Aviram.pdf

Bryant, L. (2007). Emerging trends in social software for education. In *Emerging technologies for learning* (Vol. 2, pp. 9–18). Coventry, UK: Becta. Retrieved January 13, 2011, from http://partners.becta.org.uk/upload-dir/downloads/page_documents/research/emerging_technologies07.pdf

Buckingham, D. (2007). *Beyond technology. Children's learning in the age of digital culture.* London: Polity Press.

Ching, C., Basham, J., & Fang, E. (2005). The legacy of the digital divide. Gender, socioeconomic status, and early exposure as predictors of full-spectrum technology use among young adults. *Urban Education, 40,* 394–411.

Coleman, S. (2005). Remixing citizenship: Democracy and young people's use of the Internet. London: The Carnegie Young People Initiative. Retrieved January 13, 2011, from http://cypi.carnegieuktrust.org.uk/files/Carnegie_v3LRES_0.pdf

Dlodlo, N., & Beyers, R. N. (2009). The experiences of South-African high-school girls in a Fab Lab environment. *Proceedings of World Academy of Science: Engineering & Technology, 37*, 423–430.

Erstad, O. (2006). A new direction? Digital literacy, student participation and curriculum reform in Norway. *Education & Information Technologies, 11*, 415–429.

Erstad, O. (2010). Educating the digital generation. *Nordic Journal of Digital Literacy, 1*, 56–70.

Eshet-Alkali, Y., & Amichai-Hamburger, Y. (2004). Experiments in digital literacy. *CyberPsychology & Behavior, 7*(4), 421–429.

Facer, K. (2002). *What do we mean by the digital divide? Exploring the roles of access, relevance and resource networks*. A collection of papers from the Toshiba/Becta seminar 19th February 2002. Retrieved January 13, 2005, from https://wwwcache1.kcl.ac.uk/content/1/c6/02/37/02/PAGESfromkerifacerpaper11.pdf

Gibson, S., & Oberg, D. (2004). Visions and reality of internet use in schools: Canadian perspectives. *British Journal of Educational Technology, 35*, 569–585.

Hague, C., & Williamson, B. (2009). *Digital participation, digital literacy and school subjects*. A review of the policies, literature and evidence. Retrieved January 13, 2011, from http://archive.futurelab.org.uk/resources/documents/lit_reviews/DigitalParticipation.pdf

Hargittai, E., & Walejko, G. (2008). The participation divide. Content creation and sharing in the digital age. *Information, Communication & Society, 11*, 239–256.

Ilomäki, L., & Kankaanranta, M. (2008). The ICT competence of the young. In L. Tan Wee & B. Subramaniam (Eds.), *Handbook of research on new media literacy at the K-12 Level* (pp. 101–118). Singapore: Information Science Reference.

ImpaCT2. (2001). The impact of information and communications technology on pupil learning and attainment. NGfL research and Evaluation Series. Retrieved January 13, 2011, from http://publications.becta.org.uk/download.cfm?resID=25841

Jedeskog, G., & Nissen, J. (2004). ICT in the classroom: Is doing more important than knowing? *Education and Information Technologies, 9*, 37–45.

Jenkins, H., Clinton, K., Purushotma, P., Robinson, A. J., & Weigel, M. (2006). *Confronting the challenges of participatory culture: Media education for the 21st century*. Chicago: The John D. and Catherine T. MacArthur Foundation. Retrieved January 13, 2011, from http://digitallearning.macfound.org/atf/cf/%7B7E45C7E0-A3E0-4B89-AC9C-E807E1B0AE4E%7D/JENKINS_WHITE_PAPER.PDF

Jones-Kavalier, B., & Flannigan, S. L. (2008). Connecting the digital dots: Literacy of the 21st century. *Teacher Librarian, 35*(3), 13–16.

Kiili, C., Laurinen, L., & Marttunen, M. (2008–2009). Students evaluating Internet sources: From versatile evaluators to uncritical readers. *Journal of the Educational Computing Research, 39*, 75–95.

Kucukaydin, I., & Tisdell, E. J. (2008). The discourse on the digital divide: Are we being co-opted? *UCLA Journal of Education and Information Studies, 4*(1), 1–19. Retrieved September 25, 2011, from http://repositories.cdlib.org/gseis/interactions/vol4/iss1/art6

Labbo, L. (2006). Literacy pedagogy and computer technologies: Toward solving the puzzle of current and future classroom practices. *Australian Journal of Language and Literacy, 29*(3), 199–209.

Lakkala, M., & Ilomäki, L. (2010a). Experienced teachers' pedagogical practices in teaching with technology. Paper presented at the joint Conference of EARLI SIG Higher Education and EARLI SIG Teaching and Teacher Education, 13–16 June, Kirkkonummi, Finland.

Lakkala, M., & Ilomäki, L. (2010b). *Unfolding experienced teachers' pedagogical practices in technology-enhanced collaborative learning*. Unpublished manuscript.

Lakkala, M., Ilomäki, L., & Kosonen, K. (2010). From instructional design to setting up pedagogical infrastructures: Designing technology-enhanced knowledge creation. In B. Ertl (Ed.), *Technologies and practices for constructing knowledge in online environments: Advancements in learning* (pp. 169–185). New York: Information Science Reference.

Lankshear, C., & Knobel, M. (2006). *New literacies: Everyday practices & classroom learning*. London: Open University Press, McGraw-Hill.

Lewin, C., Comber, C., Fisher, T., Harrison, C., Hawe, K., Lunzer, E., et al. (2004). The UK ImpaCT2 Project. *Education, Communication & Information, 4*(2/3), 336–340.

Luukka, M-R., Pöyhönen, S., Huhta, A., Taalas, P., Tarnanen, M., & Keränen, A. (2008). *Maailma muuttuu — mitä tekee koulu? Äidinkielen ja vieraiden kielten tekstikäytänteet koulussa ja vapaaajalla* [The world changes — how does the school respond? Mother tongue and foreign language literacy practices in school and in free-time]. Jyväskylä, Finland: University of Jyväskylä Centre for Applied Language Studies.

Mills, K. (2010). A review of the "digital turn" in the new literacy studies. *Review of Educational Research, 2*, 246–271.

Nardi, B. A., & O'Day, V. (1999). *Information ecologies. Using technology with heart*. Cambridge, MA: MIT Press.

Norris, P. (2001). Digital divide? *Civic engagement, information poverty & the internet in democratic societies*. New York: Cambridge Press.

OECD. (2010). *Are the new Millenniums learners making the grade? Technology use and educational performance in PISA*. Paris: OECD Publishing.

Pedersen, S., Malmberg, P., Christensen, A. J., Pedersen, M., Nipper, S., Graem, C. D., & Norrgård, J. (Eds.). (2006). *E-learning Nordic 2006: Impact of ICT on education*. Copenhagen, Denmark: Ramboll Management.

Pruulmann-Vengerfeldt, P., Kalmus, V., & Runnel, P. (2008). Creating content or creating hype: Practices of online content creation and consumption in Estonia. *Cyberpsychology, 2*(1), 1–8.

Rantala, L. (2010). Digital Literacies as school practices. In A. Lloyd & S. Talja (Eds.), *Practising information literacy: bringing theories of learning, practice and information literacy together* (pp. 121–141). Wagga Wagga, New South Wales, Australia: Centre for Information Studies.

Robin, B. R. (2008). Digital storytelling: A powerful technology tool for the 21st century classroom. *Theory into Practice, 47*(3), 220–228.

Ruthven, K., Hennessy, S., & Deaney, R. (2005). Incorporating Internet resources into classroom practice: Pedagogical perspectives and strategies of secondary-school subject teachers. *Computers and Education, 44*, 1–34.

Sefton-Green, J., Nixon, H., & Erstad, O. (2009). Reviewing approaches and perspectives on "Digital literacy." *Pedagogies, 4*(2), 107–125.

Taalas, P., Tarnanen, M., Kauppinen, M., & Pöyhönen, S. (2008). Media landscapes in school and in free time — two parallel realities? *The Nordic Journal of Digital Literacy, 3*(4), 240–256.

Tierney, R. J., Bond, E., & Bresler, J. (2006). Examining literate lives as students engage with multiple literacies. *Theory Into Practice, 45*(4), 359–367.

Turcsányi-Szabó, M., Bedő, A., & Pluhár, Z. (2006). Case study of a TeaM challenge game-e-PBL revisited. *Education & Information Technologies, 11*(3), 341–355.

Twist, J., & Withers, K. (2007). The challenge of new digital literacies and the 'hidden curriculum'. In *Emerging technologies for learning* (Vol. 2, pp. 27–39). Coventry, UK: Becta. Retrieved January 13, 2011, from http://partners.becta.org.uk/page_documents/research/emerging_technologies07_chapter3.pdf

van Deursen, A. J. A. M., & van Dijk, J. A. G. M. (2009). Using the internet: Skill related problems in users' online behavior. *Interacting with Computers, 21*(5), 393–402.

van Dijk, J., & Hacker, K. (2003). The digital divide as a complex and dynamic phenomenon. *The Information Society, 19*, 315–326.

Vekiri, I., & Chronaki, A. (2008). Gender issues in technology use: Perceived social support, computer self-efficacy and value beliefs, and computer use beyond school. *Computers & Education, 51*(3), 1392–1404.

Walsh, C. (2007). Creativity as capital in the literacy classroom: Youth as multimodal designers. *Literacy, 41*(2), 79–85.

6

WHAT HAUNTS THE NARCISSUS-NARCOSIS

Media Education and the Social Life of Digital Technologies

Stuart R. Poyntz

Introduction

Raymond Williams (1985) tells us a concept of mediation has been part of the English language since at least the fourteenth century. Over time, through inclusion in various systems of modern thought, three distinct uses of the term have emerged, two of which are of interest here.[1]

First, there is the sense in which mediation describes "the interaction of two opposed concepts or forces within the totality to which they are assumed to belong" (Williams, 1985, p. 205). Colloquially (but also in more positivist conceptions), this usage finds its way into unfavourable talk about our relationships with the mass media. The media's impact on our understanding of reality is often cast as an "indirect connection ... in a contrast between *real* and *mediated* relations, *mediation* being then one of the essential processes not only of consciousness but of ideology" (Williams, 1985, p. 206). In this usage, mediation is productive, but misleadingly so. The critique of ideology thus becomes a process of revealing the way experience is mistakenly organized by our representational systems. In the field of media education, this sense of the term has found greatest uptake in the privileged role afforded textual decoding in classroom practice (Morgan, 1998; Buckingham, 2003). Making sense of the social life of signs has generally meant students learn to deconstruct images in order that they might develop critical skills necessary to operate in a highly suspect media environment. Many have sympathy for these ambitions; and yet, there are also reasons to believe these forms of critical practice, like ideology critique more generally, fail to achieve the kinds of transformations educators hope for. This issue has special importance for teachers.

On the one hand, a number of researchers have observed that a "textual fixation" in media literacy tends to privilege the teacher's reading as the correct understanding of any media representation, over and above students' interpretations (Morgan, 1998, 1996; Buckingham, 2003). What is lost in such practices is a willingness to "problematize the 'will to interpretation' of media teaching itself" (Morgan, 1998, p. 124). I have argued elsewhere (see Poyntz, 2006) that this concern can become debilitating, particularly when it leads educators to refrain from interrogating how domination operates in media representations, or when it undercuts educators' willingness to foreground media that represent new forms of democratic life. Nonetheless, neither of these goals can succeed if media education only amounts to the substitution of one authoritative voice (i.e., the teacher) for another (i.e., broadly speaking, mainstream media). On the other hand, a tendency to privilege the power of texts has also discouraged an investigation into the way media operates in specific contexts of use. As a result, the inherent instability of all textual formations has been misunderstood, and the role of *situated* audiences who produce meaning in specific contexts of circulation has remained undertheorized. Because of this, while still in use in some settings, the notion of mediation as productive deception has fallen out of favour as it has increasingly become apparent that access to the real is always a function of social relations that "cannot be reduced to an abstraction of that relationship" (Williams, 1985, p. 206).

Alternatively, then, mediation is also used to describe a kind of interaction that is in itself substantial. It includes "forms of its own, so that it is not the neutral process of the interaction of separate forms, but an active process in which the form of the mediation alters the things mediated" (Williams, 1985, p. 205). In relation to digital media culture, for instance, this is to say that the dimensions and forms of experience generated within new information environments alter what it is we mean by culture in the first place. In this usage, mediation is productive, creating new practices and newly formed phenomenon specific to that experience. For media educators, this conception poses challenges because the focus now turns to the situated contexts within which media texts are used. Rather than imagining texts to be static objects susceptible to analysis in their own right, they now operate as moving targets. The meaning of these targets, in turn, is determined by the ways they are worked in specific instances of dissemination and appropriation. If attention to this problematic now forms a central part of media literacy research, in what follows, I offer a contribution to this work by examining how mediation operates in Derrida's thinking about *spectrality,* and then secondarily, in McLuhan's heuristic, acoustic space.

In *Spectres of Marx* (1994) and *Echographies of Television* (Derrida and Steigler, 2002/1996), Derrida's work calls attention to a clarification in the operation of deconstruction. This move coincides with a new and more explicit interest in the role of tele-technologies in Western society. Of interest for media educators is the way Derrida's marking of an injunctive moment within deconstruction distinguishes the notion of spectrality from the simulacrum. To be sure, this "originary performativity" in Derrida's schema is not to be thought of as a new form of presence that stands outside of representation (Derrida, 1994, p. 31). Rather, any emancipatory promise will always already be a function of the way mediation operates in digital media environments. Nonetheless, Derrida's clarification is helpful because it suggests that the potential for critical agency does not depend on anything like the authoritative voice of the teacher; rather, it is a function of the instability inherent in the production of meaning itself. In this way, spectrality offers a valuable contribution to media education by drawing attention to the way iteration calls forth an always available moment of critical performance. At the same time, attention to the spectral—in the form of digital tele-media technologies—also makes clear a limitation in Derrida's system. Mark Hansen (2000) and others (Gumbrecht and Pfeiffer, 1994; Lefebvre, 1991) have noted this shortfall, and suggested it has to do with the way Derrida's schema reduces technology to the representational, thereby ensuring that meaning operates as the final "tribunal for evaluating technology" (Hansen, 2000, p. 123). For media educators this difficulty can be translated into the problem of thinking about the materiality of technology. A turn to McLuhan's work on acoustic space will be useful at this point because his heuristic continues to offer helpful ways to delineate how cultural media constitute contemporary social life. This is to say, an encounter with Derrida and McLuhan offer media educators a way to hold different but related levels of analysis in productive tension. Both thinkers conceive of mediation as productive, and if Derrida helps us to understand how this produces a certain kind of emancipatory promise, McLuhan's work remains vital for locating this promise in relation to the dimensions of technological lifeworlds characteristic of modern society (Stevenson, 2002).

Spectrality and Absence

Within the field of media literacy, the development of global media cultures alongside the rise of new information technologies has garnered much attention. Broadly speaking, these transformations have brought to the fore a whole set of pressing issues having to do with the nature of young people's media experiences. These include: the rise of global media conglomerates and the ongoing commercialization of youth cultures; the development of interactive media and newly configured relations of production and consumption; ongoing debates about the digital divide; and, concerns about the technologizing of schools and the role of ICTs in the development of more democratic pedagogical cultures. In turn, these issues have fed a series of debates about the new configurations of childhood, and the extent to which anything like a digital generation has evolved. Questions about the nature of critical agency in an age when media cultures and young people's lives seem constantly in flux are also much debated today. In the midst of this tumult, Derrida's work on spectrality remains salient because it helps to clarify the terms on which an emancipatory critical practice might operate. At the same time, a limitation in Derrida's schema also points to the ways in which McLuhan can help media educators examine the contexts and forms of meaning constitution that operate in information societies.

By the early to mid-90s, with the publication of *Spectres of Marx* and then later, *Echographies of Television*, the work of tele-technologies became a more obvious and sustained focus in the writing of post-structuralism's most significant theorist. Derrida's challenge to the Western philosophical tradition has long drawn effect from the explosion of representational forms and systems of communication, which increasingly allow the spoken word to function "without the presence of the speaking subject" (Derrida, 1974, p. 10). Where his project largely concerned metaphysics or the search in the Western philosophical tradition for "an absolutely pure, transparent and unequivocal translatability," however, this changed with the arrival of the above texts (Derrida, 1996, p. 211). In both instances, the media are in the foreground and are understood to be forces of virtualization that produce "spectral effects." Derrida introduces his notion of spectrality in conjunction with an investigation of Marx because this new term is linked with developments in the commodity form. In fact, if spectrality recasts deconstruction in a digital age, it does so, in part, by reconceptualizing materialism in an age of deconstruction.

In the Marxist tradition, materialism operates as a manner of thinking existence whereby matter is always understood to precede and exceed our concepts. It's in this sense that Derrida identifies the logic of materialism with a logic of deconstruction. Both are what he calls, logics of demand (i.e., they refer to an excess that remains an inescapable alterity) that cannot be translated into a new order of presence. Where Derrida rejects an ontological foundationalism in Marx—a foundationalism premised on the primacy afforded notions of social labour, class and mode of production, etc.—he also argues: "Deconstruction has never had any sense or interest ... except as a radicalization ... of a certain spirit of Marxism" (p. 92). Given this, not surprisingly what distinguishes the spectral is "paradoxical phenomenality, ... [a] *non-sensuous sensuous* of which *Capital* speaks with regard to a certain exchange value" (Derrida, 1994, p. 7). At the same time, the spectral is not just another name for reified commodity experience. It "is also ... the tangible intangibility of a proper body without flesh ... [and t]his already suffices to distinguish the spectre ... from the simple *simulacrum* of something in general" (Derrida, 1994, p. 7).

The importance of the distinction between the spectral and the simulacrum will occupy us below. Here, however, Derrida's attention to television, video, and other modes of visual representation calls attention to the ways in which contemporary media culture shares characteristic features with deconstruction. In fact, the spectral might be thought of as a new kind of ontology, one where "the new speed of apparition ... the simulacrum, ... the virtual event, cyber-space and surveillance," are shaping a "democratic deficit" in Western democracies (Derrida 1994, p. 54). These developments arise because: "As it has never done before, ... techno-mediatic power ... *conditions and endangers* democracy" (Derrida, 1994, p. 54; italics in original). While not deploying spectrality as a conceptual frame, others (Sandywell, 2006; Cazden et al., 2000/1996; Stevenson, 2000) have rehearsed similar themes and concerns. Barry Sandywell (2006), for instance, notes that in a time when tele-technologies mediate life, what results is a "global risk society with its corresponding constellation of ontological insecurities and contradictions" (p. 43). *Time Magazine* may have designated the citizens of the new digital democracy as their "Person of the Year" for 2006, but, as Sandywell (2006) observes:

> Dystopian descriptions of the Web in the popular press frequently appear prefixed by the adjectives 'ungoverned' and 'unregulated'. Promiscuous information flows in cyberspace create an anarchical theatre for anti-nomian agents with subversive intentions; cyberspace is imagined as a site of dangers perpetrated by disembodied intruders and anonymous agencies. A predominant image of computerized social systems is one of fragile configurations prone to systems failure and periodic 'crashes'. In extreme forms modern technophobia involves a haemorrhaging of trust that results in cyberparanoia (for example, the post-human anxiety that the planetary matrix of interconnected computers and allied digital technology are 'thinking for us', 'taking over' our lives, and that 'virtual co-presence' replacing 'real community' is a prelude to totalitarian futures).
>
> *(p. 47)*

The half-life called the spectral well describes this new social form because it calls attention to that which makes "the present waver: like the vibrations of a heat wave through which the massiveness of the object world—indeed of matter itself—now shimmers like a mirage" (Jameson, 1995, p. 85). Derrida extends his analysis in *Echographies*, suggesting that the growing power of communication systems alter our understanding of the state, immigration, and citizenship. Spectrality thus speaks of a time "out of joint," our own time in which the media system takes "the phenomenal form of a war, a conflictual tension between multiple forces of appropriation, between multiple strategies of control" (Derrida and Steigler, 2002/1996, p. 37).

As is well known, McLuhan's media theory also traces these kinds of transformations. In his more erratic and fantastical moments McLuhan's prognostications are unhelpful. Yet, McLuhan's notion of acoustic space, helpfully delineates environmental aspects of the new material formations produced by electronic culture. In an electronic and digital age, McLuhan theorized that the dominant category of space changes. The *differential space* of the acoustic replaces the linear, visual space of print-based cultures (Lefebvre, 1991).

What results is an environment characterized by flow, one that "is spherical, discontinuous, non-homogeneous, resonant, and dynamic" (McLuhan and McLuhan, 1988, p. 33). Here, "the invisibilia of electronic communication ... constitute[s] the fundamental materiality of contemporary social and cultural production" (Cavell, 2002, p. 24). Such invisibilia resonate with the peculiar ontology described by spectrality because for both Derrida and McLuhan new digital media produce significant consequences in the way subjectivity is structured, not just in relation to cultural content but in regard to perceptual processes (Kline, Dyer-Witheford, and De Peuter, 2003). McLuhan (1994/1964) attends to these developments in remarking that electronic and digital media are "'make happen' agents, ... not 'make aware' agents" (p. 48). They operate as procedural mapping devices that render the human form discarnate by externalizing, as digital communication, what had previously been embodied forms of human experience. As but one example, the computer and other kinds of information technologies reconstitute the structure of experience by producing "a new sense of time, based on experiences of speed, reversibility, and resumability...; and, arising at the intersection of these time–space reorientations, a gradual habituation to virtual immersion, disembodied identity, and multimedia intensity" (Kline, Dyer-Witheford, and De Peuter, 2003, p. 35). Through this, "[t]he discarnate user of electric media bypasses all former spatial restrictions and is present in many places simultaneously as a disembodied intelligence" (McLuhan and McLuhan, 1988, p. 72) To return to Derrida's (1994) notion of the spectral, here, one is made into "the tangible intangibility of a proper body without flesh" (p. 7).

Spectrality as Language Effect

Where Derrida's attentiveness to the role of media in contemporary culture marks an interesting and important development in his work, this shift also coincides with a clarification "in the way in which deconstruction handles concepts in general" (Jameson, 1995, p. 75).[2] It locates a logic of impact, an intensity that is not knowledge per se, but a haunting that constitutes a necessarily inconceivable ground through which we make sense of the world. Deconstruction has always been a performative mode of thinking, which is to say, the logic of *différance* unfolds through the process of evoking the ground on which philosophical (and other sorts of) claims are made. If the spectral also works this territory, it simultaneously calls attention to a clarification in the operation of deconstruction. This is the moment in Derrida's argument, which is perhaps most interesting for media educators.

While attending to the virtual dimensions in contemporary culture, the spectral invokes the possibility of a new formation based on the "disordered plurivocity" that is an inescapable presence necessary to a properly understood deconstruction (Derrida, 1994, p. 23). To be sure, this new formation is neither a function of Hegelian Spirit nor ontological knowledge. Rather, the spectral occupies the realm of the performative. It is a kind of figured concept that Jameson (1995) notes, "is ... of a somewhat different type than those that began to proliferate in Derrida's earlier work, beginning most famously with 'writing' itself and moving through a now familiar spectrum of marked terms like dissemination, hymen, along with the inversion of this practice, which consisted in modifying a letter in a word whose sound thereby remained the same (*différance*)" (p. 79). It speaks of a breaking up of the present, but in such away that disruption operates at one and the same time as an injunction toward a new presence, one that is in constant movement, "enjoined, ordered, distributed in the two directions of absence, at the articulation of what is no longer and what is not yet" (Derrida, 1994, p. 25). What results from this is a new set of rules around meaning, such that critique as deferral also produces a new and singular movement beyond deferral, delay, postponement.

The extent to which the spectral amounts to a modification in the way deconstruction operates is perhaps most apparent when Derrida turns his attention to a notion of the just: the inescapable moment underlying the possibility of deconstruction. For Derrida, a remnant of justice lies at the jointure of the present in all its alterity. He invokes the original performativity at the heart of deconstruction as a political injunction, in other words, and links this injunctive moment with Marx's legacy. It is that which "remains irreducible, irreducibly required by the spacing of any promise and by the future-to-come ... Without lateness, without delay, but without presence, [*différance*] is the precipitation of an absolute singularity, ... even if it moves toward what remains to come, there is the pledge" (Derrida, 1994, p. 31). This pledge is what allows deconstruction to escape a "critical neoidealism" or nihilism (Derrida and Steigler, 2002/1996, p. 5), "precisely because it cannot be either narrowed-down or fixed to a single part of both of its meanings" (Trifonas, 2003, p. 227; see also Derrida, 1982; Lather, 2003; Peters, 2003). In *Echographies*, Derrida (Derrida and Steigler, 2002/1996) argues further that this moment is premised on "the experience of the other as other, the fact that I let the other be other, which presupposes a gift of restitution, without reappropriation and without jurisdiction" (p. 21). Such a formation is never guaranteed, but as an indicative force for a future where plurality flourishes, it is an injunction of possibility, a sense of weak messianic hope that Derrida links with the work of Walter Benjamin. It is an "experience of the emancipatory promise," and, as with Benjamin, it speaks in its virtual dimensions to the "spectral effects" characteristic of information technologies (Derrida, 1994, p. 59).

McLuhan's understanding of the space of critique was not conceived in relation to the operation of language, but it's interesting to note, if only in preliminary fashion at this point, the similarities between what Derrida proposes as a critical, if singular, act, and what McLuhan outlines as an embryonic strategy of critique in his 1951 text, *The Mechanical Bride*.

This text is a remarkable, if now dated examination of advertising and other kinds of "folklore" in the age of industrial man. For Stevenson (2002) it represents an early moment in McLuhan's work, where he seems fixated on media content as opposed to the constitutive force of media culture as forms of communication. And yet, even here, to examine the "whirling phantasmagoria" of media culture (2002/1951, p. v), McLuhan seemed suspicious of moral indignation and instead thought it necessary to stand in the middle of the media vortex to develop an "unprecedented self-awareness" of the movements happening around us (McLuhan, 2002/1951, p. 45). He outlines this strategy in the preface to the text as a method learned from Edgar Allan Poe's "A Descent Into the Maelstom." In the story, Poe's sailor "saved himself by studying the actions of the whirlpool and by co-operating with it" (McLuhan, 2002/1951, p. v). This method allowed McLuhan to theorize the possibility for temporary disjunctures within the movements of consumer culture. Such disjunctures arise when threads of discontinuity in the phantasmagoria become apparent (McLuhan, 2002/1951, p. v). Below, I will address how this initial strategy is turned into a more fully developed understanding of the space of critique in electronic and digital culture; the point I want to emphasize here is the way McLuhan's method for locating a critical distance inside the movements of consumer culture has a common logic with the search in deconstruction for alterity within the structures of textuality. The deconstructive moment alludes to both a past and a future and, like Poe's sailor trapped in the vortex, it can be configured as a search for "the experience of the impossible," which, in its most promising moments, is also "a radical experience of the perhaps" (Derrida, 1994, p. 35).

The way in which Derrida has fashioned deconstruction as spectrality seems of special significance for media educators. The logic of *différance* now appears complicit in interesting ways with how meaning is produced in an expansive tele-technological system. The media's ability to manifest "virtual events whose movements and speed prohibit us more than ever … from opposing presence to its representation" produces a kind of victory for the simulacrum (Derrida, 1994, p. 169). As Irit Rogoff (1998) argues, what results is a media culture increasingly characterized by a field of vision similar in kind to *différance*.

> Derrida's conceptualization of *différance* takes the form of a critique of the binary logic in which every element of meaning constitution is locked into signification in relation to the other … [This corresponds with recent media where] we have begun to uncover the free play of the signifier, a freedom to understand meaning in relation to images, sounds or spaces not necessarily perceived to operate in a direct, causal or epistemic relation to either their context or to one another.
>
> *(p. 25)*

Instead, contemporary visual culture increasingly operates through "the continuous displacement of meaning in the field of vision and the visible" (Rogoff,

1998, p. 25). *Différance* is thus a characteristic feature. As examples, Rogoff (1998) notes the relentlessly intertextual nature of contemporary perception:

> In the arena of visual culture the scrap of an image connects with a sequence of a film and with the corner of a billboard or the window display of a shop we have passed by, to produce a new narrative formed out of both our experienced journey and our unconscious. Images do not stay within discrete disciplinary fields such as 'documentary film' or 'Renaissance painting,' [in other words,] since neither the eye nor the psyche operates along or recognizes such divisions.
>
> *(p. 26)*

One way to interpret Rogoff's description is to say it helps to clarify how tentative meaning production is in regard to cultural artifacts today. It is a function of the spaces and communities within which an artifact (or text) is used, rather than something that exists only within the object itself, or within a particular discursive frame—like art history, media studies, for film studies. Derrida doesn't make reference to the same developments, and yet he is certainly clear that spectrality identifies the differential movements of virtual communication.

At the same time, the spectral locates possibilities through which new formations might result by these movements. It's in this latter sense that Derrida's talk of spectrality is so important for the field of media education. The spectral locates an *aporia*, a condition in the production of meaning that is not transcendable but which expresses contradictions within our material culture. The productiveness of this *aporia* lies in the way spectrality makes clear both the shifting nature of a reified commodity world and also the way these shifts call to the forefront a powerful new critical force within deconstruction.[3] Where spectrality speaks to a weak messianic hope, a promise of the just, it attends to the possibility of what is not yet, of what might be in our imaginings of more equitable futures.

Non-Linguistic Materiality

If these developments indicate an exciting and compelling clarification in the operation of deconstruction, one that has particular force for the work of media educators, I suggest they also draw attention to a crucial limitation in Derrida's work. This has to do with the critical role iteration is meant to play in his system. For our purposes, identifying this shortfall will also mark the point at which Derrida's schema must be supplemented by a level of analysis that attends to non-linguistic forms of mediation.

The gist of the problem is: the value of iteration as a critical operation in Derrida's work would seem to unwind as the tele-technological system itself expands. As a force of critique, the work of iteration—what Hansen (2000) call, the "constitutive technical contamination" (p. 124) in language—is premised on Derrida's understanding that speech invokes the realm of the ontological by positing a self-presence which is at the heart of metaphysics. Deconstruction, in turn, seeks to dismantle all forms of such presence. But if digital technologies increasingly transform the way meaning is constituted, or, said otherwise, if speech is increasingly electrified—as McLuhan (1994/1964) long argued—then the presence of a speaker, understood as one who summons presence through the use of textual forms, is no longer invoked in the same way. Rather, as the movement of technology reconfigures the nature of meaning constitution—including the subjectivity produced by this process—the lure of presence in language dissipates, and thus so too does the force of iterability as a locus of critique.[4]

Derrida (1974, 1986) himself recognized this tension long ago and proposed a generalization of deconstruction and "an extension of *différance* to objects other than philosophical and literary texts" (Hansen, 2000, p. 122), to what he called the "'totality of our relation to the world'" (Derrida, quoted in Hansen, 2000, p. 122). Gumbrecht (1994) suggests Derrida is able to do this by conceiving of exteriority—that is, our material relations to the world beyond texts—in terms of a kind of concreteness that inhabits language. Thus, to the extent that writing (or *écriture*) displaces presence in language by referring to an always excessive mark, a similar mode of intimation allows for the application of *différance* to the "relative exteriority" of all our material relations to the world (Gumbrecht, 1994, pp. 394–395). Or does it? The problem this move poses is the concept of matter has been textualized through the figural work of language. Others (Eagleton, 1988; Gleenblatt, 1989; Lefebvre, 1991) have noted this tendency within deconstruction, but the particular direction of Hansen's (2000) critique is important in relation to what I see as the ongoing relevance of McLuhan's work for media educators and others.

Hansen argues that in order for Derrida to extend *différance* to non-textual objects, he must deploy a notion of incompatibility in a way that circumscribes the 'totality of our relation to the world.' But to do this Derrida must also reduce technology to representational technology. Beginning in *Of Grammatology* (1974), he does this by conceiving of exteriority in terms of the technology of writing.

> If the trace, arche-phenomenon of 'memory,' which must be thought before the opposition of nature and culture, animality and humanity, etc., belongs to the very movement of signification, then signification is *a priori* written, whether inscribed or not, in one form or another, in a 'sensible' and 'spatial' element that is called 'exterior.' Arche-writing, at first the possibility of the spoken word, then of the *'graphie'* in the narrow sense, the birthplace of 'usurpation,' denounced from Plato to Saussure, this trace is the opening of the first exteriority in general, the enigmatic relationship of the living to its other and of an inside to an outside…
>
> *(p. 70)*

In this formulation, Derrida defines exteriority as "'the exteriority of *meaning*,'" which is to say, that which is outside is understood to be such in terms of the logic of signification (Derrida, quoted in Hansen, 2000, p. 126). The outside does not have any independent relationship because it is conceived of in relation to the work of the *graf*, the technical contamination that is a necessary materiality within language itself. But in submitting this manner for thinking the technological—and by this, attempting to extend *différance* to objects other than texts—Derrida has also left thought as "the tribunal for evaluating technology" (Hansen, 2000, p. 123). By this, the representational becomes the foci of analysis because technology itself has been recast as "*artificial* memory" (Hansen, 2000, p. 123). As Hansen (2000) goes on to argue:

> by taking the being of what *is* [*physis*] and making it thoroughly dependent on the metaphysics of the text (and thus on the operation of *techne*), Derrida simply effaces the very category of radical exteriority and, along with it, all traces of materiality outside the space governed by textuality.
>
> (*p. 125*)

The difficulty this creates is technology is then conceivable only in relation to meaning-creation as opposed to meaning-constitution (Gumbrecht, 1994). Through this framework, however, the exteriority of technology has been domesticated within thought, and if this seems unsatisfying it's because at some level technology is a set of material forces constitutive of a non-linguistic exteriority.

We might reframe this problem for media education in the following way: while Derrida's work with spectrality offers a compelling case for imagining the terms on which a critical agency can operate today, his schema doesn't escape a limitation that afflicts all critical projects which attend to texts as the central instantiation in meaning production. Derrida makes us aware of how tentative these instantiations are; but his schema offers no way to delineate the specific dimensions of these conditions, what we might call the materialities of situated life. The shift Hansen draws our attention to, in other words, amounts to a delinguistification in how we imagine technology in relation to the social.

Arguably, Derrida's concern for the spectral nature of tele-technologies begins to point in this direction. In fact, all I (and Hansen) have done is bring the real implications of Derridean thinking to the foreground: that is, as in other poststructuralist work, Derrida marks the transition away from the linguistic as a sufficient mode for conceiving of the materiality of our time. In registering this development, however, Derrida cannot go beyond the eclipse of language. McLuhan, on the other hand, is useful at this stage because he offers us a way to think about speech as electronic mediation (McLuhan, 1994/1964, pp. 57–60). McLuhan too was concerned with the discontinuous, fragmented nature of contemporary culture; but his attention to the acoustic as a heuristic for describing this environment draws attention to a significant level of analysis for media educators today: that is, the way in which cultural media act as forces that make certain kinds of situated life possible. Where a deconstructed notion of mediation continues to have value then, it needs to be complemented by attention to the non-linguistic materiality McLuhan addresses as acoustic space.

Mediation in Acoustic Space

There is not room to review McLuhan's theory in detail, but crucially this now unfashionable media scholar was not concerned with the way modern forms of communication act as forces of alienation because he theorized that all media are best understood as extensions of the body. This focus lead to forms of technological determinism in McLuhan's writings. Nonetheless, his texts remain instructive because unlike so much work on technology, McLuhan helps us to understand that media are more than systems of representation; they constitute forces that facilitate our ability to have specific kinds of experiences at all.

While motivated by different concerns and drawing from different intellectual traditions, the anti-humanist strain in McLuhan's work echoes with a similar tendency in Derrida's project. Media, McLuhan (1994/1964) argued, translate "experience into new forms. [For instance, t]he spoken word was the first technology by which man was able to let go of his environment in order to grasp it in a new way" (p. 57). The invention of the alphabet, he argued, accelerates this process. The alphabet translates and reduces "a complex, organic interplay of spaces into a single space. The phonetic alphabet reduce[s] the use of all the senses at once, which is oral speech, to a merely visual code" (McLuhan, 1997/1962, p. 45). This code, in turn, is crucial to the formation of societies and empires, which depend on the presence of a system of coded communication to form and translate directives, laws and organizational structures across space, in a way that speech on its own cannot. Like other more obvious kinds of technology, in other words, the alphabet constitutes certain cultural possibilities. For McLuhan, the rise of print culture extends these possibilities because print facilitates the formation of compartmentalized and specialized sensory perceptions. "Whereas oral cultures allowed the rich interplay of all the senses, print culture abstract[s] writing from speech and promote[s] the visual component of the human organism" (Stevenson, 2002, p. 123). This leads to the development of portable (books, manuscripts), rational (laws and regulations), and calculable (legers, train schedules, etc.) forms of communication that, historically, have been crucial to the formation of the nation state. McLuhan argued further that print facilitates the hegemony of individualism in Western culture because book culture requires that "reading practices are silent and attentive, that the text have an author, and that the translation of a shared collective culture is converted into one dependent upon individual forms of expression" (Stevenson, 2002, p. 123). As extensions of the senses, then, McLuhan's concern was always how technological mediation facilitates certain developments while restricting others. In this way, where Derrida aides us in identifying the instability of given meaning-structures, McLuhan is helpful for locating how media constitute meaning in the first instance.

To make sense of how technologies operate as cultural mediums, McLuhan also draws on a dynamic theory of space. For instance, he argued that the problem of the print epoch—that is, the age between the Renaissance and, roughly, the early decades of the twentieth century—is that it privileges one sense—the visual—to the exclusion of all others. Because of this, as much as print culture allows for certain developments to occur it is also biased toward static, structured forms of perception, ways of seeing that foreground linearity, distance and analytic understanding to the exclusion of concerns for context and perspective. What results is a culture of visual space in which "abstract figure minus ground" is privileged (McLuhan and McLuhan, 1988, p. 33). As in Newtonian physics, space is conceived as "an infinite container, linear and continuous, homogeneous and uniform" (McLuhan and McLuhan, 1988, p. 33). McLuhan argued these developments cause the other senses to atrophy, leading, for instance, to the sterile forms of rationalism and universalism that fed various destructive examples of imperialism and nationalism in the late nineteenth and twentieth centuries. In contrast, the space of electric and digital culture diminishes the hegemony of visual space. Contemporary media produce an environment that emphasizes context, multiplicity and the interplay of form and content through the re-immersion of the visual faculty with the other senses. More involving perceptually, the space of the acoustic privileges intertextual relations in which cultural forms "pour upon us instantly and constantly" (McLuhan and Fiore, 1967, p. 61).

Where early modern visual space is Newtonian in form, acoustic space resembles the spacetime formations of Einstein's theory of relativity. Electronic culture shortens time and compresses space because we are constantly involved, connected, and attached to information and therefore each other. In this sense, technology seems to make time bend. It also changes the relations between borders. Whether at the level of national, local, or personal interconnections, they become more porous and mutable (Sandywell, 2006). If one wanted an example of this process, the experience of identify theft is instructive.

Although not an entirely new phenomenon, one of the interesting characteristics of identity theft is it is only enacted once our discrete selves have been turned outward and realized in network form. We don't lose our bodies through the crime, we lose the substance of a self in an information age—the tissues of data through which the self is materialized. Today, the remarkable reach of data collection activities and the size of databases[5] produce mediated forms as digital bodies with porous and mutable boundaries subject more than ever to viral disruption (Sandywell, 2006). Accordingly, when identity theft occurs it is our "selves" constituted as information "bodies" in an intertextual, networked universe that is acted upon in ways that extend wildly beyond our control. As such, neither our selves nor our technology exist as discrete objects; rather as McLuhan (1994/1964) observed: "Our private and corporate lives ... become information processes" just because we have put ourselves outside of us via electronic and digital technology (p. 52). Importantly, this is not merely a linguistic process nor does it just mimic the structures of textuality. Instead, identity theft is enacted by and is symptomatic of new forms of mediation because, while this crime may amount to a deconstruction of the self, what really matters here are the new material conditions constitutive of how our selves are remade via the tissues present in new electronic connections.

Within the new spacetime formations of electronic and digital culture, McLuhan suggested that resonance functions as the dominant mode of operation/motion. As an operative dynamic, resonance is similar to the coming-and-going Derrida describes as the disjunctive/injunctive movement in deconstruction. And yet, resonance also refers to the vibrations of sound waves, an oscillation materialized as a non-linguistic form. In chemistry, resonance is used to describe the property of certain chemical compounds that have characteristics of two or more electronic structures simultaneously. This sense makes clearer McLuhan's understanding. Resonance is that which animates the acoustic; it speaks of the motion necessary for the intertextual experiences characteristic of our cultural forms. As Cavell (2002) argues, resonance "conceptualizes the break in the uniformity and continuity of space as visualized; it is a sign ... of the discontinuity of acoustic space, of the fact that it produces meaning through gaps" (p. 23). Near the end of his career, McLuhan referred to the resonant as the "fecund interval" of acoustic space (McLuhan, quoted in Cavell, 2002, p. 23). The work it does in a theory of mediation is really as a non-linguistic materialization of iterability; it draws attention to how media forms blur the boundaries between each other and create new forms of interaction and meaning by this process. The importance of this sense of resonance is evident, particularly when aligned with another dimension of acoustic space: that is, simultaneity and its place in a fractured environment.

Certainly in a digital age, because data reaches us simultaneously from all directions, "acoustic space has the structure of a sphere in which things create their own space and modify and coerce each other. Without visual stress necessary to drive the other senses 'underground' into the subconscious, their interrelatedness is constant" (McLuhan and McLuhan, 1988, p. 35). Electronic culture is thus experienced as a percept of simultaneity. McLuhan long argued that artists are the first to understand this because: "As the visual sense moves back into interplay with the other senses, it is natural that rigid chronology becomes fuzzy and uncertain. While these developments occurred in science, ... artists were articulating discontinuity and simultaneity for their own publics" (p. 45). McLuhan was especially affected by the way Joyce explored this dynamic through devices like the double-plot structure in *Ulysses*, but the work of Schoenberg on atonality, Eisenstein on montage, and the cubists on perspective would all be influential.

How McLuhan understood simultaneity to be characteristic of our time is captured nicely in his (1994/1964) aphorism: "In the electric age we wear all mankind as our skin" (p. 47). This is not merely a representational experience; rather, the speed of electronic culture pours upon contemporary subjects, "instantaneously and continuously, the concerns of all men" (McLuhan, 1994/1964, pp. 171–172). As a result, "[b]y means of translation of immediate sense experience ...[,] the entire world can be evoked and retrieved at any instant" (p. 57). Different from Derrida, in other words, McLuhan conceives of the process of simultaneity in terms of new sense ratios facilitated by the outering or externalization of our selves via non-linguistic forms of mediation. To make clear what this means, an example is helpful.

Think, for instance, of the opening of the 2003 U.S.-led war in Iraq. It's tempting to talk about this period in terms of the marketing of mass persuasion and the nature of the representational experience this produced (Rutherford, 2004). And of course, this remains vital, not least for media education. But in thinking about these new representational experiences, we also encounter a new form of embodiment or meaning constitution, which, for instance, begins to collapse older dichotomies (between producer/audience, actor/receiver, journalist/soldier). In recalling certain aspects of the way TV and journalism functioned during the initial phase of the war, for instance, Sarah Boxer (2003) writes:

> With the war rolling ahead on television, you the viewer [were] made a part of the invading army, ... [and] just as the audience [felt] a part of the army, the army [became] part of the audience. American troops on an aircraft carrier [watched] CNN to see how the war [was] playing and progressing. Soldiers [were] watching other soldiers on television. [Meanwhile,] there [was] general confusion as to who [was] acting and who [was] watching ... [A]t the crux of the confusion [was] the traditional eyewitnesses to war, the journalists, 'embedded' with the troops. [Were] the television cameras the witnesses of war, or [were] they part of the weaponry? Or both?"

Of course they were both, and it is in this sense that they, and the troops/audiences watching/acting in the war, mark a change in *both* the representation of conflict, and the concurrent sense ratios made possible by video-phones, fractured television screens, and cable news channels with global reach. If, as McLuhan (McLuhan and McLuhan, 1988) offered, we—audiences and soldiers, journalists and troops—all "hear from all directions simultaneously" this is made possible by technological developments which produce new forms of embodiment (p. 35). Images, sounds, and text interact together and engage us as never before, such that resonant, simultaneous movement becomes the ground on which meaning is constituted. But once this happens, it's necessary to address these mediations beyond the terms of representation, if only because this is not merely a language effect. Rather, the wavering of the present is lived through newly embodied forms, including a whole set of reconstituted physiological sensations.

This last point brings us to a final dimension of McLuhan's understanding of acoustic space; that is, the space of critique afforded within this environment. McLuhan spoke of a *space* of critique in relation to the acoustic because, like Derrida, he understood that the possibility for critical acts could not rest on the shoulders of a humanist subject. Where Derrida helps us to locate a critical agency in a post-humanist world, however, McLuhan's concern for technological mediation focuses attention on where moments of crisis and change are likely to occur.

McLuhan located possibilities for the critique of new media by attending to the way these cultural forms alter the ratios of older media. He captures this idea when he (1994/1964) notes: "The effect of radio is visual, the effect of the photo is auditory. Each new impact shifts the ratios among all the senses" (p. 64). Because of this: "The hybrid or the meeting of two media is a moment of truth and revelation from which new form is born. For the parallel between two media holds us on the frontiers between forms that snap us out of the Narcissus-Narcosis. The moment of the meeting of media is a moment of freedom and release from the ordinary trance and numbness imposed ... on our senses" (p. 55). What McLuhan's getting at here is that where the development of new technologies tends to numb users/audiences, if only because of the novelty and possibility offered by new experiences, these changes simultaneously create moments of crisis and opportunity in relation to older media experiences. As a result, affordances are created for new forms of critical practice. Interestingly, of late, media education researchers (see Burn and Durran, 2006; Burn and Parker, 2003; Burn et al., 2001) have turned their attention to the way new digital media change young people's relation to older media like film and television. What they are finding is that technologies like digital video editing software allow young people to anatomize filmic and televisual language. By this, youth are able to experience the provisional nature of meaning production because the display of an edit in an editing software's interface is governed by what Manovich (2001) calls the principle of variability: that is, "media objects in a database [are only ever] held in a temporary configuration by algorithmic instructions" (Burn and Durran, 2006, p. 281). This variability in turn makes clearer the opportunities students have to express forms of pleasure and notions of critique in relation to their own socio-cultural context. In this way, film and television turn more than ever from fixed texts to provisional and variable resources for meaning production, resources that can be constantly reframed to address one's needs, desires, and commitments.

Of course, McLuhan's communication theory is not without significant problems.[6] Where I have avoided a discussion of these, it is because my intent has been to suggest ways in which media education can benefit from an encounter with McLuhan and Derrida. Today, media literacy is concerned with how to conceive of critical agency without privileging the authoritative voice of the teacher. Researchers are also concerned with how to delineate the characteristics of new digital media as specific forms of mediation. While certainly not exhausting these issues, I suggest that an encounter with Derrida and McLuhan offers significant resources that afford media educators ways of putting levels of analysis in productive tension. In the end, this provides us with the kinds of cognitive maps appropriate to the complex nature of contemporary culture.

Notes

1   Mediation can also mean: "finding a central point between two opposites, as in many political uses" (Williams, 1985, p. 205). I am not concerned with this use of the term for reasons that will become obvious below.

2   *Spectres of Marx* offers the most detailed analysis in this regard; however it is interesting to note how often *Echographies of Television* draws on this modification and clarification of *différance* in discussing tele-technologies. For instance, see pp. 6, 10, 11–13, and 21 in *Echographies*.

3   In regard to this argument, Derrida's (1994) particular reading (pp. 151–161) of the relationship between use value and exchange value in Marx is significant. Derrida's central point here is that use value and exchange value are inseparable from each other. Simultaneity is a characteristic of their becoming because use value cannot forge the sociality that is essential to the commodity form on its own. But if this is so, Derrida suggests, use value cannot exist as a pure form. Rather, in order for the phantasmagoria characteristic of the commodity form to exist, it must have begun "before ... exchange value, at the threshold of the value of value in general ... The said use value of the ... ordinary sensuous thing, ... the wood of the wooden table concerning which Marx supposes that it has not yet begun to 'dance,' ... must indeed have made a start, however minimal it may have been, on an idealization that permits one to identify it as the same through possible repetitions" (Derrida, 1994, p. 160). For Derrida, this reworked relationship between use value and exchange value alters our conception of alienation and the utility of an ideology critique underwritten by commodity fetishism. Use value and exchange value are here understood to mediate each other and thus to share more than a totality to which they both belong; in fact, they each live in the others' home. As such, while it may not be possible to pose the critique of ideology by opposing presence to its representation, this does not mean that a kind of critical agency is impossible. It's just not the agency guaranteed by authority (of a teacher, for instance) or transparency.

4   I would like to thank Dr. Richard Cavell for helping me to see the force of this argument.

5   For instance, while it is often claimed that the Internet is "'the largest artifact in the known universe'" (Sandywell, 2006, p. 43), Wal-Mart has such vast collections of demographic information on its customers that their databases are understood to be equivalent in size to three times all the information circulating on the Internet (Hays, 2004).

6   On this see Stevenson, 2002, for a helpful and judicious examination of the weaknesses in McLuhan's theory.

Bibliography

Boxer, S. (2003, April 3). "McLuhan's messages, echoing on iraq". *New York Times*. Late Edition – Final. Retrieved March 23, 2004, from http://web.lexis-nexis.com.universe/document?_m=74455977e924d5c5a2cb1e70a8bb6ad5

Buckingham, D. (2003). *Media education: Literacy, learning and contemporary culture*. Cambridge: Polity.

Burn, A., Brindley, S., Durran, J., Kelsall, C., Sweetlove, J., & Tuohey, C. (2001). 'The rush to images': A research report in digital filmmaking and the moving image. *English in Education*, *35*(2), 34–48.

Burn, A., & Durran, J. (2006). Digital anatomies: Analysis as production in media education. In D. Buckingham & R. Willett (Eds.), *Digital generations: Children, young people, and new media* (pp. 273–293). Mahwah, NJ: Erlbaum.

Burn, A., & Parker, D. (2003). *Analyzing media texts*. London: Continuum.

Cavell, R. (2002). *McLuhan in space: A cultural geography*. Toronto: University of Toronto Press.

Cazden, C., Cope, B., Fairclough, N., Gee, J. P., Kalantzis, M., Kress, G., et al. (2000/1996). A pedagogy of multiliteracies: Designing social futures. In B. Cope & M. Kalantzis (Eds.), *Multiliteracies: Literacy, learning and the design of social futures* (pp. 9–37). London: Routledge.

Derrida, J. (1996). Semiology and grammatology: Interview with Julia Kristeva. In P. Cobley (Ed.), *The communication theory reader* (pp. 209–224). London: Routledge.

Derrida, J. (1994). *Specters of marx: The state of the debt, the work of mourning, and the new international* (Peggy Kamuf, Trans.). New York: Routledge.

Derrida, J. (1986). *Memoires for paul de man* (C. Lindsay, J. D. Culler, & E. Cadava, Trans.). New York: Columbia University Press.

Derrida, J. (1982). "*Différance*" (Alan Bass, Trans.). In *Margins of philosophy* (pp. 3–27). Chicago: University of Chicago Press.

Derrida, J. (1974). *Of grammatology*. (Gayatri Chakravorty Spivak, Trans.). (Corrected Edition). Baltimore: Johns Hopkins University Press.

Derrida, J., & Stiegler, B. (2002/1996). *Echographies of television: Filmed interviews*. (Jennifer Bajorek, Trans.). Cambridge: Polity Press.

Eagleton, T. (1988). Capitalism, modernism, and postmodernism. In D. Lodge (Ed.), *Modern criticism and theory: A reader* (pp. 384–398). London: Longman Group.

Greenblatt, S. (1989). Towards a poetics of culture. In H. A. Veeser (Ed.), *The new historicism* (pp. 1–14). London: Routledge.

Gumbrecht, H. U. (1994). A farewell to interpretation (W. Whobrey, Trans.). In H. U. Gumbrecht & K. L. Pfeiffer (Eds.), *Materialities of communication* (pp. 389–402). Stanford, CA: Stanford University Press.

Gumbrecht, H. U., & Pfeiffer, K. L. (Eds.). (1994). *Materialities of communication*. Stanford, CA: Stanford University Press.

Hansen, M. (2000). *Embodying technesis: Technology beyond writing*. Ann Arbor: University of Michigan Press.

Hays, C. L. (2004, November 14). What they know about you. *New York Times*, pp. 3, 9.

Jameson, F. (1991). *Postmodernism, or, the cultural logic of late capitalism*. Durham, NC: Duke University Press.

Jameson, F. (1995 Jan./Feb.). "Marx's purloined letter." In *New left review*. No. 209. 75–109.

Kline, S., Dyer-Witheford, N., & de Peuter, G. (2003). *Digital play: The interaction of technology, culture, and marketing*. Montreal: McGill-Queen's University Press.

Lather, P. (2003). Applied Derrida: (Mis)reading the work of mourning in educational research. *Educational Philosophy & Theory*, *35*(3), 257–270.

Lefebvre, H. (1991). *The production of space* (D.Nicholson-Smith, Trans.). Oxford: Blackwell.

Manovich, L. (2001). *The language of new media*. Cambridge, MA: MIT Press.

McLuhan, M. (2002/1951). *The mechanical bride: Folklore of industrial man*. Boston: Beacon Press.

McLuhan, M. (1997/1962). *The Gutenberg galaxy: The making of typographic man*. Toronto: University of Toronto Press.

McLuhan, M. (1994/1964). *Understanding media: The extensions of man*. Cambridge, MA: MIT Press.

McLuhan, M., & McLuhan, E. (1988). *Laws of media: The new science*. Toronto: University of Toronto Press.

McLuhan, M., & Fiore, Q. (1967). *The medium is the message*. Harmondsworth: Penguin.

Morgan, R. (1998). Provocations for a media education in small letters. In D. Buckingham (Ed.), *Teaching popular culture: Beyond radical pedagogy* (pp. 107–131). London: University College London Press.

Morgan, R. (1996). Pantextualism, everyday life and media education. *Continuum: Journal of Media and Cultural Studies, 9*(2), 14–34.

Peters, M. A. (2003). Derrida, pedagogy and the calculation of the subject. *Educational Philosophy & Theory, 35*(3), 313–332.

Poyntz, S. (2006). Independent media, young people's agency, and the promise of media education. *Canadian Journal of Education, 29*(1), 154–175.

Rogoff, I. (1998). Studying visual culture. In N. Miroeff. (Ed.), *The visual culture reader*. (pp. 24–36). New York: Routledge.

Rutherford, P. (2004). *Weapons of mass persuasion: Marketing the war against Iraq*. Toronto: University of Toronto Press.

Sandywell, B. (2006). Monsters in cyberspace: Cyberphobia and cultural panic in the information age. *Information, Communication & Society, 9*(1), 39–61.

Stevenson, N. (2002). *Understanding media cultures: Social theory and mass communication* (2nd ed.). London: Sage.

Stevenson, N. (2000). The future of public media cultures: Cosmopolitan democracy and ambivalence. *Information, Communication & Society, 3*(2), 192–214.

Trifonas, P. P. (2003). Toward a deconstructive pedagogy of différance. In P. P. Trifonas (Ed.), *Pedagogies of difference: Rethinking education for social change* (pp. 220–235). London: Routledge Falmer.

Williams, R. (1985). *Keywords: A vocabulary of culture and society* (rev. ed.). New York: Oxford University Press.

7

WIKILEARNING AS RADICAL EQUALITY

Juha Suoranta and Tere Vadén

Introduction

At the end of his latest magnum opus *In Defense of Lost Causes* (2008), Slavoj Zizek lists the four antagonisms that, in his view, will not be solved or overcome by Capitalism. Not surprisingly, the first in the list is ecology, where the possibility of crisis is connected to the second antagonism: techno-science in the guise of biogenetics. New forms of apartheid (new walls between the wealthy West, and poverty and agony vegetating in the world's shanty towns, *favelas*, skid rows, barrios, and ghettos) is the third antagonism, the fourth being that of intellectual property (echoing Michael Hardt's and Antonio Negri's ideas of the commons; see Zizek 2008, 421–425.) It is the last of these antagonisms which we take as our starting point by studying the question of intellectual property and open access not from the juridical point of view but from the point of view of education as a core commons. In this respect we believe that living and learning in the Wikiworld—the already existing world of free resources, software and collaboration on the net (see Suoranta & Vadén 2010)—marks the unprecedented possibility to change our individualized and alienated ways of being and learning in the world into something more humane and more just. In this respect it is our contention that what we have called "wikilearning" is a new paradigm of learning at the same time as it is a means—perhaps even a weapon—in the hands of the majority of the people in their struggle to break free from the chains of the formal machinery of corporate and state-governed learning.

A working definition of wikilearning could be as follows: (1) the group is self-organized and volunteer (in opposition to pupils and students as captive audience in the school settings); this naturally includes the option of starting new groups (so-called forking), (2) all (study) materials are available on the basis of open access (content is created under copy left licenses, if licenses are needed at all), and (3) everybody has equal possibility for contributing, commenting and working on the materials right from the start. An additional condition could be (4) to limit wikilearning to activities that are mediated by computer networks (in practice, the Internet), but that seems an unnecessary move, as the point of wikilearning is also to disseminate the practices out of the cyberworld into other spheres of life. Wikilearning can also be defined using a pedagogical maxim launched by the French philosopher Jacques Rancière (1991): "Teach what you don't know." The maxim represents the ultimate equality between students and teachers, between people, as it does not take into account any distinctions like age, previous schooling history, or gender that are often taken as a basis of pedagogical rank. Thus wikilearning in its ideal form and full fruition but also in its many practices signifies radical equality between different people, and differs drastically from the politically regulated and curriculum-directed schooling systems governed by the state.

Institutional Education and Ideological Calls

National educational systems maintained by nation states are characteristically closed top-down organizations, and in the recent world of vast opportunities of learning they seem to forestall more than allow "opportunities for people to learn from each other" (Preskill & Brookfield 2009, 24). As ideological power structures, or in French philosopher Louis Althusser's terms, ideological state apparatuses, schools (including corporate universities) have classical overdeterminate structures which produce individual subjectivities. As such, schooling systems also fit Althusser's description of an ideological state apparatus in their capacity to present a "call" to the individual as a subject: "the category of the subject is constitutive of all ideology, but at the same time and immediately I add that *the category of the subject is only constitutive of all ideology insofar as all ideology has the function (which defines it) of 'constituting' concrete individuals as subjects*. In the interaction of this double constitution exists the functioning of all ideology, ideology being nothing but its functioning in the material forms of existence of that functioning" (Althusser 1971). Another way to say this is that the formal, systemic education is the ideological field as organized by the field of power. The ideological-educational matrix "calls out" the subjects by offering them various discursive positions and possibilities of agency penetrated by the institutional power of the state itself.

According to John Holloway (2005) "the state is not just a neutral institution but a specific form of social relations that arises with the development of capitalism. And, that it is a form of social relations that is based upon the exclusion of people from power, that is based on the separation and fragmentation of people." This we know from other analyzes, too. From the critical point of view the emphasis must be placed on the multi-layered socio-political structure of learning in state education: the key point is to realize how learning is regulated politically, and how it is in the service of dominant politics in society. In the formal learning processes of schooling both teachers and students become sub-ordinates with only relative autonomy. Althusser (1971) poses a crucial question, "What do children learn at school?", and provides the following answer:

> They go varying distances in their studies, but at any rate they learn to read, to write and to add—i.e. a number of techniques, and a number of other things as well, including elements (which may be rudimentary or on the contrary thoroughgoing) of 'scientific' or 'literary culture', which are directly useful in the different jobs in production (one instruction for manual workers, another for technicians, a third for engineers, a final one for higher management, etc.). Thus they learn know-how. But besides these techniques and knowledges, and in learning them, children at school also learn the 'rules' of good behaviour, i.e. the attitude that should be observed by every agent in the division of labour, according to the job he is 'destined' for: rules of morality, civic and professional conscience, which actually means rules of respect for the socio-technical division of labour and ultimately the rules of the order established by class domination. They also learn to 'speak proper French', to 'handle' the workers correctly, i.e. actually (for the future capitalists and their servants) to 'order them about' properly, i.e. (ideally) to 'speak to them' in the right way, etc. To put this more scientifically, I shall say that the reproduction of labour power requires not only a reproduction of its skills, but also, at the same time, a reproduction of its submission to the rules of the established order, i.e. a reproduction of submission to the ruling ideology for the workers, and a reproduction of the ability to manipulate the ruling ideology correctly for the agents of exploitation and repression, so that they, too, will provide for the domination of the ruling class 'in words'. In other words, the school (but also other State institutions like the Church, or other apparatuses like the Army) teaches 'know-how', but in forms which ensure *subjection to the ruling ideology* or the mastery of its 'practice'.

On the other hand, it is said that schools and educational institutions are among the few places in which it is possible to learn to participate in politics (Bauman 1999, 170), and also to learn certain skills of counterhegemony, although it is usually the case that teachers are forced to live a double life by being at the same time both the agents and the targets of ideological power. Most often schools follow curricula (whether national or more local) which are political documents to the core. Therefore, to act politically, or to be a political player in the field of education, a teacher should take that document as part of society's political programming, and not as an innocent handbook or as a substantial cornerstone of their work. Ideally, they should encourage their students to political meta-learning, to critically examine the foundations of curricula, its themes and subjects. That is, they ought to encourage their students to the development of a political awareness. Some try to this with notable heroism, perhaps leaving the curriculum aside and concentrating on the principles and practices of liberatory pedagogy while others claiming they do not care about politics (unfortunately, not realizing the long-term consequences of this position) ignore the question, or are socialized only to obey the rules of the given ruling ideology in their teacher training.

Of course, in principle (and in rare cases also in practice) teachers have power over their work (relative autonomy) and they execute their daily tasks independently from party politics or other ideological direction, but it is often the case that this is done in quite naive a manner or only in apparent independence: political and policy changes remain unnoticed. By saying this we are not referring to the individual teacher's thoughtlessness as such, her fault or error, but to the very fact that the ideological nature of the educational system does not reveal itself to political analyzes easily, and the structural forces opposing attempts to practice political meta-learning and raise political awareness are sometimes too great to overcome. Thus an important question is: "Can the teachers be expected to promote democratic practices in classrooms, when they representatives of the dominant power and at the same are its subordinates?" (Tomperi & Piattoeva 2005, 258). From Althusser's (1971) point of view, this is mission impossible:

> I ask the pardon of those teachers who, in dreadful conditions, attempt to turn the few weapons they can find in the history and learning they 'teach' against the ideology, the system and the practices in which they are trapped. They are a kind of hero. But they are rare and how many (the majority) do not even begin to suspect the 'work' the system (which is bigger than they are and crushes them) forces them to do, or worse, put all their heart and ingenuity into performing it with the most advanced awareness (the famous new methods!). So little do they suspect it that their own devotion contributes to the maintenance and nourishment of this ideological representation of the School, which makes the School today as 'natural', indispensable, useful and even beneficial for our contemporaries as the Church was 'natural', indispensable and generous for our ancestors a few centuries ago.

We cannot help thinking that every teacher needs skills and courage to acknowledge and question her political roles and ideological contexts in the digital age. Otherwise there is a danger of disconnect between students and teachers in that the latter group lags too much behind in their media and other literacies compared to the group of students (see Levin & Arafeh 2002). As so many times repeated in the already vast literature of critical pedagogy, critical position of educational workers is the bedrock for the democratic society. As Stephen Preskill and Stephen Brookfield (2009, 14) state, "perhaps the most important element of learning leadership [and to be a teacher, a father, a colleague, a scholar, we might add], however, is being open to learning from the people around you and letting them see how crucial this is for your own practice and development." That is why we now turn to another world of learning outside the reality of formal schooling and its ideological practices.

Wikilearning

Formal schooling assumes that there is always someone who knows in the end, someone who knows what others should know and acquire, someone who knows the meaning of things, and what is meaningful to know. In Lacanian-Zizekian terms this is the Big Other (see e.g., Zizek 2008). There is no more fundamental rationale for the modern schooling than this Big Other who "knows in advance." Using the terminology of Jacques Rancière the assumption of the Big Other refers to the pedagogical myth: it divides the world in two by supposing a socially constructed division of power, as well as a lower and higher intelligence. Writes Rancière (1991, 7):

> [The pedagogical myth] says that there is an inferior intelligence and a superior one. The former registers perceptions by change, retains them, interprets and repeats them empirically, within the closed circle of habit and need. This is the intelligence of the young child and the common man. The superior intelligence knows things by reason, proceeds by method, from the simple to the complex, from the part to the whole. It is this intelligence that allows the master to transmit his knowledge by adapting it to the intellectual capacities of the student and allows him to verify that the students has satisfactorily understood what he learned.

Of course, in everyday life it is impossible and unnecessary to live such a myth since learning occurs in the course of action and participation, that is, when something must be done, and, therefore and by the same token, learned. In the everyday world we very often seem to learn by ourselves, from our parents and guardians, and from our peers. Therefore we are inclined to think as adult education theorist Griff Foley (1999, 1) who contends that for him "the most interesting learning occurs informally and incidentally, in people's everyday lives. And some of the most powerful learning occurs as people struggle against oppression, as they struggle to make sense of what is happening to them and to work out ways of doing something about it."

Let us illustrate the ideological nature of formal education by an example that also leads directly to the particularities of wikilearning. As we saw in the quote from Althusser, above, the emphasis of formal learning is on usefulness: the key is to constitute and set to work subjectivities that are useful and minimally disruptive to the ruling ideology. In the current economico-political climate, the requirement of usefulness and effectivity has gained ever more momentum, the state demanding greater transparency and more precise target-ing of educational resources. "Employability" is one of the current buzzwords for this utilitarian function of formal education (see Moore 2009).

From the narrow point of view of "employability," any surplus of educa-tion is a at best a benign side-effect, at worst a waste of taxpayers money. As Terry Wrigley (2007, quoted in Moore 2009, 243–244) says, "capitalism needs workers who are clever enough to be profitable, but not wise enough to know what's really going on." Conversely, for the radical consciousness such a surplus is necessary, as observed already in the 1970s by Rudolf Bahro:

> The production of surplus consciousness that is already in train spontane-ously must be vigorously pursued in an active way, so as to produce quite intentionally a surplus of education which is so great, both quantitatively and qualitatively, that it cannot possibly be trapped in the existing struc-tures of work and leisure time, so that the contradictions of these struc-tures come to a head and their revolutionary transformation becomes indispensable.
>
> *(Bahro 1978, 404, cited in Gorz 1997, 89)*

One field for the surplus of education is, precisely, so-called informal educa-tion happening in a very natural *ad hoc* manner in everyday life; for instance, when pupils at school learn important lessons of life from their peers. Such informal learning extends beyond the school-hours, when the kids engage, for instance, in various activities on the Net, chatting, playing, gaming, and so on. It is this unregulated and, from the perspective of formal education, unneces-sary learning that forms the basis of the Wikiworld.

The Internet is one such field of open learning where we "common people" not only seek and share information but also create new knowledges and image new possibilities without anyone giving us orders or homework, without any-one's specific pedagogical or other authorization, and without usual patterns of classifications such as age, skills, gender, or ethnicity. Undoubtedly the most important example of wikilearning so far has been the Wikipedia and its sister projects such as Wikiversity.

Open wiki projects, such as Wikipedia and Wikiversity, take their form over time. They are, first of all, online communities that are responsible for building their own culture and way of operating. Because of this, when an open wiki project is started, it is hard to know what it will finally become. Still, open wiki projects do not develop independently because they are embedded in specific socio-cultural contexts. Because of their free and open nature—anyone may join—their context changes over time depending on the socio-cultural demographics of active community members (Leinonen, Vadén, & Suoranta 2009).

Both Wikipedia and Wikiversity are based on people's joint efforts in learning (call it folk knowledge, common wisdom, or collective intelligence). Besides the obvious fact that Wikipedia and its kinds are the largest informal educational apparatuses ever and as such represent the ultimate and quite coincidental (at least from the point of view of formal education) achievement in lifelong learning and popular education, they demonstrate the power of the collective learning in an ethical and very straightforward way. As put by David Runciman (2009): Wikipedia has turned into a relatively reliable source of information on the widest possible range of subjects because, on the whole, the good drives out the bad. When someone sabotages or messes with an otherwise sound entry, there are plenty of people out there who see it as their job to undo the damage, often within seconds of its happening. It turns out that the people who believe in truth and objectivity are at least as numerous as all the crazies, pranksters and time-wasters, and they are often considerably more tenacious, ruthless and monomaniacal. On Wikipedia, it's the good guys who will hunt you down.

The aim of Wikipedia is to set information available to everyone and to serve every learner who has access to the Internet. Wikilearning can be characterized as a Rhizome like in Sylvano Bussotti's notation in his composition entitled "Rhizome" (Five Pieces for David Tutor [1959]; Deleuze & Guattari 1987, 3). The notation is paradigmatic in its nonhierarchy if compared to typical "notations" of a well-ordered curriculum. Rhizome's staff does not determine playing; it arises, develops and lives organically.

It is important to note that the Wikipedia is explicitly a free encyclopedia, not a "comprehensive" or "reliable" one; these qualities are mere side-effects of freedom. Freedom here is understood in the sense of "free speech." Everyone is from the outset free to contribute to and edit on the articles in the Wikipedia. This ideal embodies in a great way the sense Ranciére gives to the universality of notions like egality (social and political equality). For Ranciére egality is not the goal of our actions, for instance, in education, it is rather the starting point; we act on the ground that everyone already is equal. The freedom of Wikipedia, together with its copyleft licence, which gives the users freedom to copy, modify and redistribute the material, given that the redistributed version is also copylefted, provide a social setting for the Ranciérian universality.

This social setting (free speech and copy left) is supported by the technological side of wiki software. A "wiki" is simply a web page (originally the name for the software underlying the web page) that can at any time by edited, and that automatically keeps track of the versions, and allows for the addition of new pages. Usually a wiki also has a tab for discussions, where the editions and additions can be deliberated on. Consequently, the wiki has become the dominant technology of knowledge creation, documentation, negotiations on knowledge, and so on. Epistemologically, a wiki page has interesting qualities: it has a visible history and a genealogy that can be seen. At the same time, with its "edit" button, it presents itself not as immutable "it is written"–

knowledge, but as provisional, fallible and collective, thus giving rise to a need of critical reflection on the uncertainty of knowledge. By combining these socio-technological properties of wikis (free speech, copy left, universality as a starting point, editability and version tracking) with the surplus of informal education we get the notion of *wikilearning*.

Characteristics of Wikilearning

It is possible to sketch dimensions—a typology—that characterize certain key differences between wikilearning and learning in formal settings such as school. At least the twelve aspects shown in Table 7.1 should be noted.

Radical Openness and "Disorganization" of Learning vs. Politically and Economically Regulated School Learning with Top-down, Ready-made Curriculum

Wikilearning is a radically open and dis- and unorganized in the sense that it is not regulated by laws or education policies, it is not part of a nation state and its educational system, but an independent activity. It does not exist in a written curriculum. However, as Scott Lash (2002), among others, has pointed out, the disorganizational nature of networked communities can be very effective. For

TABLE 7.1 Comparing Wikilearning and School Learning

Wikilearning	School Learning
Radical openness and "disorganization" of learning	Politically and economically regulated school learning with top-down, ready-made curriculum
Voluntary participation	Compulsory participation
Radical inclusiveness	Economically and culturally determined exclusiveness
Peer-to-peer (p-2-p) interaction	Teacher- and tutor directiveness
Reflective uncertainty	Unreflective certainty
Evaluation and synthetization	Listening and (rote-)memorizing
Cooperation and sharing	Evaluation of individual achievements
People's collective intelligence, knowledge as an aggregation	Schooled elite's expert knowledge, knowledge as a body of learning
Problem-based learning	Subject-based learning
Folksonomy	Taxonomy
Local, contextual ad hoc-learning	Predestined learning goals and achievements
Radical equality	Equal opportunities

instance, the informal volunteer organization provides a framework for such intricate distributed knowledge work as developing the GNU/Linux operating system.

Voluntary Participation vs. Compulsory Participation

Whereas wikilearning occurs in free participation, school learning is not only compulsory, but also governed and regulated by the federal government and/or the state, and teachers and adminstrators as "disciplinary experts" who not only decide what and how students ought to be learnt but also shape curriculum and assessment standards (Greenhow, Robelia, & Hughes 2009, 248). The voluntarity of wikilearning extends to all levels; the decision to participate or not, the intensity and mode of participation are all voluntary.

Radical Inclusiveness (Wikipublics, Wikipublicity) vs. Economically and Culturally Determined Exclusiveness (Mainstream Media, Counterpublics)

In order to participate in the mainstream media you have to have certain qualities in your possession. It is not enough to be able to read and write and speak. You also have to have a degree, that is, educational and cultural capital. Often a permission of some kind is needed, and often the permission is not granted in a neutral way, but may need connections, money, qualifications, etc. In addition, mainstream media is heavily dependent on both its owners and the flow of advertisement money. Both facts point to the same direction: mainstream media cannot be too controversial if it wants to sell and make a profit. Like the mainstream media, alternative media with their counterpublics have their own rules of participation, too, which exclude or include. Participation in wikilearning is much more inclusive activity: only basic literacy and computer skills are needed.

Peer-to-Peer (p-2-p) Interaction vs. Teacher and Tutor Directiveness

Wikilearning occurs in a peer to peer mode, that is, by learning from each other, and helping each other to learn. Importantly, the p-2-p structure allows also giving without taking and taking without giving, i.e., it is not reciprocal. Thus peer pressure is kept to a minimum. This might sound like a dream, or a never fulfilled utopia, but it is actually embedded in the use of the wiki technology itself. Where school learning "technology" is written according to the habits and traditions of didactics and pedagogy (teacher-centered, student-centered pedagogy and so forth), and these habits and traditions are also embodied in school buildings and classrooms designs etc., wikilearning is based on voluntary self-aggregation of the participants with their productive assets. These assets are both immaterial and material: immaterial as brain power and cooperation (or "participatory processing") with other users, and material as access to computer and to the digital networks (Bauwens 2009, 123).

Reflective Uncertainty vs. Unreflective Certainty

One general wikilearning principle is that of reflective uncertainty. Wiki information should not be taken for granted, because wikis are editable and the current edit may be erroneous if not outright malicious. However, the history of edits can, at least in principle, be traced back to the beginning. This, of course, is a dramatic difference between wiki-information and printed information. Wikipedia's edit and history buttons potentially increase learners' skills in critical media literacy in comparison to textbooks' qualities to augment unreflective certainty. Gradually, by using wiki type pages, users learn to mentally expect and anticipate the structures of editability and genealogy also on other pages, including those of books. Thus, the reflective uncertainty of wikified information leaks also to other areas of knowledge.

Evaluation and Synthetisation vs. Listening and (Rote-)Memorizing

In wikilearning it is crucial to negotiate on information and knowledge (e.g., in wikis' discussion areas and so-called coffee rooms) in contrast to school learning, which emphasizes hearing and listening, and rote memorizing the things teacher has taught. Wikilearning includes information searching and comparison of different sources of information as opposed to school learning's text book approach.

In addition communication and information exchange in wikilearning are not based on the model of sender and receiver, but on suggestion and evaluation. Take an ethnographic look to the classroom: in a traditional classroom the activities are speaking, listening, making notes, filling workbooks. The wikilearners are widely distributed, and the activities are typically computer-mediated. However, the difference is bigger on the level of cognition and experience. Speaking, listening and making notes correspond to the cognitive activities of conveying information and memorising. When an open source developer receives a piece of new code (a patch) the point is not to memorise or even to use it, but to evaluate it, and synthesise it with possibly several versions of the existing codebase. (It is also noteworthy, that in the hacker world, there is a militant ethos of evaluating the patch, the hack, and not the submitter, the author of the patch). Ideally, all activity in wikilearning has this quality of evaluation and integration, rather than delivering and memorising. This quality of learning can be seen especially in young people's learning as Greenhow et al. (2009, 251) point out: "Contradicting traditional pedagogical models in which students submit their works to one authoritative source (the instructor) and receive feedback from that source, today's learners expect to participate in evaluating as well as in being evaluated and to share work and feedback among their peers."

Cooperation and Sharing vs. Evaluation of Individual Achievements

Wikilearning is based on doing and creating together. The idea is that no one can achieve alone what can be achieved together. In wikilearning individuals' learning achievements are not measured, criteria external to learning activity itself are not used. The value of a learning activity will be judged only by the participants themselves based on their different motivations of participation (utility, fun, communality, etc.).

People's Collective Intelligence vs. Expert Knowledge of the Schooled Elite

A wiki page aggregates the common pool of information by the editors of the page. It is not the property or achievement of any one participant in the group and could not be written by any one editor. The wiki software is built for this kind of aggregation, not for the publication or dissemination of pre-existing knowledge. Furthermore, the process of aggregation does not have a pre-defined endpoint. The aggregate is always freely available and subject to further uses, editions, modifications and additions. This promotes a radical plurality of information, compared to the gated or closed forms of expert information relied on by formal education.

Problem-based Learning vs. Subject-based Learning

The motivation for wikilearning is based on voluntarism, therefore the artificial boundaries of subjects (such as maths, literature, etc.) do not have to be replicated. The motivation of each participant is in one way or another *internal*—based on the desires and problems of everyday life. This is, again, in clear contrast to formal education which is often compulsory and in which individual learning tasks are often externally motivated (by the need to get good grades, to be a good pupil, etc.).

Folksonomy vs. Taxonomy

Connected to the point above, the material in wikilearning is categorised and interconnected by ways which the users find meaningful, not in the categories of expert definitions or institutional classifications. The tags and hyperlinks created by users eventually build a folksonomy, in which both the basis for the classification (the ontology) and the classification itself emerge without expert validation either before or after the fact. Thus folksonomy supplants the more familiar taxonomies where the new always gets subsumed under the old.

Local, Contextual Ad Hoc Learning vs. Predestined Learning Goals and Achievements

Wikilearning responds to local and contextual needs. In the anthropology on open source software developers, one of the earliest groups that have embraced wikilearning to the full, this phenomenon is called "scratching your own itch"; developers typically develop software that they themselves need or want to learn about (see Raymond 1999). Consequently, also the process and duration of learning are based on this real-world need, unlike in formal schooling where pre-existing goals have to be achieved and where performance is evaluated with regard to rigid benchmarks.

Radical Equalities vs. Equal Opportunities

As discussed above, wikilearning is based on radical equality in the sense that with regard to wikilearning everyone already is equal—the starting point is the freedom of everyone to participate, create, use the materials, etc. Wikilearning is not regulated by academic degrees and does not intend to produce a rival hierarchy or order of rank. In fact, typically, the hierarchy in a disorganisation is also task-based, contextual, informal and susceptible to rapid changes.

The Impact of Wikilearning: Radical Equality Comes to the School

Let us return to radical equality once more. The point of starting from the idea of equality in learning is, of course, not the naive presupposition that right from the outset everyone would have the same dispositions, capacities, skills, etc. The idea of radical equality is not a description of empirical facts, but rather a principle that structures action. For example, consider a doctor facing a person who is ill. The doctor may base his response to the patient based on various qualifications, such as whether the person is insured or not, whether or not she belongs to the group of people that the doctor is responsible, and so on. Alternatively, by assuming the position of radical equality, the doctor may structure his response by assuming the equality of all patients. Or consider a refugee or a migrant from the poor South to the rich West. Typically, the bureaucracy responds to her by demanding different qualification and documents that may or may not prove that she is entitled to this or that service or benefit. Again, the point of radical equality would be for the bureaucrat to structure her action so that the refugee/migrant already is equal to any fully documented citizen.

By analogy, the processes of wikilearning are structured so that they "call out" the equality of all participants. No external consideration limits access. This is the counter-ideological move. Learning is geared toward the qualities of co-operation, Habermasian negotiations and deliberation, and, most importantly, towards a plurality of knowledges.

In terms of education, this means the demolition of teachers as authorities, the sources or catalysts of learning. It is possible—even desirable—to teach that which you do *not* know! (see Suoranta 2008). Ranciére turns the tables by suggesting that it is the educator (the "explicator") who needs the idea of the uneducated, not the other way around. The educator "calls out" the uneducated: "It is the explicator who needs the incapable and not the other way around; it is he who constitutes the incapable as such. To explain something to someone is first of all to show him he cannot understand it by himself" (Rancière 1991, 6). Here we find the knot that ties wikilearning as radical equality to social justice: "We know, in fact, that explication is not only the stultifying weapon of pedagogues but the very bond of the social order. Whoever says order says distribution into ranks" (Rancière 1991, 117).

Of course, wikilearning can also be seen from a different, more critical vantage point: it too has its own ideological traps and hidden assumptions which state that in the free world of learning a learner becomes docile knowledge-skill worker who is willing to serve as a servant of creative economy; she is active and interactive 24/7, media savvy, flexible, and reflective. On this dark side of wikilearning, the learner becomes her own task-master who has internalized the needs of the market to the point where all requirements on her skills and time have been outsourced to herself. Here wikilearning has been appropriated as a hyper-effective part of the utilitarian educational machine.

The answer to this danger is not to step away from wikilearning, but to inject it with a purpose that is dialectically both internal and fundamentally alien to the utilitarian goals. What we have in mind is, of course, again, the surplus of education that is both spurred on by capitalism itself (as entertainment, edutainment, lost generations, etc.) and feeds on the gaps in capitalism (there are innumerable wikis on alternative economies, self-subsistency, self-help, DIY culture, etc.).

What of the relationship between formal education and wikilearning? Naturally, seeing the hypercompetitive allure of wikilearning, schools everywhere want to align themselves with its promise, presenting themselves as "formal learning with a human face"; as schools who are on the forefront of social media, web 2.0, and so on. There are numerous reasons to be skeptical of this development. The structures of formal education (compulsory attendance, division of subjects, division between teachers and students, need to give grades to individuals, etc.) strongly counteract any attempt to inject wikilearning into schools.

In order to really align former formal education with wikilearning, we have to go all the way. In practice this would mean that schools fully embrace the

Wikiversity as a global platform of learning. By now it is clear that digital information and communications technologies create new forms of interaction and learning which do not exist without those technologies, or were not obvious in the earlier stages of those technologies (Liff & Steward 2001, 340). But as Leinonen et al. (2009) note:

> There is a chance that Wikiversity will become one of the most important online education sites on the Internet with a great impact on global capacity building. But it is possible that Wikiversity will slowly vanish when the first pioneering volunteers realize that running an online education site requires more than masses of editors of wiki pages.

This is where the "heroes of formal schooling" have a revolutionary possibility: by assuming the position of radical equality they can open up the learning processes in which they and their co-learners (be they "pupils" or "colleagues") are engaged, and at the same time take part in creating educational resources beyond the commodified educational market. Free software already exists, free encyclopedia exists, and the next wave is free education.

Conclusions

What we have wanted to understand and emphasize is that Wikiworld is a site for multiple voices necessary for the democratic struggle for global justice. And actually we are imagining even more for we acclaim that, if allowed, common people, the great majority, will use Wikiworld most effectively, and it is our task as affluent parts of the population to fight with them in terms of open access. We define Wikiworld as collectively distributed network and wikilearning as shared meaning-making as an opponent to the traditional model of schooling based at least partly on elite's often well-hidden "hatred of democracy" (Rancière 2007). From this perspective the ideas of the wikiworld and wikilearning can be hard to digest for those who see them only as adjuncts to the capitalist market and capitalist schooling. Thus, we are inclined to think as *mujerista* theologian Ada María Isasi-Díaz (2008, 382), who focuses especially on the standpoint of poor women:

> the poor and oppressed are better able to imagine another way of understanding and dealing with reality, a way that can make us all realize that every one of us must struggle against oppression. I am in no way claiming that poor women are intellectually more capable or morally superior. The claim for privileging the understandings and praxis of poor women has to do with what it means to know reality. Being involved in the material mediations of reality, taking responsibility for reality, and changing reality are intrinsic elements of knowing reality. Because changing reality is central to knowing reality, those who are privileged are necessarily less

inclined to change reality than those who have little or nothing to lose by changing it. The fact is poor women and all the oppressed must change reality if they (and the rest of us) are to survive.

The wikiworld is about changing the premises of living in the world. Wikilearning belongs to everyone. And thus the questions of learning freedom and democracy and changing the world are always questions about power, the use of power, and the capacity to do things in a given political and social circumstances with other people. As prominent social theorist John Holloway (2005) has stated, "power means our capacity to do things. This power, it seems to me, is always a social power, simply because the doing of one person always depends on the doing of others. It is very difficult for me to imagine a doing which would not be dependent on the doing of other people. It is clear that our doing here at the moment depends on the doing of hundreds or thousands of people who created the technology we are using, who created the concepts we are using."

Where some social theorists have doubted the potential of critical educational practices as tools for changing the world (see Holst 2002, 78–79), others, like Rancière, have answered the question affirmatively. From our point of view, the question has been wrongly posed since education, society and politics are always inseparable and intertwined; they are woven into each other in the level of people's everyday learning. Thus it is not useful to decide the question by theorizing it in advance; theorization depends upon the social practices in the area of wikilearning and the surrounding social world. The question is only how learning and its complex, ideological and hegemonic relations are defined and arranged in societies. For us the emancipatory practice of wikilearning is the cradle of radically equality.

References

Althusser, L. (1971). *Lenin and Philosophy and Other Essays* (Trans. B. Brewster). New York: Monthly Review Press. Retrieved from http://www.marxists.org/reference/archive/althusser/1970/ideology.htm

Bahro, R. (1978). *The Alternative in Eastern Europe*. London: New Left Books.

Bauman, Z. (1999). *In Search of Politics*. Stanford, CA: Stanford University Press.

Bauwens, M. (2009). Class and Capital in Peer Production. *Capital & Class, 97*, 121–141.

Deleuze, G., & Guattari, F. (1987). *A Thousand Plateaus. Capitalism and Schizophrenia*. Minneapolis: University of Minnesota Press.

Foley, G. (1999). *Learning in Social Action. A Contribution to Understanding Informal Education*. London: Zed Books.

Gorz, A. (1997). *Farewell to the Working Class*. London: Pluto Press.

Greenhow, C., Robelia, B., & Hughes, J. E. (2009). Learning, Teaching, and Scholarship in a Digital Age. *Educational Researcher, 38*(4), 246–259.

Holloway, J. (2005). *Change the World Without Taking Power*. Retrieved from http://eipcp.net/transversal/0805/holloway/en

Holst, J. (2002). *Social Movements, Civil Society, and Radical Adult Education*. Westport, CT: Bergin & Garvey.

Isasi-Díaz, A. M. (2008). Se Hace Camino al Andar [The Road is Made by Walking: What the Future Demands of Women-Centered Theologies]. *Feminist Theology, 16*(3), 379–382.

Lash, S. (2002). *Critique of Information.* London: SAGE.

Leinonen, T., Vadén, T., & Suoranta, J. (2009). Learning In and With an Open Wiki Project: Wikiversity's Potential in Global Capacity Building. *First Monday, 14*(2). Retrieved from http://firstmonday.org/htbin/cgiwrap/bin/ojs/index.php/fm/article/viewArticle/2252/2093

Levin, D., & Arafeh, S. (2002). *The Digital Disconnect. The Widening Gap between Intenet-Savvy Students and their Schools.* Washington, DC: Pew Internet and American Life Project. Retrieved from http://www.pewinternet.org/Reports/2002/The-Digital-Disconnect-The-widening-gap-between-Internetsavvy-students-and-their-schools.aspx

Liff, S., & Steward, F. (2001). Communities and Community e-Gateways. In T. Teoksessa Keeble, L. Leigh, & B. Loader (Eds.), *Community Informatics. Shaping Computer-Mediated Social Relations* (pp. 324–341). London: Routledge.

Moore, P. (2009). UK Education, Employability, and Everyday Life. *Journal for Critical Education Policy Studies, 7*(1). Retrieved from http://www.jceps.com/?pageID=article&articleID=151

Preskill, S., & Brookfield, S. (2009). *Learning as a Way of Leading. Lessons from the Struggle for Social Justice.* San Francisco: Jossey-Bass.

Rancière, J. (1991). *The Ignorant Schoolmaster. Five Lessons in Intellectual Emancipation.* Stanford, CA: Stanford University Press.

Rancière, J. (2007). *Hatred of Democracy.* London: Verso.

Raymond, E. (1999). *The Cathedral and the Bazaar.* Sebastopol, CA: O'Reilly.

Runciman, D. (2009). Like a Boiling Frog. The Future of Wikipedia. *London Review of Books 31*(10). Retrieved from http://www.lrb.co.uk/v31/n10/runc01_.html

Suoranta, J. (2008). *Jacques Rancière on Radical Equality and Adult Education.* Encyclopaedia of Philosophy of Education. http://www.ffst.hr/ENCYCLOPAEDIA/doku.php?id=jacques_ranciere_on_radical_equality and_adult_education

Suoranta, J., & Vadén, T. (2010). *Wikiworld.* London: Pluto Press.

Tomperi, T., & Piattoeva, N. (2005). Demokraattisten juurten kasvattaminen. [Rasing the Democratic Roots]. In T. Kiilakoski, T. Tomperi, & M. Vuorikoski (Eds.), *Kenen kasvatus? [Whose Education]* (pp. 247–286). Tampere, Finland. Vastapaino.

Wrigley, T. (2007). Rethinking Education in an Era of Globalisation. *Journal for Critical Education Policy Studies, 5*(2). Retrieved from http://www.jceps.com/index.php?pageID=article&articleID=95

Zizek, S. (2008). *In Defense of Lost Causes.* London: Verso.

8

LEARNER VOICE AND LIVED CULTURE IN DIGITAL MEDIA PRODUCTION BY YOUNGER LEARNERS

Implications for Pedagogy and Future Research

John Potter

The concerns about the widening gap between the activities of youth in school and at home in the countries of the developed world have been widely reported in both mainstream media and academic commentary. I am including YouTube in the mainstream media for the purposes of this argument. A widely viewed YouTube video such as "A Vision of School Students Today" (Wesch, 2007), which includes a series of slow fades through a lecture hall with students holding up placards which call for a greater engagement on the part of the teachers in their schools, holds the possibilities and potentials of digital media, as represented by the productive use of the Internet for social networking, communicative and educational activity.

In popular commentary on the subject, authors such as Mark Prensky (2005) invoke the concept of "digital native" to describe the situation of children and young people in the wider society. Older people are "immigrants" who speak in strange accents and whose brains are wired only for older cultures. Far from bemoaning the state of popular culture, others such as Steven Johnson (2005) maintain that popular culture is making us smarter. From a more academic perspective both Mimi Ito and Henry Jenkins celebrate participatory culture, with Jenkins and his colleagues (2006) identifying very many ways in which productive engagement with new media introduces sophisticated and multiple new skills and dispositions. Meanwhile Ito's (Ito et al., 2009) youth are capable of deep immersion in activities, multitasking, developing and refining their skills. These enthusiastic authors are countered somewhat by other commentators such as Nicholas Carr (2010) who has published work claiming to show that heavy Internet users are having their brains wired differently by long engagement with many screens, moving from task to task, recognising the idea that sophisticated multitasking activity is possible but at the cost to deeper, reflective thinking. Certainly this meme, in Lankshear and Knobel's (2006, p. 128) sense of a "contagious pattern of thought," has taken root in mainstream press in many countries, including the United States, where a recent supplement of the *New York Times* reported that youth were "Wired for distraction: Struggling to learn in a flood of texting, web surfing and games" showing in interviews in the article how good grades do not follow night after night of multitasking with social networking sites and more (Richtel, 2010).

Recently, at the inaugural conference of the Media Education Association in the UK in November, 2010 (MEA, 2010), a number of presenters concerned themselves with the pedagogical challenges presented by working with young people in a range of settings in an era of profound and rapid media and cultural change Whilst there was a familiar ring to many of the papers, a notable shift was occurring in the field which signalled a genuine attempt at dialogue between previously separate communities. Technologists and social media commentators presented alongside teachers, teacher educators and consultants. The common theme in many sessions seemed to be how to take account of participatory culture in the new media age. Meanwhile, in his keynote, Henry Jenkins debunked many of the common tropes and misconceptions held about the issue. "Digital natives" as a concept got short shrift with Jenkins pointing out that even if that analogy held true, immigrants to new worlds always bring useful artefacts and traditions from the old world into the New World when they arrive there; the implication being that slower forms of textual engagement and comprehension may be things to value for at least some of the tasks with which youth and others are engaged.

Nevertheless, the analogy by Prensky (op. cit.), whilst imperfect has at least been useful in fuelling a debate about a real issue. This is not about the "natives" and "immigrants" as such but about the relations between *all* social actors in the field of education and learning in the new media age. For all the roles in schools, the advent of wider access to digital media age has encompassed huge changes in the artefacts, practices and social arrangements around cultural production (Lievrouw and Livingstone, 2006). We are all swimming in technology and media culture and all of us; even teachers, as well as students, children, parents, social commentators and academics are wrestling with the same issues. For pedagogy this means considering how to engage fully with participatory culture, how to refine educational systems so that they do not leave the very real skills and dispositions being displayed by children and young people outside the school gate.

Certainly as educational consultant Sir Ken Robinson (2010) and many other commentators point out school systems in both the developed world and in the developing world are undergoing rapid reform in the light of such developments as media technologies, mobile learning, and the all pervasive online experiences. The school curriculum in many countries, as one of a number of legacies of colonialism, is designed around a 19th-century industrial-pedagogical model. Robinson and others suggest that in successful countries, there is space for innovation and support for a technological and media driven revolution in the curriculum and its mode of delivery. Many educators who may previously have considered themselves to be in the didactic mode of teaching with technology are taking what has been described as the "mediatic turn" (Friesen and Hug, 2008). In doing this they are seeking to enact in a real pedagogical setting many of these suggestions and notions presented by David Buckingham in his attempts to describe how we can, should, and even must move beyond thinking about technology and fetishising its artefacts and into an engagement in the curriculum with media culture (2007).

Where the curriculum organisation in a country enables the creative combinations of subjects into projects and themes, there is a corollary with the way both business is done, and problems are solved in the world beyond the classroom. Students learn how to combine and recombine many different sources; they learn how to critique and how to be critical users of these sources. In the UK, the most recent pronouncements on the curriculum by the new education Secretary suggests that there is going to be a pause in attempting to join this world revolution and a backward set of steps to the 19th century model mentioned above. Again, and it is perhaps a debate worth having, this is about a deeply felt need by traditionalists to return to what is assumed to be a long vanished but reliable and successful set of methods in teaching and learning, centred around "subjects" and "facts." The connection to cultural theory in this meme returns us to the middle of the century before last and the pronouncements of Matthew Arnold, describing education as being about communicating the "Best that has been thought and said in the world" (2009).

As the debates continue there is a pressing need for researchers to report from the various settings around the world. Whilst many, such as those who reported at the MEA-organised Media Literacy Conference (MLC2010) described above, are concerned with older children, there is a pressing need for a similar engagement with younger learners. It is no longer the case that 11 years is the starting point of an engagement with media culture. How are the new media cultures to be accounted for in educational spaces? What is the likely interface with home in the new media age? How will pedagogy change? What are the consequences if nothing changes?

Two recent research projects may prove useful in framing thinking about how to approach younger children. Both were designed to explore ways of working with younger children's media cultures in a productive sense within the confines of the regulated school curriculum and its buildings and spaces. Each of the case studies attempts to present a different strand which is nevertheless inter-related in trying to build an understanding of how educational designs can reflect changes in material and media culture. In turn it might be possible to locate ways in which these changes could drive curriculum reform as well as future research in the field.

The work described in the sections which follow is predicated on the assumption that is not reasonable to assume that studies of youth and older children are the only places to look in trying to understand the interface between interactions with popular culture at home and the curriculum in school. In the UK, studies by Sonia Livingstone and colleagues over a number of years (Livingstone, 2009) have explored the opportunities and risks by younger children with increased engagement in online environments and new media and have shown that the opinions and actions of younger learners is a rich field of research. Younger and younger children are entering education systems with wide experiences of popular culture and media, including the productive use of new media.

The first project presented here explored the differences between children's experience of new media technology at school and at home. The methodology attempted to connect to the wider themes of the project by engaging with children's own media production in the form of video and audio recordings in the field. The findings in this study suggested that the desire to engage with the "learner voice" approach was representative of a wider need to see experience of popular culture reflected and acknowledged within pedagogy. This approach also suggests that it might be possible for teachers themselves to research the learner voices of the children and young people in their care. The methodology is simple and easily replicated and yields extremely interesting results about the inter-relationship between children as views of their own learning and the wider media culture.

In the second project, fieldwork was carried out in two schools among children taking part in video projects on themes of self-representation and identity. The findings in this study suggested that this new media literacy practice can be metaphorically conceived as a form of "curatorship" in the organisation of digital media assets and that this connects to an important set of dispositions and skills in lived culture which might be profitably and usefully explored in pedagogical reforms.

Hearing the Learner Voice: Using Student-generated Video and Audio in Research

Research which connects culture, media and pedagogy is emerging which looks at the structures and opportunities for agentive behaviour in participatory culture (Ito et al., 2009; Livingstone, 2009). The research project, Learners and Technology 7–11 (Selwyn, Potter, and Cranmer, 2008) aimed to explore these structures and opportunities within, between and outside school and home settings. Data was collected in primary schools in five settings in the UK from children in the upper age range. A questionnaire completed by 612 pupils and focus group interviews formed the more traditional research methods employed in the work. However, in order to further the aims of a project exploring issues of agency in the uses of new technology and media, the researchers were concerned to involve the pupils themselves in the data collection. Thus they also collected drawings of future ICT uses by 355 pupils, *pupil led* focus groups, online elicitation of pupil generated content, audio and video data generated by pupils within the school.

At the end of a series of visits to schools and many, many hours of analysis of audio and video data, it was possible to draw conclusions around the locus of control of the curriculum and children's desire for change and greater control over their use of technology in the school setting. The children were not surprised about the differences between home and school and neither did they have any great expectations for change. Nevertheless, as the researchers concluded:

> Despite the slightly prosaic nature of some of the responses, it would be unwise to dismiss these responses as uninformed and unimaginative. Indeed, we would contend that these depictions of a desired future reflect many of the tensions underlying children's current engagements with ICTs in school. Specifically we would contend that the data in this report provide a telling insight into the issues underlying pupil's understandings of ICT and schools. In particular many of the responses reflect clearly the restrictions of the schools and the (relative) freedoms of the home, as well as the oppositional relationship between the 'work' of learning in school and the 'play' of using digital media at home.
>
> *(Selwyn, Potter, and Cranmer, 2008, p. 28)*

It is true to say that not all of the data collection methods achieved the ambitious aims of the project. The online elicitation was held up and ultimately thwarted by the difficulties in the ways in which school culture allowed or did not allow access to external sites. However, the student initiated video productions were much more successful and the student-led focus groups more successful still; making media where the locus of control of the research fell much more into the hands of the children seemed to be highly successful. Videos in two of the project schools were directed and shot by pupils as young as 8 or 9. Most of these clips were filmed handheld and in mid shot or close-up on a child or pair of children, with the questions asked from behind the camera. This had the effect of freeing up dialogue between children familiar to each other as well as allowing researchers to look for other key markers in gesture and choice of framing when applying multimodal analysis to the texts afterwards (Kress and Van Leeuwen, 2001; Burn and Parker, 2003). However, pupil-led talk is not necessarily the norm in schools in the settings at this point in time where a legacy of years of teacher-talk centred methods has taken its toll. Certainly the evidence on many of these videos backed the assertion that pupils wished to construct an answer which was school-focused and school-expected and that they were indeed playing out the roles they should. It took control of the camera to free up the learner-researchers and provoke deeper thinking on the subject.

In other videos it was obvious that higher levels of media production experience were reflected in the richness of the responses. Certainly, pupil-led talk was richer in their productions with children frequently moving off-script and being confident to follow a line of thought. This helped to create a series of "fly on the wall" documentary-style productions which allowed the interviewers to assume the role of investigative journalists. The four videos on school use in this particular setting featured interviews of children at work in a computer suite, playing curriculum-based games, assembling slide presentations as well as talking to each other about sites which they visited inside and outside school.

The videos which examined the issue of home use took the form of focus group discussions, led by pupils. They used some of the techniques which the researchers had employed, building on answers in the style of a semi-structured interview and, in most cases, allowing for discussion to take place. One example concerned the different uses of websites and social networking and alluded directly to the subversive nature of the activity at home compared to school. The speaker concealed his mouth as he revealed himself to be a regular user of the social networking site, Piczo, which was blocked in school and discouraged at home. The speaker was well aware of the fact that the research video was being made in school by his friends and could be seen by teachers and researchers. He was keen to reveal his use of this site, yet in the gesture of partial disguise of his voice, he was signalling that he is aware that doing so is effectively transgressive. His playful gesture of concealment showed awareness of the watching children, teachers and researchers and of his position as a particular kind of social actor in the setting.

This data from the interviews was analysed alongside the children's drawings and surveys and focus groups in which the children were trained as facilitators and left to work on their own. Across all available artefacts there was, as stated above, evidence of the disconnect between home and school uses of new media technologies. There was a desire for change expressed many times in each of the available modes which was constrained and shaped by the social and pedagogic functions of the school. Nevertheless, pupil engagement with the process suggested that they had a sophisticated understanding of the ways in which the social spaces operate and how their new media use differs in the context of home and school. The desire for change did not spring so much from wanting to engage less with the formal curriculum, as might be imagined by following the "digital natives" argument (Prensky, op.cit.), so much as from a wish to bring some of the skills and processes used outside school back into the setting. Permission was sought in their illustrations packed with such pleas, for gaming and other new media entertainment to be allowed into school, but, for the most part, alongside and incorporated into the settings.

It is important to note that the attempt to hear the "learner voice" on these issues was based on a democratic, participatory and emancipatory view of research design with learners as proposed by Michael Fielding (2004). He suggested four stages of learner engagement with activities in school. At the most basic level learners are used simply as a data source, assessed against normative targets. The next stage is to think of learners as active respondents to questions and to listen and analyse the responses that they give in particular settings where they have the freedom to discuss aspects of their learning. The third level positions learners as co-researchers with increased involvement in the learning decisions taken by teachers. Finally, with learners as researchers themselves, partnership is the dominant motif in activities with student voice leading the way. In this case the skills and dispositions of lived culture where students are more generative and active outside of school have a corollary with the activities which they are required to undertake inside school. The research in this project was conducted somewhere between the third and fourth levels described by Fielding.

In the opening sections of this chapter I made reference to a belief that all social actors in the setting should be represented. We were therefore interested in discovering which aspects of the discussion would be welcomed by the teachers of these children, how (or whether) they would they see their role changing and also how they would reposition teaching and learning with media in school. In this we were going to the heart of going to the heart of much of the discussion at the MEA-organiszed MLC event mentioned in the opening sections. There was a cautious but positive welcome to the greater use of new media in other areas of the curriculum, in other subjects. Teachers themselves are actors in the outside world where technology and media are part of material and lived culture.

In particular teachers welcomed bringing into the open some aspects of teaching and learning with websites, where there was more discussion about what is true on a site, about what is true or likely about what somebody says in a comment and so on. One might expect to see the discussion elide with the debates on e-safety and this indeed what happened with remarkable commonality and candour in the views expressed from the school, regulatory side. Indeed the only aspects of the opinions of the learners and their proposed solutions which were not popular with teachers and which were viewed negatively in the curriculum going forward included the limiting factors of the curriculum itself.

It would seem from these discussions that our confirmation of differences between children's use of technology at home and their experiences at school was not news to any of the teachers. However, the ways in which the teachers then went on and conceived being able to 'work with' children's home uses of ICT (rather than simply ignoring them) was surprising and interesting. Although many were aware of children's ICT interests and skills, most teachers did not feel fully competent and confident to reach across the divide and make use of these skills in the classroom. Children's home use was certainly not an unknown quantity, but was not known enough to be made full use of in the classroom.

Much more discussion of this project occurs elsewhere (Selwyn, Potter, and Cranmer, 2010) for this chapter the key elements to take from it are that:

- Learners require a space which gives them a voice on issues of internet and new media use from an early age;
- Video production of interviews and audio recording of their own groups is a dynamic and replicable methodology which unlocked how media are perceived more widely inside and outside school.

Digital Video Production, Autobiography and Curatorship

Student-generated video by younger learners in another context entirely forms the basis of the second project discussed in this chapter. In this case the production was not framed by an overarching investigative enquiry by outsiders. In this case the content of the videos was much closer to the fourth level of learner voice research proposed by Fielding (op. cit.) with children as researchers of their own learning and context. This study analysed the process and the productive output of a video project by young learners in two primary schools in which freely authored videos were conceived as a commemorative piece about their time in the school, celebrating spaces, relationships and memories; in the case of one group, this was just before leaving those spaces and relationships. The project has been discussed and written about at a micro level of individual video pieces (Potter, 2005, 2010) as well as the macro overview of the whole enterprise within the parameters of a (completed) doctoral study (Potter, 2009).

A factor in the project, which was common across all productions made in the schools, was the way in which the videos themselves made aspects of the children's past lives and current development beyond the curriculum visible where previously they had been invisible. In representing identity at the moment in time in which the production was shot and edited the learners were also, in addition to responding to the commission to curate an aspect of their lives, putting down a marker of their changing identity. This is a powerful and slightly different conception of video making in school, making use of the cultural capital (Bourdieu, 1986) which the children were able to employ in structuring their pieces and representing themselves. What emerged, beyond the forms produced themselves was a new way of examining the relationship of autobiographical modes of expression to the wider, lived culture.

Active, agentive curatorship of media resources in production may be said to enable previously invisible processes around growing and changing to be represented in media remixes and reformulations. In this there is a degree of accordance with aspects of theories of identity (Goffman, 1990; Giddens, 1991;

Merchant, 2005) as well as with those of learner or student voice (Fielding, op. cit). The authenticity of these voices may be difficult to prove and highly contested, as perhaps in the project outlined in the previous section, but, allowing for these debates, a key aim was to find a way to analyse carefully the video productions, as well as the associated interview responses, to see if activities and artefacts close to the lived culture of the learners were permitting control and curatorship of media assets. In this, it was important to adopt the view of active assimilation of such assets as derived by those working in the field of new media literacies (Robinson and Turnbull, 2005). However, the study aimed to pursue a different goal, investigating this active assimilation in terms of a kind of "curatorship" of media assets, implying collection, assembly and exhibition. This positioned the curatorship of media assets, self-produced (as in the actual shots in the video) or collected from other sources (the music, other images) as an active skill and disposition which bridges literacy practices and identity representation and is both evident and inherent in children's media production.

Whilst an adapted form of multimodal analysis was used to unlock the modes in the productions (Burn and Parker, 2003) there were further frameworks drawn from media literacy and socio-cultural theory (de Certeau, 1984; Foucault, 1984; Bourdieu, 1986) which enabled a rich account to be constructed about the purposes, skills and dispositions of the learners as they represented their identity. With some of the similarities in form in evidence in the children's video productions, including parody of news and interviews, or anarchic free play interspersed with more obviously narrative forms, there were clear distinctions in terms of the successful use of expressive qualities across all of them. It was also possible to locate aspects of Street's proposed model of "ideological" literacy (Street, 2003) across all these practices, in the children's rich engagement with the medium in so many forms. Thus one child was able to name teamwork as a key component in his vision of himself as a new literacy practitioner in digital video production; others gave interviews fully in role as famous directors; one girl quietly describes her joy at finding herself undaunted in the many possibilities of editing when others couldn't cope. Equally, there are times where this awareness breaks down or arrives too late in the day, as with some children regretting that they only saw the potential of the medium and their relation to it, after they had finished.

Gee's "affinity spaces" (2004) in which people successfully take part and make meaning inside groups or networks has something to offer the discussion of the children as new literacy practitioners, certainly in so far as some of the defining characteristics of this concept are apparent in relation to the videos. Affinity spaces, which Gee suggests are usually found in networks outside of formal school structures, offer opportunities to access higher order thinking skills. Even though these video projects took place within school, the children concerned were operating in a "third space" beyond the curriculum at a point in the school year where they had completed formal engagement with testing and were soon to leave. They had opportunities to participate in the project off timetable. Perhaps they illustrated a way to create the kinds of opportunities which Gee outlines, within the school environment. Affinity spaces have eleven characteristics in Gee's original conception, and these projects exemplify six of them as follows (from proposals by Gee, 2004, with each characteristic quoted in italics):

- a *"common endeavour"* is established in the brief at the beginning of these projects, with its high stake emphasis on self -representation;
- there is no attempt to separate children into skill sets and to establish mastery of some over others, *"newbies and masters and everyone else share common space"*;
- in the editing of the pieces, *"content is transformed by interactional organisation"*—the children bring in media assets to be added to the production and discuss their place;
- *"intensive and extensive knowledge are encouraged"*—thus children may value each other's ability to work *intensively* with a specialised part of the process, with editing for example at the same time as *extensively*, for example, by bringing in an idea for the overarching narrative;
- *"tacit knowledge is encouraged and honoured"*—such that even if not articulated in words, people's individual contributions are incorporated in the form of their tacit understanding of form and their generation of new ideas for content, even where this is sometimes hard to express
- *"there are many different forms and routes to participation"*—this takes account of the different roles in production in new media; the affinity space in production fosters engagement by a wider group across different skill sets for different lengths of time, at different times.

Some of these issues have also been addressed specifically in relation to younger learners (Marsh, 2004; Larson and Marsh, 2005) in arguing for a wide and inclusive definition of, and engagement with, new literacies; which takes into account the range of practices undertaken by young people with new technologies in the home and at school, such as we have seen in these productions. Marsh (2004) also points out that the necessary inter-disciplinary engagement between these domains is still in its earliest stages, certainly where the youngest learners in the education system are concerned.

Evaluations of media production by children and associated instructional texts have sometimes focused exclusively on teaching formal aspects of narrative and editing concepts, drawn from the tradition of film language (Barrance, 2004). Whilst these are important elements to consider in pedagogy around the construction of meaning it is no longer the only way of framing the subject for learners. In an era in which the short video form is growing rapidly, made and exchanged online, and sits alongside other media assets, readily appropriated and exchanged, we need a way of understanding children's engagement with digital video as a rapidly changing social literacy practice in the experience of new media and popular culture (Tyner, 1998; Street, 2003; Marsh and Millard, 2006). In the view of Sefton-Green (2005) and Buckingham (Buckingham, 2003) we further need to align this with a socialised view of creativity which is much more closely connected with group work, situated peer-review and an awareness of group roles in cultural production than with individual auteurs and the realisation of a personal expressive goal.

It is possible that, instead, building on viewing and evaluation in the very public spaces of YouTube, would allow an eliding of the process of media production with the end-product more closely. Writers are already commenting on the ways in which such spaces are changing the nature of the process of composition and consumption of media texts and are becoming a form in themselves, based more on cultural resonance and exchange (Davies and Merchant, 2007).

As the short forms become more common and are perhaps used in social spaces in school contexts in ways suggested by some commentators (Davies and Merchant, 2007, pp. 61–63) it should be possible to layer in teaching and learning about structures and the expressive possibilities of media forms over time, alternating analysis and production as suggested by Burn and Durran (2007) adapting them for younger children, and working in self-representational activities, such as those suggested by this study.

Many of the videos depend on the organisation of particular patterned communication which reflects the children's lived social experiences up to that point; how they have found their voice and exhibited the general, performed self in the spaces of the school. To an extent, this is how the children organised their 3-minute videos. They are not simply organising the scenes in their videos as memes, Lankshear and Knobel's "contagious patterns of thought" (op. cit.) but also as personal communications, which reflect their ways of being in the world as part of a cultural construct (Bourdieu, 1986). Recording these ways of being involved engaging with it as a practice and a process which involved assembly of the resources needed to represent both the anchored and the transient forms of identity (Merchant, 2006) in a variety of spaces for different purposes and audiences.

The aspects of "curatorship" which suggest themselves as new literacy practices entail the conflation of many skills and attributes into one, all of which involve being literate and functioning in new media. Curating, as a verb, incorporates many sub-components and actions; it suggests at least the following: *collecting, cataloguing, arranging and assembling for exhibition, displaying.* Some of these, as we have seen, have been posited as actions which are taken by young children in assembling their physical collections (for example, of toys), and refracted through the lens of new media in other studies (Mitchell and Reid-Walsh, 2002; Pahl, 2006).

First, *collecting* resources or media assets: This refers to assets that you create yourself and save, such as video clips, sound files, still images and more. Equally, it could be assets collected from family and friends. These could be in many forms, such as comedy, parody, news, drama, documentary, tutorial video. The assets may have been gathered in from TV broadcast, mass media, re-edited and posted for direct quotation and re-purposing. These could take the form of very small clips, barely lasting more than a few seconds or even parts of seconds, up to much longer sequences. They could take the form of sound from a favourite mp3 file or CD track, recorded from the immediate environment, downloaded or ripped from a music library. Furthermore, they can, as in the case of many of the videos in this study take the form of re-enacted and re-imagined media assets. It was possible to see in these productions, these re-enactments are themselves intertextual references which are collected, played with and incorporated (Potter, 2009).

Second, *cataloguing*: As the children discovered, it is much harder to edit in digital video without knowing where your various media assets are, what they are called and what they contain in the way of meaning-making resource. At the time you come to edit, you need to be able to locate the files you have made, the files you wish to include, the audio and any still images and so on. You need to know where these are on your computer or elsewhere. They need to have been organised and catalogued, tagged for their location in ways that are meaningful to the producers themselves. The software will ask for the location at some point, so that you can import it into the new exhibition. And with social software and online spaces for sharing media assets of course, the cataloguing is for others as their tagging and organisation is for you, to be shared and incorporated into new exhibitions and spaces. This has already been noted as an area for potential development as both skill set and resource in educational settings, developing learners' capacity for working with user-generated folksonomies as opposed to author-generated taxonomies (Davies and Merchant, 2007). This has also recently emerged as a research focus by the *Futures of Learning* new media study group in the United States in work directed by Anne Balsamo under the heading *Virtual Museums: Where to Begin?* (2009) in practical application development in the global tagging of web artefacts by end users in *"Steve: The Museum Social Tagging Project"* (SteveProject, 2009)

Third, *Arranging and assembling*: These skills are those of planning for elements to be in dialogue with one another, to suggest specific meanings by their location and juxtaposition in the timeline of the video, on the screen, in the production when it is complete. This is an active process of working with intertextuality, using the tools in the software to assemble a coherent whole—not necessarily a narrative whole, but a coherent and cohesive whole which stays together for the overarching purpose of the project, of lasting or short duration, and which communicates something of the original intention.

All of these skills map onto those suggested by Jenkins and Gee earlier, and suggest an active authoring practice within lived culture. Curatorship as defined above for new media and identified in these productions incorporates elements of Jenkins' "new skills", such as *Play, Performance, Appropriation,*

Collective Intelligence, Transmedia Navigation and *Networking* (Jenkins et al., 2006). It further suggests an active engagement with Gee's "affinity spaces" in that it features a conception of all of the following at some level ...

> ... "common endeavour" (in which) ... content is transformed by interactional organisation ... intensive and extensive knowledge are encouraged ... tacit knowledge is encouraged and honoured ... there are many different forms and routes to participation ...
>
> *(Gee, 2004, pp. 77–89)*

Miller wrote how, in this respect, digital media create their own "sensual field" which respects "the larger integrity of connections between the media it incorporates" (2008, p. 71). This "integrity of connections" is an important concept because it suggests a set of organising principles. The particular kind of production in new media dictates these to an extent so that, in the examples of new media in these studies, the short moving image form has its own conventions, the breaking of which results in incoherence and lack of a viable representational form. Where it works, however, it allows users to control, select and publish aspects of their performed, recorded self in new media; and we can see here an essential life skill; the management of resources and assets made for, by and about us in a range of media, as posited in recent work which focuses specifically on the digitisation of personal memories in media assets (Garde-Hansen, Hoskins, and Reading, 2009; Williams, Leighton John, and Rowland, 2009).

The children were making productions at some speed in a medium in which they had previously had little expressive experience as producers, as distinct from their experience as consumers (Buckingham, 2003). Their relative levels of success were high on their own terms as was their appreciation of how they employed a variety of forms in pursuit of a video which satisfied the brief of self-representation in a space. And around all of this was the fact the work was located within the productive media and cultural experience of the children.

Implications for Future Research and Pedagogy in Media Culture, Pedagogy and Younger Learners

Two sorts of implications emerge from the projects described in the preceding sections. These are concerned respectively with pedagogy and with research and, to an extent, with a conflation of the two, in which learning and teaching are seen as processes which themselves have an accordance with research; recording phenomena and processes which were previously invisible and attempting explanations which attempt to make them knowable and visible.

From a pedagogical standpoint, the findings from the "learner voice" project in the first of the two sections above suggest a need to develop forms of classroom technology provision which fit better with the needs, values and experiences of young people. This rather prosaic and reductive finding nevertheless conceals some important detail about the ways in which digital media culture is becoming a field in which skill sets and dispositions are developed by younger and younger learners outside school. In the project, over time, in their expressive modes in the video output they provided, the texts, practices and social arrangements of recording and capturing ideas became a facilitator of richer, qualitative data comprehensible by unlocking the many modes which underpinned both the form and content of what was being said. In bringing this forward in their work, the children were thoughtful, articulate and constructive, demonstrating perhaps that they merited a genuine participatory role in the access to media technology in the setting.

Nevertheless, the work described was an acknowledged "snap-shot", suggesting that more is needed in the way of follow-on research which attempts to hear the "learner voice", and connect with children's media cultures and pedagogy. This needs perhaps to be longitudinal in nature and cover the full age-range of pupils (focusing especially on early years and the transition from primary to secondary school).

On the basis of the second piece of work reported, the autobiographical-curatorial video explorations, one replicable piece of pedagogy is also the basis for research itself, namely, the finding of rich sources of data through self-representational work with younger learners in educational settings. This finds a corollary in print literacy where thematic work around the self is often the earliest writing experience in schools. It moves this experience into an expressive mode in media with which the children are already familiar. Pedagogical input could be threaded in alongside opportunities to make short, simple self-representational texts alongside frequent review and evaluation, demonstrating not merely the function of the tools but how certain juxtapositions and appropriations produce different meanings. This is an argument essentially about placing media literacy activities at the heart of pedagogy with even very young learners. Both projects reported above point to a powerful and as yet largely untapped resource for moving forward with research and pedagogy at the interface between young children and their learning in the digital age.

References

Arnold, M. (2009). *Culture and Anarchy* (reprint of 1869 text). New York: Oxford University Press.

Balsamo, A. (2009). *Virtual Museums: Where to Begin?* Accessed July 7, 2009, at http://futuresoflearning.org/index.php.

Barrance, T. (2004). *Making Movies Make Sense*. Cardiff: Media Education Wales.

Bourdieu, P. (1986). *Distinction: A Social Critique of the Judgement of Taste*. London: Routledge.

Buckingham, D. (2003). *Media Education: Literacy, Learning and Contemporary Culture*. Cambridge: Polity.

Buckingham, D. (2007). *Beyond Technology: Children's Learning in the Age of Digital Culture*. London: Routledge.

Burn, A. and Durran, J. (2007). *Media Literacy in Schools*. London: Paul Chapman.

Burn, A. and Parker, D. (2003). *Analysing Media Texts*. London: Continuum.

Carr, N. (2010). *The Shallows: What the Internet Is Doing to Our Brains*. New York: W.W. Norton and Co.

Davies, J. and Merchant, G. (2007). 'Looking from the Inside Out: Academic Blogging as New Literacy'. In M. Knobel and C. Lankshear (eds.), *A New Literacies Sampler* (pp. 61–63). New York: Peter Lang.

de Certeau, M. (1984). *The Practice of Everyday Life*. Berkeley: University of California Press.

Fielding, M. (2004). 'Transformative Approaches to Student Voice: Theoretical Underpinnings, Recalcitrant Realities'. *British Educational Research Journal, 30*(2), 295–311.

Foucault, M. (1984). *The Foucault Reader*. London: Penguin.

Friesen, N. and Hug, T. (2008). 'The Mediatic Turn: Exploring Consequences for Media Pedagogy'. In K. Lundby (ed.), *Mediatization: Concept, Changes, Consequences* (pp. 61–63). New York: Peter Lang.

Garde-Hansen, J., Hoskins, A., and Reading, A. (eds.) (2009). *Save as ... Digital Memories*. London: Palgrave.

Gee, J. P. (2004). *Situated Language and Learning: A Critique of Traditional Schooling*. New York: Routledge.

Giddens, A. (1991). *Modernity and Self-identity: Self and Society in the Late Modern Age*. Cambridge: Polity.

Goffman, E. (1990). *The Presentation of Self in Everyday Life* (new edition). London: Penguin.

Ito, M., Baumer, S., Bittanti, M., boyd, D., Cody, R., Herr-Stephenson, B., Horst, H. A., Lange, P., Mahendran, D., Martinez, K. Z., Pascoe, C. J., Perjel, D., Robinson, L., Sims, C., and Tripp, L. (2009). *Hanging Out, Messing Around, and Geeking Out: Kids Living and Learning with New Media*. Cambridge, MA: MIT Press.

Jenkins, H., Clinton, K., Purushotma, R., and Robison, A. J. (2006). *Confronting the Challenges of Participatory Culture: Media Education for the 21st Century*. Chicago: MacArthur Foundation.

Johnson, S. (2005). *Everything Bad is Good for You: How Popular Culture is Making us Smarter*. London: Allen Lane.

Kress, G. and Van Leeuwen, T. (2001). *Multimodal Discourse: The Modes and Media of Contemporary Communication*. London: Arnold.

Lankshear, C. and Knobel, M. (2006), *New Literacies: Everyday Practices and Classroom Learning*. Maidenhead, Berks, UK: McGraw Hill Education/Open University Press.

Larson, J. and Marsh, J. (2005). *Making Literacy Real: Theories and Practices for Learning and Teaching*. London: Sage.

Lievrouw, L. H. and Livingstone, S. (eds.) (2006). *The Handbook of New Media* (updated student edition). London: Sage.

Livingstone, S. (2009). *Children and the Internet*. Cambridge: Polity.

Marsh, J. (ed.) (2004). *Popular Culture, New Media and Digital Literacy in Early Childhood*. London: Routledge.

Marsh, J. and Millard, E. (eds.) (2006). *Popular Literacies, Childhood and Schooling*. London: Routledge.

Media Education Association (MEA). (2010). *MLC 2010:* The Media Literacy Conference, Queen Elizabeth Conference Centre, London, November, 2010 (organised by the Media Education Association and The Centre for the Study of Children, Youth and Media, London Knowledge Lab, Institute of Education, University of London)

Merchant, G. (2005). 'Electric Involvement: Identity Performance in Children's Informal Digital Writing'. *Discourse: Studies in the Cultural Politics of Education, 26*(3), 301–314.

Merchant, G. (2006). 'Identity, Social Networks and Online Communication'. *E-Learning, 3*(2), 235–244.

Miller, D. (2008). *The Comfort of Things*. Cambridge: Polity.

Mitchell, C. and Reid-Walsh, J. (2002). *Researching Children's Popular Culture: The Cultural Spaces of Childhood*. London: Routledge.

Pahl, K. (2006). 'An Inventory of Traces: Children's Photographs of Their Toys in Three London Homes'. *Visual Communication, 5*(95), 95–114.

Potter, J. (2005). '"This Brings Back a Lot of Memories"—A Case Study in the Analysis of Digital Video Production by Young Learners'. *Education, Communication & Information,* 5(1), 5–23.

Potter, J. (2009). *Curating the Self: Media Literacy and Identity in Digital Video Production by Young Learners* [thesis]. University of London, London.

Potter, J. (2010). 'Embodied Memory and Curatorship in Children's Digital Video Production'. *Journal of English Teaching: Practice and Critique, 9*(1), 22–35.

Prensky, M. (2005). 'Listen to the Natives'. *Educational Leadership, 63*(4), 8–13.

Richtel, M. (2010, Nov. 21). 'Wired for Distraction'. *New York Times.* Available at http://www.nytimes.com/2010/11/21/technology/21brain.html.

Robinson, K. (2010). "RSA Animate—Changing Education Paradigms". YouTube. Available at http://www.youtube.com/watch?v=zDZFcDGpL4U

Robinson, M. and Turnbull, B. (2005). 'Veronica: An Asset Model of Becoming Literate'. In J. Marsh (ed.), *Popular Culture. New Media and Digital Literacy in Early Childhood.* London: Routledge.

Sefton-Green, J. (2005). 'Timelines, Timeframes and Special Effects: Soft and Creative Media Production'. *Education, Communication and Information, 5*(1), 99–110.

Selwyn, N., Potter, J., and Cranmer, S. (2008). *Learners and Technology: 7-11 End of Project—Full Report.* Coventry, UK: BECTA.

Selwyn, N., Potter, J., and Cranmer, S. (2010). *Primary ICT: Learning from Learner Perspectives.* London: Continuum.

SteveProject. (2009). *Steve: The Museum Social Tagging Project.* Accessed July 7, 2009, at http://www.steve.museum

Street, B. (2003). 'What's "New" in New Literacy Studies? Critical Approaches to Literacy in Theory and Practice'. *Current Issues in Comparative Education, 5*(2), 77–91.

Tyner, K. (1998). *Literacy in a Digital World.* Mahwah, NJ: Erlbaum.

Wesch, M. (2007). 'A Vision of School Students Today'. YouTube. Available at http://www.youtube.com/watch?v=dGCJ46vyR9o

Williams, P., Leighton, J., and Rowland, I. (2009). 'The Personal Curation of Digital Objects: A Lifecycle Approach'. *Aslib Proceedings: New Information Perspectives, 61*(4), 340–363.

9

WIKIPEDIA IS THE NEW PUBLIC LITERACY

A Case Study in the Field of Philosophy

John Willinsky

In writing about the cultural degradation brought on by mass participation in the publishing potential of the Internet, Andrew Keen snidely notes in his book *The Cult of the Amateur*, "and then there is Wikipedia, an online encyclopedia where anyone with opposable thumbs and a fifth-grade education can publish anything on any topic from AC/DC to Zoroastrianism," which is for Keen "the blind leading the blind—infinite monkeys providing infinite information for infinite readers, perpetuating the cycle of misinformation and ignorance" (2007, p. 4). To substantiate what he sees as *Wikipedia*'s abysmal record, he cites a Forbes' article, jumping from the lack of education among contributors to its tendency of, as he puts it, "deceptively spreading corporate propaganda." The Forbes reporter was able to detect from the public record that *Wikipedia* keeps all edits that someone at Wal-Mart had deleted from the company's entry, as Keen misquotes the story, "the line about underpaid employees making less than 20 percent of the competition" (ibid.).[1]

However wrong Keen gets it in this case, *Wikipedia*'s reliability as a source of knowledge continues to remain an open question. Students are warned not to cite *Wikipedia* in their papers, as if any student would be advised, after fifth grade, shall we say, to quote from any encyclopedia instead of consulting original studies or at least sources like *Forbes* and the *New Yorker* as Keen does (Jaschik, 2007). Still, others have pointed out how *Wikipedia* continues to be beset by factual mistakes and awkward writing, with the errors that are pointed out corrected by Wikipedians far too quickly for most readers to enjoy seeing them for themselves (Read, 2006). Wikipedians, as the eight million registered writers and editors contributing to this work would be known, have also responded to these obvious concerns about accuracy by placing a series of admonishing tags at the top of entries. One reads, "This article is a stub" ("You can help

Wikipedia by expanding it"), while another is "The examples and perspective in this article or section may not represent a worldwide view of the subject" ("Please improve this article or discuss the issue on the talk page"). Then there are the tiny superscripted annotations, placed discretely at the end of an unsubstantiated claim, that read "citation needed."

Yet it strikes me as remarkably shortsighted to continue to judge this massive social phenomenon of people coming together to the world's largest free and open encyclopedia of human knowledge solely on the basis of its accuracy.[2] What needs to be considered is how it represents yet another Internet-spawned manifestation of what has been called, in the case of open source software, *an impossible public good* (Weber, 2004, p. 9, citing Marc Smith and Peter Kollock). The (previously) impossible nature of this public good, now so freely shared, is also found in the *open access* movement in research and scholarship (Harnad et al., 2008; Willinsky, 2006), and the *open educational resources* initiative (Caswell, Shelley, Hensen, and Wile, 2008), both of which are opening the realm of learning to far wider access.

In that sense, Keen (2007) has it wrong again when he mocks *Wikipedia* as "a cathedral of knowledge" (p. 20). It has no such pretense and so very openly is a work in progress that it is all the more educational. When Don Fallis poses the question in his "epistemology of Wikipedia" as to "whether people are more (or less) likely to acquire knowledge as a result of a particular institution," the answer is that people are more likely to learn new things not only about what they are looking for, but about the nature of knowledge through this openness (2008, p. 1663). The openness of the entries, discussion and history of the entries, the endless efforts to get it right, to find the warrant and backing, to establish a way of conveying ideas. The process is now being greatly aided by the openness of scholarly and educational resources, and in this study, as well as a previous one (Willinsky, 2007), I examine how *Wikipedia*, as a newly emerged site of public learning, is drawing on the university, as a traditional site of knowledge, with a new level of public access to research and scholarship.

My focus is on *Wikipedia*'s use of the *Stanford Encyclopedia of Philosophy* (SEP) as one of the leading innovative and open projects in the academic community. SEP was begun in 1995 by Edward N. Zalta at Stanford's Center for the Study of Language and Information (Perry & Zalta, 1997). Zalta set out to create a "dynamic" encyclopedia that combined peer review with ongoing updating and revision. Entries offer internal and external link to related materials, as well as access to the author's homepage and email. SEP is intended to be "useful both to professional scholars and the general public" (ibid), and as an important part of that, it is entirely free to read online. That it is free has been made possible by a variety of grants, with a current program to have it funded by an endowment, with support from research libraries and philosophy departments. SEP is a new sort of knowledge resource. It is not only free but peer-reviewed and periodic, updated and archived. Some authors prepare entries as free of directly cited secondary literature as the *Encyclopædia Britannica*; others offer entries as heavily footnoted as any scholarly work in the humanities.[3] SEP is not published by a press, but is copyrighted by the Metaphysics Research Lab in the Center for the Study of Language and Information at Stanford University, as well as by its authors. At the time of this study, SEP had 1,026 entries on philosophic figures and concepts (while adding a half-dozen or so entries a month) and was receiving roughly half a million hits a week.

This study considers how Wikipedians are using SEP. It examines the links in *Wikipedia* that lead to entries in SEP and the extent to which those links are used (over a two-week period). This earlier study I conducted of *Wikipedia*'s use of freely available research established that a very small proportion (2 percent) of *Wikipedia* entries had links to research that could be read by readers who did not hold a membership in a research library (1970). The study also demonstrated that relevant research was freely available or open access for 60 percent of the *Wikipedia* entries in the study's sample.[4] This study examines in some detail how one particular open access resource, namely SEP, can contribute to *Wikipedia*.

2.0 Method

This study of *Wikipedia*'s use of SEP was made possible by the close cooperation of the editors at the *Stanford Encyclopedia of Philosophy*. After discussing the intent, scope, and design of the study with Principal Editor Edward N. Zalta and Senior Editor Uri Nodelman, both provided both helpful suggestions to improve the study and the weblogs for SEP over a two-week period (in which the IP addresses had been encrypted to protect the identity of users). The information provided to us on the weblogs identified that set of users who had arrived at SEP by clicking on a link in *Wikipedia*. The weblogs, for the two-week period between June 22 and July 5, 2008, revealed, after some cleaning up of the data, where in *Wikipedia* people clicked on a link leading to SEP, and where that link led to in SEP.[5]

This data did not tell us how long readers spent in SEP nor, of course, what sense they were making of the SEP entries they encountered. But it did tell us that readers of an entry on Aristotle or Politics in *Wikipedia* were clicking on links leading to SEP. At the very least, we might assume that a click through to SEP indicated an interest in the reference that was being made in the text of the entry or under External Links, if not an interest in learning more about the topic. It did tell us that in cases where the SEP link in *Wikipedia* was clearly identified as *Stanford Encyclopedia of Philosophy*, that readers were pursuing a more specialized source of knowledge, if not an official academic resource. In addition, *Wikipedia*'s advanced search capacities through "Wiki Searching External Links" provided data on where SEP links had been placed in *Wikipedia* and where they led, so that I could judge both readers' responses to the initial work done by Wikipedians with links to SEP and discussions of those links on the talk pages.

The numbers that describe links from *Wikipedia* to SEP are bound to seem miniscule compared to Wikipedia's astounding statistics, whether for entries, languages, readers, or Wikipedians. Yet in this one area of philosophy how SEP is cited by Wikipedians and which of those citations are used by readers throw further light on the process of learning to which these new works contribute, and the something more to that learning that can arise because of these connections.

3.0 Results

3.1 *SEP References in* Wikipedia

At the time of this study, 1,741 of Wikipedia's entries contained one or more links to 942 entries in the *Stanford Encyclopedia of Philosophy*, for a total of 2,263 links. To put that in proportion, Wikipedians were connecting their work to slightly over 80 percent of the 1,026 entries that made up SEP at that time (with additional links to archived earlier editions of SEP).[6] The vast majority of the links were connecting entries that were about ideas such as Truth and Causality, as well as Pleasure and The Meaning of Life, as opposed to specific philosophers such as Kant and Descartes. The *Wikipedia* entry with the largest number of links to SEP was Aristotle, with 14 links to SEP (Table 9.1). It was followed by the *Wikipedia* user page devoted to the Wikipedian Simfish who had embedded 13 links to SEP on his page, and then by the entry for Truth with 10 links to SEP.[7] The entry in SEP most often cited by *Wikipedia* is Libertarianism, with 15 links, followed by Atheism and Agnosticism and Classical Logic (Table 9.2).

TABLE 9.1 *Wikipedia* Pages with the Most Links to SEP

Wikipedia *Pages*	*SEP Links*
Aristotle	14
User:Simfish	13
Truth	10
Immanuel Kant	9
Causality	8
Computational Epistemology	8
Philosophy of Physics	8
Politics	8
Rene Descartes	8
Epistemology	7

TABLE 9.2 Stanford Encyclopedia of Philosophy entries most often cited in *Wikipedia*

SEP Links	Wikipedia *Pages*
Libertarianism	15
Atheism and Agnosticism	14
Classical Logic	14
Copernicus	13
David Hume	13
Ontological Arguments	13
William Godwin	12
Karl Marx	12
Friedrich Nietzsche	12
Zeno's Paradoxes	12
Karl Popper	12

Note: The URL for SEP itself, although not counted as an SEP entry for purposes of this table, is included 72 times.

3.1.1 The Aristotle File

The *Aristotle* entry in *Wikipedia* is a substantial piece of work, at close to 9,000 words long, with edits on this page continuing to take place on a daily basis during the course of this study.[8] *Wikipedia* rates the entry B-class on by the *Wikipedia* Version 1.0 Editorial Team, which means "No reader should be left wanting, although the content may not be complete enough to satisfy a serious student or researcher." The entry itself dates back to April 21, 2003, when, at 3,000 words, it was largely devoted to the philosopher's biography, with the text largely lifted without attribution and only minor changes from the *Catholic Encyclopedia* (Turner, 1907). A small amount of space was given to his method and a summary of three criticisms of his work. The bibliography did contain links to what was already a rich set of Aristotle's works freely available online, principally through Virginia Tech. There was little commentary, then, with biography as background and the links to the actual works of Aristotle the extent of it. There was little commentary on Aristotle's work and no references to commentary or interpretations of this work or of Aristotle's important place in the history of philosophy.

The current Wikipedia article on Aristotle includes well-referenced summaries of his work in physics, metaphysics, biology and medicine, as well as practical philosophy.[9] At the top of the entry, it offers readers a baseball card-like sidebar with his picture, birth and death dates, along with his "school" and "notable ideas." At the end of the entry, after the List of Aristotle's Works, References, Further Reading, and See Also, there is a list of External Links made up of "Collections of Aristotle's Works," which are available in English and the original Greek from five websites, and "Articles on Aristotle," which includes links to the Aristotle entries in the *Internet Encyclopedia of Philosophy* and the *Catholic Encyclopedia*.[10] These two links are followed by a set of links to thirteen entries in SEP that bear on Aristotle's work: Scholarly surveys of focused topics from the *Stanford Encyclopedia of Philosophy*: articles on Aristotle in the Renaissance, Biology, Causality, Commentators on Aristotle, Ethics, Logic, Mathematics, Metaphysics, Natural philosophy, Non-contradiction, Political theory, Psychology, and Rhetoric.

This set of SEP links in *Wikipedia* did not include the obvious SEP entry for Aristotle himself, but rather sought to extend *Wikipedia*'s reach by providing links to the various SEP Entries devoted to different aspects of this peripatetic philosopher's work.

SEP also turns up in one of the 51 "References" or footnotes that operate as hyperlinked footnotes in the *Wikipedia* entry on Aristotle, at the end of the statement: "In a similar vein, John Philoponus, and later Galileo, showed by simple experiments that Aristotle's theory that the more massive object falls faster than a less massive object is incorrect."[11] Reference 12, which simply reads *Stanford Encyclopedia of Philosophy*, leads directly to the section on Philoponus' theory of impetus in the SEP entry on John Philoponus, by Christian Wildberg. Wildberg points out that while Philoponus' theory is based on a misguided sense of a kinetic force being imparted to falling or thrown objects, it did lead Philoponus to experimentally test and disprove Aristotle's conclusion about the differing speeds of falling bodies, much as Galileo did centuries later. Wildberg's entry for Philoponus provides a substantial list of primary and secondary sources, while nothing is listed under "Other Internet Resources" except "please contact the author with suggestions."[12]

3.1.2 Citing SEP in Wikipedia Discussion Pages

SEP also proved useful to Wikipedians in the discussion pages that accompany each page in *Wikipedia*, where they included 216 links to SEP (representing roughly 10 percent of the links from *Wikipedia* to SEP). Foremost among the discussions in which SEP figured was the one that accompanied the *Atheism* entry. SEP was cited 18 times over the course of an extensive discussion that overshadowed the 10,000-word entry itself, with the discussion running to dozens of archived pages that were, in some case, well over 20,000 words of back and forth among Wikipedians. In the course of this extensive "talk," J. J. C. Smart's SEP entry *Atheism and Agnosticism* comes up repeatedly.

When, for example, Wikipedian Brian reaches the point of exasperation at one point in the discussion on *Atheism*—"this is getting ridiculous, repeating the same arguments over and over"—he reaches for "one of the most well-known atheist philosophers, and his entry in the *Stanford Encyclopedia of*

Philosophy (comprehensive as expected)." Smart, who is himself the subject of a *Wikipedia* entry, is then cited for his statement that "atheism means the negation of theism, the denial of the existence of God."[13] At another point in the Atheism discussion, Adraeus, who works with the WikiProject Philosophy group, describes how she or he "spoke with 84-year-old Dr. John Smart of Philosophy who wrote the Atheism-Agnosticism entry in the *Stanford Encyclopedia of Philosophy*" to clarify a point in dispute about whether "the weak definition of atheism is the product of the freethought movement." Smart "responded that at the time of writing he was unaware of the distinctions."[14]

Another discussant, in objecting to the deletion of what was said to be a poorly written and clumsy section, responds emphatically that "the removed text was A DIRECT QUOTE from *Stanford Encyclopedia of Philosophy*" (with a link to Smart's SEP entry *Atheism and Agnosticism*). Someone responds that the SEP cite was a copyright violation (having perhaps yet to learn about "fair use"), while another points out that "SEP entries are written from the perspective of the authoring philosopher" while "our job as *Wikipedia* editors is to use whatever resources available to us to provide objective contributions to our encyclopedia." This discussant does allow that "you can, however, quote SEP entries if you provide citation."[15] One Wikipedian points out how Smart introduces Wittgenstein's notion of "family resemblance" (as a way of relating agnosticism and atheism),[16] while more than once in these discussion pages Smart's definition of atheism is cited ("'atheism' means the negation of theism, the denial of the existence of God").[17]

Yet what must stand as the ideal instance of SEP's contribution to the construction of *Wikipedia* entries comes, oddly enough, in the discussion page for Bobby Jindal, current governor of the state of Louisiana. Considerable discussion is given over to how best to represent and reference Jindal's stance on abortions. Jindal is, in his own words, "100 percent against abortion, no exceptions," and the question for Wikipedians working on his entry is how to represent this stance in relation to its consequences for women's health. The discussion deals at some length with the teachings of the Catholic Church, of which Jindal is a member.[18]

At one point in this discussion, DanielZimmerman states that Jindal could support an abortion if it was the result of a "double effect," in which the abortion took place as a result of another vital, life-saving procedure: "Here is another source," he goes on to write, "that describes the double effect and shows that under Catholic law, direct abortions are prohibited even if it is to save the life of the woman."[19] He then cites, as a "verifiable source" from Alison McIntyre's SEP entry *Doctrine of Double Effect* a hypothetical example in which a doctor who opposes abortion nonetheless operates on a pregnant women with cancer, which he knows will result in the loss of the fetus.[20]

This leads Ferrylodge, who disagrees with DanielZimmerman's position that the Jindal entry should include this qualification of the no exception rule, to apparently read the SEP entry. For Ferrylodge points out how McIntyre notes the limitations of just such common examples of the double effect doctrine, and cites McIntyre on the very hypothetical example that has just been quoted by DanielZimmerman: "It is hard to find a principled ground" McIntyre writes, "for drawing this distinction [between intended and unintended abortion in the case of the doctor and woman with cancer] that could serve as a guide to moral judgment."[21] SEP becomes, in this case, a guide to moral distinctions based on doctrine that are made and that can be challenged. It serves as a common text for the two Wikipedians to clarify their stances.

The month-long debate between the two continues down the page, until it is finally resolved with a compromise that allows Jindal's stance on abortion-without-exception to stand, but with additional information on exactly what the governor said as cited in the source that is used to verify the conclusions about Jindal's stance on abortion: "Thanks for working with me," DanielZimmerman writes to Ferrylodge, "to find a good solution to make this a better article."[22] And on my part, let me commend the educational quality of these exchanges, through the interpretative twists, marshaling of arguments ad evidence, right down to the encouraging comments.

3.2 Readers' Use of Wikipedia's SEP Links

To first summarize the use of the SEP links that are embedded in *Wikipedia* over the two-week period in question, it appears that *Wikipedia* readers clicked on SEP links 13,363 times.[23] Of the 2,262 SEP links that had been placed in *Wikipedia* by various editors, over half (1,248) were clicked at least once during the two-week test period (and 355 of them were clicked ten or more times during this two-week period). *Wikipedia* readers visiting the SEP entry *Machiavelli* 246 times, which topped the list (Table 9.3). Yet even the 216 links to SEP buried amid the discussion pages were clicked on 16 occasions, suggesting that readers and editors are returning to this aspect of *Wikipedia*, a few months or years after the point was originally made.

Of the 1,026 entries that made up the SEP at the time of the study, 780 were visited by *Wikipedia* readers at least once, with close to half of SEP entries visited once a day on average. However you look at it, *Wikipedia* readers took advantage of the SEP links, doing so, one may presume, to either extend what they could learn about the topic at hand or at least see what authority *Wikipedia* rested on and what more was available on this topic.

To look at this use in more detail, SEP itself was the site most frequently visited by *Wikipedia* readers, and the link leading to SEP's homepage (see Table 9.2) is, by far, the most common SEP link in *Wikipedia* (Table 9.3). That readers went to have a look at this encyclopedia of philosophy itself might be taken as an expression of interest about educational resources on the web. The weblogs indicate that most of these readers came to SEP from the *Wikipedia* entry for

TABLE 9.3 SEP Pages Most Frequently Visited from Wikipedia over a Two-Week Period, with Number of Links to the SEP Pages Found in Wikipedia

SEP Page	Visits	Links
Stanford Encyclopedia of Philosophy	496	72
Machiavelli	243	4
Definition of Art	103	1
Ethics	100	1
Philosophy of Economics	99	4
Critical Theory	98	5
Propositions	88	1
Respect	87	5
Principia Mathematica	85	7
Existentialism	80	4

the Stanford Encyclopedia of Philosophy, with a good number also coming, as well, from the *Wikipedia* entry for Philosophy, in which SEP is the first External Link (although it is not listed among the 26 "Reference Works" listed under "Further Reading" for the Philosophy entry).

Otherwise, the closely grouped array of the top five visited SEP entries display an interesting cluster that ranges from the politics and historical figure of Machiavelli, to the far more abstract definition of art and the concept of ethics, back to the political philosophy of critical theory. Among the top visited SEP entries (that is, apart from the SEP homepage) none is to be found in the SEP entries with the most links in *Wikipedia* (Table 9.2). That is, readers' use of these SEP links was somewhat independent, with the exception of SEP itself, of how often editors to *Wikipedia* cited particular SEP entries.

The Machiavelli entry in *Wikipedia* contains two links to SEP's entry on Machiavelli, which is also cited in the *Wikipedia* entries for Politics and Virtù. With Virtù, *Wikipedia* has a short 80-word entry describing the concept which Machiavelli used to cover those qualities needed to advance the state (not always virtuous by any means). The link to SEP under Virtù leads directly to the relevant section of the Machiavelli SEP entry, where Carey Nederman explains the concept in relation to Machiavelli's concepts of power and fortune. *Wikipedia*'s entry for Politics makes considerable use of SEP, with editors providing linking to its entries Authority, Confucius on Politics, Plato's Ethics and Politics in The Republic, Aristotle's Political Theory, Machiavelli, Locke, Mill, and Marx. When the *Wikipedia* entry on Politics comes to discuss Machiavelli, it includes a quotation from the opening of the SEP Machiavelli entry on a clearly intriguing point about the man's stance: "Machiavelli did not invent

'Machiavellianism' and may not even have been a 'Machiavellian' in the sense often ascribed to him."

The same delicate point about Machiavelli comes up in the opening paragraph of his *Wikipedia* entry: "His work, particularly in *The Prince*, made his name synonymous with ruthless politics, deceit and the pursuit of power by any means. The validity of that reputation is disputed." And while that ends the paragraph all too abruptly, the *disputedness* statement is footnoted with a reference to the albeit mislabeled, *Stanford Dictionary of Philosophy* which leads to Nederman's SEP entry. It is the same SEP entry that is listed under External Links in *Wikipedia*'s Machiavelli entry.[24] Yet I find the use of SEP in footnotes especially effective, as it offers readers what is still a rare experience of being able to immediately follow up with a current and esteemed consideration of the point being made. With both the Politics and Machiavelli entries, SEP is used to support a point of disputed reputation. Machiavelli's bad rap is discussed again later in the *Wikipedia* entry on the statesman, his reputation largely redeemed by the editor quoting Anthony Parel (1972) in footnote to the effect that "the authentic Machiavelli is one who subordinates personal interests for the common good ... setting aside personal interests in making sacrifices for the common good" (or, more precisely, I would think, *for the state*). The Parel quote is an excellent choice as it highlights the needed distinction between Machiavelli's reputed and actual stance. In contrast, the SEP footnotes, while they would be improved by the briefest of annotations that spoke to the question at hand, still hold an advantage over the Parel footnote by providing a gateway to Nederman's much fuller consideration of Machiavelli.[25] As to why the links to the Machiavelli entry in SEP tops the list of links that readers pursued, it may seem obvious enough in these desperate political times when state interests seem to overrule public concerns. Not the least of it was the June 10, 2008, publication of *Machiavelli's Shadow: The Rise and Fall of Karl Rove* by Paul Alexander.

The third most frequently visited SEP page by *Wikipedia* readers in this study was an External Link in the entry for Art that read "The Definition of Art entry in the Stanford Encyclopedia of Philosophy by Thomas Adajian." This model of reference clarity was not the only link to the definition of art in the entry. Under Further Reading, a small boxed-off section reads "Look up *Art* in the *Wikionary*, the free dictionary." The *Wikionary* definition of *art*, begins with "Human effort to imitate, supplement, alter, or counteract the work of nature." The entry for Art itself in *Wikipedia* includes a definition in the second paragraph of the entry, followed immediately by a disclaimer around definitions: "Generally art is a (product of) human activity, made with the intention of stimulating the human senses as well as the human mind; by transmitting emotions and/or ideas. Beyond this description, there is no general agreed-upon definition of art." Still, readers have on reaching the end of the *Wikipedia* reached for further insight into what defines art. The other entries under

External links seem to lack the focus of the SEP one: "Art and Play from the Dictionary of the History of ideas" seems narrow by comparison, and it is not immediately apparent what an "In-depth directory of art" is, to take two other of the seven entries.

The SEP entry for the Definition of Art by Thomas Adajian does not provide any easy answers for art collectors or students. It begins, "the definition of art is controversial in contemporary philosophy" and concludes with a quotation by Kendall Walton stating that "it is not at all clear that there words—'What is art?'—expresses anything like a single question ..." Of course, we do not know how far readers went with this 6,000-word SEP entry, after arriving there via *Wikipedia*. But if they only read the first sentence and looked away, they would have had a taste of what philosophy makes of the world. And to suggest that 50 people a week somewhere in the world just might do that in the course of their day seems slight enough but not insignificant from an educational perspective.

A final instance of relatively frequent SEP use comes from René Descartes, whose entry in *Wikipedia* led to 229 visits to SEP. What distinguishes the SEP links in this entry is how well the bridge from the *Wikipedia* entry to the wealth of materials on Descartes in SEP was set up (Figure 9.1). The *Wikipedia*'s External Links for Descartes begin with a set of "General" entries, which include Descartes' works online, followed a second set grouped under Stanford Encyclopedia of Philosophy. Each link leads to a substantial essay by a different philosopher, not least of which is the entry Descartes and the Pineal Gland (the seat of the soul and the organ of thought for Descartes) by Gert-Jan Lokhorst. However, the most popular of the Descartes pages in SEP for *Wikipedia* readers was the entry Descartes' Epistemology (97 visits), followed by Descartes' Theory of Ideas (62 visits).

Stanford Encyclopedia of Philosophy

- Descartes' Epistemology ☑
- Descartes' Ethics ☑
- Descartes' Life and Works ☑
- Descartes' Modal Metaphysics ☑
- Descartes' Ontological Argument ☑
- Descartes and the Pineal Gland ☑
- Descartes' Physics ☑
- Descartes's Theory of Ideas ☑

FIGURE 9.1 SEP links in the Descartes entry in *Wikipedia*.

4.0 Discussion

What I am referring to as the educational quality of *Wikipedia* has much to do with the stance that its editors are taking on knowledge. It is a stance that sets *Wikipedia* apart in what I find an encouragingly educational way. The learning that I am concerned with here takes place on a peripheral basis, that is, out of the corner of the readers' eye, barely noticed and perhaps only after reading about this or that *Wikipedia* feature in another setting. *Wikipedia*'s increasing emphasis on verifiability and documentation only further exposes learning's apparatus.[26] It exposes the degree to which knowledge is the product of learning, and as such often subject to *editing, discussion, history*, those three *Wikipedia* muses that hang as tabs over every entry. This learning has to do with *Wikipedia*'s openness, not just openness to editing, but openness to discussing the editing at a level of detail that far exceeds the entry being discussed, and openness to the history of the editing so that the process of making an entry is subject to review and further discussion. This amounts to a statement about knowledge. It represents an epistemic stance.

As Fallis has argued in some detail, *Wikipedia* is not about the newly established wisdom of crowds (2008, p. 1670). *Wikipedia* entries are not some sort of unconscious expression of what is collectively known, of the sort Prediction Markets use to accurately second-guess election results (Sunstein, 2006). Rather, the *Wikipedia* entries considered here, at least, represent the hard and concerted work of people, many of them members of the Wikiproject Philosophy group. Still, there is a further educational risk arising from this appreciation of *Wikipedia* as a labor the love of knowledge. It could well lead people to assume that *Wikipedia* represents this open and always-formative, often-contested approach to knowledge way, in a way that stands apart (from knowledge proper, that is, from the certain, fixed, and well-formed knowledge arrived at by academics and other experts, and publicly fronted by, for example, *Encyclopædia Britannica*. Thus I find that even the favorable judgments of Wikipedia—as when Fallis finds it "sufficiently reliable" and "more verifiable than most other information sources" (2008, p. 1667)—miss the parallels in the tentative and formative nature of learning in both public and academic realms, as well as their increasing openness. The focus on verifiable reliability does little to encourage the educational value of strengthening connections between the two realms.

While *Wikipedia*'s use of SEP has been the focus of this study, I should make it clear that the links to scholarly work are happening in more than philosophy (Table 9.4). For example, in August of 2008, arXiv.org, an archive of high energy physics papers, as well as to a lesser degree mathematics, computer science and other fields, recorded 10,000 visits from *Wikipedia* readers, led by an interest in super symmetry and the Large Hadron Collider.[27] Like SEP, arXIv.org provides open access to all articles, while other research sites being used by *Wikipedia* editors, such as PubMEd, operate as indexes to articles, a growing number of which are freely available, while still the largest number of

TABLE 9.4 Scholarly Resources Used by Wikipedia Editors, with Approximate Number of Items Associated with Resource and Number of Links in Wikipedia to the Resource

Scholarly Site	Type of Resource	Total Items	WP Links
Open Access Scholarly Articles			
SEP	Peer-reviewed philosophy encyclopedia	1,026	1,300
SSRN	Repository of social science working and published papers.	164,000	1,000
arXiv.org	Repository of working and published papers in high energy physics and other sciences	500,000	5,000
Citeseer	Index of scientific papers, principally in computer sciences	768,000	1,200
Abstracts with Some Open Access Articles			
RePEc	Repository and index to economics published and unpublished papers	510,000	500
PubMed	Life sciences index to published literature	6,000,000	5,000
SAO/NASA ASD	Smithsonian Astrophysical Observatory data system and digital library of articles	7,200,000	7,000
Subscription / Pay-Per-View Access			
JSTOR	Digitized back issues of journals from across the disciplines	2,000,000	4,500
ScienceDirect	Journal articles and books from Elsevier, the largest scientific publisher.	9,000,000	2,400
CrossRef *	Publishers' identifier system for journal articles	32,000,000	181,600

* CrossRef's Digital Object Identifiers (DOI) are used by journals in PubMed and ScienceDirect, leading to overlap in these counts, as well as by Highwire Press journals, which make 2 million articles free, largely some period after publication.

references to scholarly materials remain linked to subscription or pay-per-view services. The increasing degree to which *Wikipedia* is proving a public bridge to these new scholarly resources, as itself part of the educational project of this work, has yet to figure in discussions of *Wikipedia*'s reliability and accuracy.[28]

It is fortunate indeed that efforts are underway on a number of fronts, from federal legislation to university policies, to increase the degree to which the scholarly literature is freely available for such purposes, and many articles are now available in open access archives or through open access journals (Harnad et al., 2008; Willinsky, 2006). While I do not want to discourage anyone from going to the public library to pile on the books from the further reading lists for Aristotle, Machiavelli, and Descartes, I have previously argued, in ways that I hope this study of SEP reinforces, that *Wikipedia* editors would do well to use, wherever possible, references that readers can begin reading at a click (Willinsky 2007).[29]

In this case, *Wikipedia* editors have already drawn on 80 percent of the entries in the *Stanford Encyclopedia of Philosophy*, and readers are using the vast majority of those links to consider a particular aspect of a philosopher's work, as we saw with Aristotle, and to see how philosophers deal with such puzzling questions as *what is art*. If it is not always a good thing for reference works to cite other reference works, in this case it makes perfect sense.[30] SEP's comprehensive reviews of philosophical topics and figures provides *Wikipedia* readers with the next step up, letting them in on how philosophers talk to other students of philosophy. The openness and intersection of these two enterprises, however that openness differs, only increases the opportunities to learn about the nature of what we know and how we know it. What could be more philosophical than that? It is what I most find most encouraging about the uncertain pursuit of knowledge in this new realm.

Notes

1   It is an unfortunate example to use to demonstrate that *Wikipedia* is destroying "our culture, and our values," not only because it is not an instance of the blind leading the blind, nor because Keen's line that "making less than 20% of the competition" is so in need of professional editing, but because what Hessel wrote in *Forbes* was that "an employee, also identified by a Wal-Mart IP address, cut a line stating the megaretailer paid its employees 20% less than its competitors did" (Hessel, 2006). Nor does Keen note that in 2005 a "Criticism of Wal-Mart" was initiated in *Wikipedia*; as I write, it is now running to 9,000 words. *Encyclopaedia Britannica*, in its 224 word entry does note: "Extreme growth has not occurred without controversy; Wal-Mart has been variously criticized for contributing to urban sprawl and for perpetuating low wages. Its merchandising practices are nonetheless emulated by other retailers, and Wal-Mart continues to gain popularity with customers around the world" (Wal-Mart, 2008). It is only because Wikipedia makes its edits public that such deletions were detectable by tools others have developed (see wikidgames http://wired.reddit.com/wikidgame/?s=top).

2   In 2007, the Pew Internet and American Life Project found that a third of American adults who go online consult *Wikipedia* (Rainie & Tancer, 2007). It also found that nothing else comes close in terms of "educational and reference websites" traffic, as does *Wikipedia*, which receives 24 percent of the traffic (followed by Yahoo Answers at 4 percent).

3   To take two entries discussed in this paper, SEP's main entry on Aristotle by Christopher Shields has 27 footnotes, some with links to other of the SEP entries on Aristotle, while the entry for Philoponus have no footnotes, even when reference is being directly made to the secondary literature: "Nowadays, Philoponus is often celebrated for having been one of the first thinkers to reconcile Aristotelian philosophy with Christianity." I take this level of additional source-documentation, which is unevenly applied in SEP and *Wikipedia* entries, to reflect a repositioning of both works. And while it is tempting to contrast a scholarly journal and encyclopedia as different forms, from the first year of the *Philosophical Transactions* in 1665, there has a repackaging of each year's issues into a volume with an index that turned it, in effect, into an encyclopedia.

4 Björk, Roos, and Lauri, for example, have calculate that 20 percent of scholarly literature's output in a given year is freely available online through open access journals, archives and personal websites (2008).

5 The SEP weblogs originally contained 17,724 records of users coming from *Wikipedia* to SEP. The logs were then rid, for purposes of this research, of (a) computer-generated traffic from bots and crawlers (836 records), (b) any doubling of records through a redirect that took users from one URL to another in SEP (3,297 records), and (c) records without an identifiable source and/or target (188 records). This left a total of 13,363 records of users moving from *Wikipedia* to SEP.

6 While this is a study of how readers of *Wikipedia* come to SEP, it can be pointed out that SEP contains 17 entries with linked references to *Wikipedia* entries, largely under "Internet Resources," with a link, for example, in the SEP entry for Time leading to *Wikipedia* entries for Eternalism, Philosophy of Space and Time, and Presentism.

7 Simfish includes a list of SEP entries among his lists of things that interest this contributor who has done some 300 edits to *Wikipedia* since 2004. Simfish casts himself on his blog as "a teenager who is very thoughtful and who has a lot of respect for the natural and social sciences" Simfish/InquilineKea's Thoughts (undated) http://simfishthoughts.wordpress.com/about/.

8 The editing at the time of this writing is being done by, among others, DionysosProteus, a lecturer in drama in London by his own account; Nev1, a "content adder" who specializes on Machester-related entries: SmackBot that automatically checks and corrects standardized features such as the use of "External links" (rather that "External Link"); RainbowOfLight, a self-described "grammar Nazi"; and RichardVeryard, a graduate of Open University.

9 One still feels that the entry could use the eye of a sharp editor, when you come across expressions such as "Aristotle is one of the most important founding figures in Western philosophy" (to call him a founding figure surely makes "one of the most important: redundant) and to say that "he was the first to create a comprehensive system of Western philosophy" suggests anachronistically that he fashioned something that did not come into existence, as an idea even, until well over a millennia had passed.

10 The Aristotle entry for the *Internet Encyclopedia of Philosophy* has as its concluding line: "The author of this article is anonymous. The IEP is actively seeking an author who will write a replacement article," while the *Catholic Encyclopedia* entry starts out, "The greatest of heathen Philosophers ..." (Turner, 1907).

11 These items are listed in the entry as "Notes," but are referred to as "footnotes" in the *Wikipedia* style guideline Citing Sources, and will be called such in this article: "These [references, footnotes, parenthetical reference] are the most common methods of making articles verifiable. A Wikipedia editor is free to use any of these methods or to develop new methods; no method is preferred."

12 *Wikipedia* co-founder Jimmy Wales, has recently spoken of how *Wikipedia* entries have been improve as they are "more detailed, more accurate, hopefully better written, fleshed out more, with ... two or three footnotes to tell you where to go and check it" (Young, 2008, p. A18). In May, 2005, for example, the *Wikipedia* entry on Aristotle, which was by then over 5,000 words, was without footnotes or any links to SEP. The 51 footnotes that currently accompany the Aristotle entry may *tell you where to go and check*, but with the reference to SEP (as well as to Aristotle's will and Cicero's *Academica*), *Wikipedia* takes the reader directly there in a click, whether to a discussion of Aristotle disproven theory of falling bodies, or to the primary sources (courtesy of Google Books and Project Gutenberg).

13 http://en.Wikipedia.org/wiki/Talk:Atheism/Archive_33

14 http://en.Wikipedia.org/wiki/Talk:Atheism/Archive_14

15 http://en.Wikipedia.org/wiki/Talk:Atheism/Archive_22

16 http://en.Wikipedia.org/wiki/Talk:Atheism/Archive_27

17 http://plato.stanford.edu/entries/atheism-agnosticism/. SEP wasn't only deployed on *Wikipedia* discussion pages to cast light on the big ideas. It could be used, as well, for exercise in

scholarly pedantry. During May 2008, there was a 5,000 word discussion that accompanied the *Wikipedia* entry *On the Jewish Question* on whether "the" should be capitalized in Karl Marx's essay, http://en.*Wikipedia*.org/wiki/Talk:On_the_Jewish_Question.

18 http://en.Wikipedia.org/wiki/Talk:Bobby_Jindal. Biographical entries of the living are a particularly sensitive area for Wikipedia and its policy is "that editors must take particular care about adding biographical material about a living person" and that there is to be "no original research" (reiterated in the "biographies of living persons policy"), which becomes an issue when Jindal's well-known stance is cited without backing by, to further quote the policy, "reliable, third-party, published sources." http://en.Wikipedia.org/wiki/ *Wikipedia*:Biographies_of_living_persons. On the critical incident behind this policy, see Wikipedia Tightens the Reins (2005).

19 http://en.Wikipedia.org/wiki/Talk:Bobby_Jindal

20 http://plato.stanford.edu/entries/double-effect/

21 http://plato.stanford.edu/entries/double-effect/

22 The Jindal entry in *Wikipedia* on this point currently reads: "He opposes abortion without exception. However, he does not condemn medical procedures meant to save the life of a pregnant woman that would indirectly cause the termination of the pregnancy." Each sentence is backed by two footnotes that include quotations from the local media.

23 The 13,363 clicks came from 10,960 IP addresses. A terminal in a library would have a fixed IP address with many users in the course of a day, just as some users would have a single IP address in their homes, for example.

24 At least one reader expressed appreciation for the SEP link in the discussion page for the entry, after much discussion of the poor quality of writing in the entry: "I am glad the Stanford text/link is here, at the bottom—the best I've seen in a while ... Now, that's a well written text on M.!!! ;) :)"

25 The SEP footnote for Machiavelli was edited out of the entry shortly after I complete the analysis presented here along with the sentence that it accompanied—"the validity of that reputation is disputed"—as David Rundle replaced the while lot with "Whatever Machiavelli's own intentions (and they remain a matter of hot debate), his name became synonymous with ruthless politics, deceit and the pursuit of power by any means." While I am not able to tell from the data whether anyone use this footnote, I was able ascertain that of the three footnotes in the *Wikipedia* entry for Pascal's Wager leading to SEP, two of them were used four times by readers, with one of them leading to a footnote in the SEP entry.

26 *Wikipedia* has Policy and Style Guidelines on Verifiability, Verification Methods, Citing Sources, Referencing for Beginners, WikiProject for Citation Cleanup, and a number more.

27 Simeon Warner, personal communication, September 8, 2008.

28 Take as an example the WikiProject devoted to Molecular and Cellular Biology, whose 200 members seek to "create and perfect articles ... on subjects that are discussed at the primary and secondary school level," with the idea that "the perfect article is complete, but accessible to a secondary school student." In the process, one of their members has built a ProtienBox-Bot, an automated script that has already created 9,000 Wikipedia entries for mammalian genes, populating those pages not only with the appropriate symbol, description, function, genomic location, and structure, but with a handful of "Further Reading" references (contributing to the high number of CrossRef links in Table 9.4). If the bot was able to select open access articles for the *Wikipedia* entries, then from my perspective it would increase the degree to which the entry is "accessible to a secondary school student."

29 Recently, Google Scholar made finding an open access version all the more easy by indicating in its search results which links lead directly, without subscription or credit card, to a PDF or HTML file.

30 The step avoids a common self-referential issue when reference works cite each other, which reduces their claim to being a guide to some aspect of the world; on the *Oxford English Dictionary* and this matter, see Willinsky (1994).

References

Aristotle (2006). Overview. *Internet Encyclopedia of Philosophy.* http://www.utm.edu/research/iep/a/aristotl.htm

Björk, Bo-C., Roos, A. and Lauri, M. (2008). *Global annual volume of peer reviewed scholarly articles and the share available via different Open Access options.* Proceedings of the ELPUB2008 Conference on Electronic Publishing, Toronto, Canada. Retrieved from http://www.oacs.shh.fi/publications/elpub-2008.pdf

Caswell, T., Shelley Henson, S., Jensen, M. and Wile, D. (2008). Open Educational Resources: Enabling universal education. *The International Review of Research in Open and Distance Learning, 9*(1), http://www.irrodl.org/index.php/irrodl/article/viewArticle/469/1001

Cicero. (2005). *Academica.* (James S. Reid, Ed.). London: Macmillan, 1874. Gutenberg Project. Retrieved from http://www2.cddc.vt.edu/gutenberg/1/4/9/7/14970/14970-h/14970-h.htm #BkII_119

Fallis, D. (2008). Toward an epistemology of Wikipedia. *Journal of the American Society for Information and Science Technology, 59*(10), 1662–1674.

Harnad, S., Brody, T., Vallieres, F., Carr, L., Hitchcock, S., Gingras, Y., Oppenheim, C., Hajjem, C. and Hilf, E. (2008). The access/impact problem and the green and gold roads to open access: An update. *Serials Review, 34*(1), 36–40.

Hessel E. (2006, September 19). Shillipedia. Forbes. Retrieved from http://www.forbes.com/business/forbes/2006/0619/056.html

Jaschik, S. (2007, January 26). A stand against Wikipedia. *Inside Higher Education.* Retrieved from http://www.insidehighered.com/news/2007/01/26/wiki

Keen, A. (2007). *The cult of the amateur: How blogs, MySpace, YouTube, and the rest of today's user-generated media are destroying our economy, our culture, and our values.* New York: Doubleday.

Parel, A. (1972). Introduction: Machiavelli's method and his Interpreters. In Anthony Parel (Ed.), *The political calculus: Essays on Machiavelli's philosophy* (pp. 3–28). Toronto: University of Toronto Press.

Perry, J. and Zalta, E. N. (1997). *Why philosophy needs a "dynamic" encyclopedia.* Unpublished paper, Center for the Study of Language and Information, Stanford University. Retrieved from http://plato.stanford.edu/pubs/why.html

Rainie, L. and Tancer, M. (2007). *Wikipedia users.* Unpublished Data Memo. Washington, DC: Pew Internet & American Life Project.

Read, B. (2006). Can Wikipedia ever make the grade? *Chronicle of Higher Education, 53*(1), A31–A35.

Sunstein, C. R. (2006). *Infotopia: How many minds produce knowledge.* New York: Oxford University Press.

Turner, W. (1907). Aristotle. In *The Catholic encyclopedia.* New York: Robert Appleton.

Wal-Mart. (2008). Retrieved September 28, 2008, from *Encyclopædia Britannica Online* at http://search.eb.com/eb/article 9396483

Weber, S. (2004). *The success of open source.* Cambridge, MA: Harvard University Press.

Wikipedia Tightens the Reins. (2005, December 5). *Wired.* Retrieved from http://www.wired.com/science/discoveries/news/2005/12/69759

Willinsky, J. (2007). What open access research can do for Wikipedia. *First Monday, 12*(3). Retrieved from http://www.uic.edu/htbin/cgiwrap/bin/ojs/index.php/fm/article/view/1624/1539

Willinsky, J. (2006). *The access principle: The case for open access to research and scholarship.* Cambridge, MA: MIT Press.

Willinsky, J. (1994). *Empire of words: The reign of the OED.* Princeton, NJ: Princeton University Press.

Young, J. (2008, June 13). Wikipedia's co-founder wants to make it more useful to academe. *Chronicle of Higher Education, 54*(40), A18.

10

THE FUTURE OF LEARNING AND THE VIRTUAL LIFE OF KNOWLEDGE

Robert Luke and Peter Pericles Trifonas

> ... we know that it is unwise to put too much faith in futurology.
>
> *(Jean-François Lyotard)*

Published in 1979, Jean-François Lyotard's *The Postmodern Condition: A Report on Knowledge* has left an indelible imprint on the humanities, social sciences, and the "science of research" in general. The epistemological trajectory of disciplinary fields such as sociology, philosophy, applied ethics, linguistics, political science, history, "literary studies," and education, to name but a few, was forever altered by the appearance of this text and the self-proclaimed mission of its writer to reexamine the "condition of knowledge in the most highly developed societies" (Lyotard, p. xxiii). As Fredric Jameson noted in the "Forward," *The Postmodern Condition* can be considered a polemic against the Habermasian notion of a *"legitimation crisis"* that takes into account the negative consequences of the new views of scientific research and its paradigms, opened up by theorists such as Thomas Kuhn and Paul Feyerabend. What is unique about Lyotard's rendering of the postmodern is the openness of the critical vision of the legitimacy of knowledge structures in the postindustrial era that is presented. It is synoptic and yet not totalizing. Perhaps, because, Lyotard explains with respect to the authority of his vision in *The Postmodern Condition*,

> the author of the report is a philosopher, not an expert. The latter knows what he knows and what he does not know: the former does not. One concludes, the other questions—two very different language games. I combine them here with the result that neither quite succeeds.
>
> *(Lyotard, p. xxv)*

This revelation of authorial intentions regarding his method of writing, including the motivation behind its production, will guide the reading of the text. This chapter will consider perspectives on technology, knowledge, and *learning in virtual* as a type of postmodern "futurology." Or a speculative discourse of the imagination concerned with engaging the empirical manifestations of present knowledges as forms of being or becoming, but also projecting the shadowy dimensions of their unimaginable ethical effects in *a time-yet-to-come,* which is now and *after now.*

Postindustrial society exhibits signs of postmodern culture, Lyotard explains. Not only because the reality of a temporal disjunction engenders liminal perspectives on knowledge but because the nature of episteme becomes redefined in accordance with the "problems of translation" (Lyotard, 1979, p. 3) between repositories of knowledge. A question we must ask is: Can truth be reduced to an archive? Is it possible? Yes. Knowledge is nothing if it is not grounded upon a record of data which is taken as the demonstrable evidence of the self-certainty of truth. In order to secure its future, culture depends upon the possibility of referring to stable archives of meaning to endow understanding with the evidence of empirical value. The failings of memory require the demonstrable proof of a past and a future to enable the possibility of a genealogical rendering of human experience whereby knowledge can be reproduced and therefore ready to be learned.

Language intervenes, however, to destabilize the ground of meaning-making. Knowledge is thus exteriorized and transformed into the more general category of "information"—its "use-value" not withstanding the effects of representation that mediate for the limitations of human understanding by giving way to the instrumentality of technological reason. Still, Lyotard states that "Scientific knowledge is a kind of discourse" (1979, p. 3) Which is true. Knowledge is not a technology. Narrative cannot be instrumental. We must consider the significance of Lyotard's statement regarding scientific knowledge with respect to language and technology.

Epistemological doubt settles in between the apparatus used for the technical manipulation of information and its archival containment as signs of understanding. Representation deforms, denatures, and supplements the originary eidetic structures of conceptual formations. It is crucial to recognize the semantic elision that Lyotard makes—but does not specifically state—between the archiving of knowledge and the constitutive means and methods of doing so. The paradigmatic shift from discourse to technology changes the social and epistemological definitions of research and truth. Not to mention the cognitive preconditions of learning. The speculative dimension of reason comes into question after the instrumental push of technology to recode human experience according to its own nature is made. And yet, learning requires creativity and imagination. It is moved forward by epistemological curiosity—the quest for infinite human progress—and not the inculcation of procedural outcomes that render subjectivity as the products of coded instructions performed via electronic commands. Lyotard is enamoured neither by the prospects of a "cyborg subjectivity"—and the potential it foresees for a new information society—nor, by the vision of a learning culture that prioritizes the ethical value of the digital enterprising of knowledge. He details how research in such an epistemological milieu will begin to be legitimated according to the power of information as a commodity to be used by nation-states "in the world wide competition for power" (Lyotard, 1979, p. 5). Lyotard's predictions about the future of knowledge here are uncanny. He states that because of the miniaturization of technology and the increase in computing power, "learning is translated into quantities of information" (p. 4). These "bytes of knowledge"—channeled by finite systems of translation with discreet programmable languages—will produce highly directed areas of inquiry. Consequently, the legitimacy of research is to be determined in accordance with its potential viability to serve "industrial and commercial strategies on the one hand, and the political and military strategies on the other" (p. 5). The field of scientific inquiry narrows drastically when it is tied to the circulation of capital. Basic or fundamental research becomes shaped in relation to the interests of multi-national corporations and nation-states vying for control of information. In a postmodern age, where knowledge is reinterpreted as information—and its value is determined by the capacity to incite exchanges between social actors—Lyotard can speculate how learning is also in a position to be commodified in the public sphere. Education therefore no longer becomes the sole "purview of the State" (p. 5) but is determined through the socio-economic and ideologico-political forces that structure and mercantilize knowledge. An information society will be predicated and grow through the open exchange of information on a global scale. Lyotard was perhaps the first modern philosopher after Martin Heidegger to predict the future impact of technology on knowledge without referring to more recent inventions such as the World Wide Web and the Internet. The flow of information supersedes and overrides the quality of the information made available. Learning here, means learning to learn the virtual life of knowledge and how it can be used to accomplish specific outcomes.

What does it mean to "learn the virtual Life of knowledge"? What does it mean to learn how to live online, or within online spaces? How is the transition from traditional modes of learning to those mediated by new technologies affecting the way(s) in which learning is constructed? To start with, lifelong learning trends are evolving out of the "any time any place" ubiquity afforded by the use of new educational technologies, specifically the World Wide Web and the Internet. These technologies' capabilities offer greater flexibility for place-independent learning and for the evolution of new pedagogies. Within this conception of learning to learn the virtual life, the predominant issues centre on information and media literacy, online learning, the nature of virtual space, and a kind of archaeology or history about the evolution of online media themselves. Other important aspects include the notion of accessibility and the practical problems include ways in which we can encourage those not already predisposed to it to get online, to learn to live the virtual life.

A corollary to this issue is the fact that learning is no longer considered a discreet issue undertaken in specific locations (i.e., schools); rather, learning takes place in many places and in many contexts (Giroux & Simon, 1989; Nolan & Weiss, in press). Expanding the research question to include a generalized overview of Learning Environments brings to light the location of schooling and the nature of learning with the integration of the 'everyday.' This concept is the location of the networked society, and within postmodern geography, "there is a new spatial form characteristic of social practices that dominate and shape the network society: the space of flows. The space of flows is the material organization of time-sharing social practices that work through flows. Flows are the purposeful, repetitive, programmable exchanges and interactions between "social actors in the economic, political, and symbolic structures of society (Castells, 1996, p. 412). Thus to learn and live in the space of flows is to live within the fluid architecture of interrelatedness and connectivity, where process replaces product centred education. Within this new conception of place and space and the learning that works its way through it, we can come to understand the connections between the real and the virtual; "The space of flows is not placeless, although its structural logic is. It is based on an electronic network, but this network links up specific places, with well-defined social, cultural, physical, and functional characteristics" (Castells, 1996, p. 413). These characteristics constitute the ground of the networked society, upon which the effects of education operate.

Digital Literacy and Learning to Learn Online

The question of Learning the Virtual Life is a matter of using new technologies to meet the learning needs of people in the new information economy. Central to constructing a curriculum of learning (to learn) online is the idea of developing digital literacies as a foundational concept towards constructing learning within online learning environments. While the term *information literacy* resonates largely within the library community, referring to teaching the skills required to use information technologies, this definition has been expanded recently to include the broader conception of media literacies. Kellner (2000) explores the idea that "students should learn new forms of computer literacy that involve both how to use computer culture to do research and gather information, as well as learning to perceive the computer as a cultural terrain which contains texts, spectacles, games, and new interactive multimedia requiring new modes of literacy" (p. 206). It is therefore important that "genuine computer literacy involves not just technical knowledge and skills, but refined reading, writing, research, and communicating ability that involves heightened capabilities for critically accessing, analyzing, interpreting, and processing print, image, sound, and multimedia material" (Kellner, 2000, p. 206). Foregrounded here is the idea of *critical* information literacy as forming the ground upon which the effects of learning (to learn) online are situated. I use this terminology after McLuhan (1964), who has given rise to most of the basis for current research into virtuality and virtual learning itself. Most of McLuhan's (1964, 1962) work concerned the transcendental nature of things electric, and the majority of researchers in the emergent and overlapping fields of cybercultural studies, computer assisted learning theories, network architecture and learning environments have at some time used this as a starting point. At the most basic level, it is McLuhan's imaginative (re)construction of life in the virtual space of the global village that has formed the theoretical underpinnings as well as cultural subconscious of where we are today in learning online.

The pervasiveness of technology in contemporary culture underscores the need for education to integrate new literacies within extant curricula. Rendering the technology transparent makes it an accepted part of the curriculum of everyday life. However, it is also important to infuse this curriculum with a critical awareness of this media, to question the ground upon which media's effect lie. At the heart of the lie is the fact that "Schools operating within the industrial age model of education do not provide working and learning environments that support the autonomous and independent contributions befitting life in an information age society" (Fanning, 2000). More to the point, "the autonomous and responsible initiative needed for success in contemporary society centers on the individual's role in collaboration, information sharing and cooperative dialogue. Learners rarely practice these skills in most modern schools. This condition is in discord with the demands of a postindustrial, postmodern society" (Fanning, 2000). With the changing face of education and the firm establishment of the principles of life-long learning pervading all aspects of culture (including and perhaps especially corporate culture), it is imperative for educational policy and practical curricula to more fully integrate multiple literacies—particularly critical literacies—within the broader structure of learning. These concepts can be grouped together under the rubric of digital literacy.

The concept of digital literacy includes not only the skill to use information technologies (broadly defined as any technology that mediates the use of information), but also the requisite skills to decode, contextualize, and critically evaluate this information (Rheingold, 1993). The most recent addition to this aspect of literacy has been the concept of universal design, or accessibility, with respect to physically and/or learning disabled persons. With 20% of the population (54 million people in the U.S. alone; Waddell, 1999) suffering from some sort of physical or learning disability, any inquiry into the nature of learning the virtual life must take into account the fact that for these people this is drastically different. In fact, blind users of online learning environments can offer significant insights into how people construct cognitive maps of online areas, in that this process of cognition and cognitive mapping is much more explicitly defined with blind users. It should, however, be noted that there are also significant differences in the way blind users ultimately interact with computer environments, as they tend to be much more linear and hierarchical because of the inherent necessity to follow a linear pathway through the online structure. Any conception of learning to learn online must include aspects of accessibility, particularly as it relates to the construction of curricula in this area, as all curricula must be inclusive. There is a significant gap in the curricular research regarding accessibility, which my own research is addressing in conjunction with the concept(s) of critical media literacy and what I term access*Ability*: enabling learning through technology.

Access*Ability*: Enabling Technology for Life-Long Learning

The Canadian government has recently enacted policy to ensure that legislation providing access to persons with disabilities is applied to digital media, following the World Wide Web Consortium's (W3C) Website Accessibility Initiative (WAI) guidelines (http://www.cio-dpi.gc.ca/clf-upe/1/1_e.asp). It is expected that voluntary compliance on the part of all online education providers will happen as a matter of course and in keeping with the evolving standards of the WWW. "However, even though web accessibility guidelines exist, some administrators consider campus-wide initiatives to standardize the creation of web materials a costly time-consuming task that is difficult to enforce" (Hricko, 2000, p. 393). Hricko notes how "post-secondary institutions are reluctant to allocate funding for the training and resources needed to assist educators in modifying and creating acceptable web materials" (p. 393). It is therefore imperative to seek ways to encourage the accessible design of web materials from their first iteration. It is also "important that post-secondary institutions provide the necessary training, resources, and tools to develop accessible web materials" p. 398).

Just as buildings are built with accessibility factored into their architecture from the ground up, so too must WWW and Internet architecture factor in accessibility initiatives from the outset to ensure equitable access to online resources. The true democratizing potential of digital media (WWW, Internet) can be realized with accessible technology, as it does in fact provide a kind of transparent levelling of the playing field because it increases access for those who might otherwise be prevented from attending educational institutions. People with physical and/or learning disabilities are encouraged to become producers of information, and not just passive consumers. Adaptive technology allows for the potential to become active participants in learning and the economy in general. As Harrison and Vekar (2000) point out, "positive feedback from their peers can encourage students with learning disabilities to become even more active" (p.16), and this is so with the physically disabled as well. Outreach and educational programs benefit the disabled communities by offering "improved self-confidence and self-esteem, enhanced social skills and computer proficiency, as well as greater motivation for continued skill development" (Harrison & Vekar, p. 15). Ensuring accessibility in course designs that utilize online technologies will ensure that the wider population benefits from these programs. The very design of accessible online programs offers disabled persons an avenue to pursue distance education where none might have existed before. Technology directly benefits online learning by providing access to life-long learning programs to those at risk of being left out of these programs in the first place.

The idea of access to information and communication technologies (ICT) is two-sided, in that there are both politics and logistics to consider. The politics of access can be defined as ensuring everyone has access to ICT and information literacy programs. The logistics of access refer to those who are disabled in some way and need specifically designed web sites and hardware and software in order to ensure they can use ICTs. It is reasonable to assume that some people will fall into both categories, and also that some who access under "normal" conditions may gradually need adaptive technology in order to continue this access, for as people age, sight, tactile/haptic/motor control may be lost or diminished resulting in increased need for adaptive ICTs (Porter & Jutta Treviranus). With an aging population comes increased demand for more accessible web design and adaptive computer technologies to meet growing physical and learning cognitive disability to accommodate lifelong learning principles. By building in "electronic curbcuts" from the ground up, online education programs ensure they meet the principles of universal design and so are not exclusionary. In many ways the issue of accessibility is being pioneered in the United States, for the most part because the U.S. has more legislation protecting the rights of persons with disabilities. There is no legislation in Canada, outside of the Human Rights legislation, that gives disabled persons protection against this exclusion (see Harrison, 2000).

As Cynthia Waddell (1999) points out, "we have not fully addressed the linkage of the individual with the Internet community as a whole. Rapid changes in the Internet environment require that we examine not only the end-user workstation needs but also the technology barriers emerging beyond the computer workstation." What this means is that there are broader issues with respect to access and living in a culture increasingly dominated by various mediating technologies. Issues of access and accessibility—the politics and logistics of access—are pervasive. According to Waddell: "This barrier is systemic and must be addressed in our policies as well as in our education and outreach." Waddell continues, "The digital divide will continue to expand if this issue is not addressed in our research, education and outreach. As the rapid development of new web applications continues, it is necessary to ensure that new barriers are not erected to effective communication and commerce."

Online education providers must ensure that their online curricula are accessible to all of the population: "By directing our research and policy directives to address these problems, we will overcome the digital divide and ensure full participation in the global digital economy."

Another aspect of accessibility is the ability to use online media as a ground upon which to pursue life-long learning. Ensuring and enshrining access is the ground upon which media's effects permeate into the broader fabric of culture, echoing McLuhan's premise that the "medium is the message." That is, we need to encourage access to using the media itself, but also a cultivation of critical media awareness that will allow for the consumption of information to progress towards the production of knowledge. Developing critical literacies allow us to engage with the larger technologically mediated world and to take responsibility for learning from this vast and inchoate matrix of information that comprises the WWW. As Langford (1998) says, "the mere ability to read and to write is being translated into the ability to read, write, and to develop the capacities to understand, absorb, assimilate, and digest the images being transmitted electronically with the added capacity to communicate these images electrographically." The ability to use online media in order to access educational programs ensures a technological "self-efficacy" (Dusick, 1998, p. 11). The emphasis is not just on being able to read and use information, but to be able to integrate it with critical thinking skills and "metacognitive processes" that encourage engagement within life-long learning. This is especially relevant if we are to engage the wider population within the rubric of life-long learning, as there are sectors of this population that must first be encouraged to pursue education in and of itself, and then be taught the critical literacy skills required to access it.

People should not just be passive consumers of information, as "The essence of this technological culture for the individual lies in his or her capacity to access, comprehend and interpret information independently and use it efficiently" (Fanning, 2000). Interpreting information means bringing it into context and producing meaning and relevance within individual or community relevance. Fanning reminds us that "technology has become more than a set of tools to be picked up and used when a person decides he or she needs them. It has become a required medium that mediates experience in most aspects of peoples' lives." It is this aspect of mediation that is important when considering how aspects of accessibility and information literacy can affect life-long learning programs. Accordingly, "we need to develop new literacies to meet the challenge of the new technologies, and literacies of diverse sorts—including an even more fundamental importance for print literacy—are of crucial importance in restructuring education for a high-tech and multicultural society" (Kellner, 2000, pp. 196–7). In order to be effective and accessible, education must take issues of access and critical media literacy into account when designing programs that utilize any advanced media. These programs must also acknowledge other barriers to pursuing education, including "cultural, social, familial, personal, or financial barriers" (Fusch, 2000).

Access*Ability* means providing an inclusive, accessible environment for learning that might otherwise be closed to people with physical and/or learning disabilities. Enabling technology has two distinct meanings. The first is that technology is enabling to those with disabilities, generally referred to as accessible. The second is the fact that technology enables different conceptions of education: it mobilizes or is mobilized to construct digital pedagogies. ICT can allow access to educational opportunities for a wider audience, especially with asynchronous online delivery of curricular materials. But rather than just using online media to deliver course materials and to perhaps facilitate communication between students and instructors, these media have the potential to radically alter the very pedagogy that underlies the provision of distance education. The effect of using technology in life-long learning programs is an enhanced understanding of the ground of these media themselves; that is, an understanding of how these media operate with and in the larger context of a learning culture. Technological transparency refers to this effect, and the notion that the ubiquitous use any given technology will make this technology transparent, an accepted facet (or fact) of media for communication. In short, a transparent technology becomes a ground of media effects.

Toward Technological Transparency

It is well known that changes in media radically alter the ways in which we learn to conceive of ourselves in our environment. With the current advent of new ICT use in education, we are in the midst of a radical paradigm shift commensurate with the emergence of "Gutenberg's Galaxy" and the introduction of the printing press (Privateer, 1999; Simerly, 1999). Accordingly, these new media are instigating new pedagogies, what Privateer (1999) calls "'digital pedagogies,' new ways of educating more consistent with the nature of contemporary technologies than with prior management models" (p. 61). Privateer shows how education has largely been constrained by an Enlightenment notion of information processing: the rote assemblage of factual data that is then re-presented as knowledge. By detailing how new technologies can challenge and produce change within traditional notions of learning, Privateer encourages us to rethink what skills will be necessary for people entering the 21st century. Skills such as information and knowledge management, connected intelligence building, and group management skills are brought to the fore under contemporary rubrics of institutional change and learning.

Privateer's analysis "invites us to rethink traditional notions of the cost-benefit ratio of higher education" as it is effected by new technologies (1999, p. 68). Similarly, Simerly (1999) also says "it is important for us to develop viable institutional responses to these very genuine concerns involving technology-enhanced education at a time when there are also multiple demands on our resources for many other high priority items deemed necessary to produce quality education" (p. 40). Simerly echoes Privateer's call for an institutional policy shift that will take advantage of recent media developments as well as the intellectual apparatus that is concomitant with this technological change. Both writers acknowledge that the cost of providing a technology-enhanced education go much further than the cost of hardware and software: "There are also many personnel expenses associated with long-range plans to utilize technology-enhanced education" such as help desks, systems administrators, and the need to provide upgrading as each software iteration is introduced into the electronic classroom (Simerly, 1999, p. 44).

Simerly (1999) also notes that "it is important to consider the existing institutional culture when planning a major change effort such as technology-enhanced education" (p. 46), a point Privateer also makes. This cannot be understated, for understanding how people will react to a forced institutional change can effect how successful an implementation of change will be. For example, older teachers and professors may have little or no familiarity with new technologies, and will certainly be resistant to the idea that these challenge their position of authority. This is the crux of the transposition of policy on which Privateer focuses. The currently evolving knowledge based culture is "characterized by digital (that is, networked processes) rather than analogic (that is, linear processes)" modalities (Walshok, 1999, p. 77). This shift, from a product to a process oriented education, is reflected in the needs and uses of ICT in education. While there exist in many institutions those people already using or more disposed to using ICT in the classroom, these early adopters need crucial institutional support (Privateer, 1999). Early adopters need the support of administration in order to offer their students the technological transparency skills that come with using these media as a matter of course or within the general processes of learning and learning to learn online (see Martine and Freeman, 1999).

Life-long learning and collaborative learning principles are especially "facilitated by the networked computer" (Harrison & Vekar 2000, p. 2), and are reflective of the ways in which current culture lives and works. Thus, education that takes advantage of technology reflects the larger cultural narrative, while at the same time offering avenues of learning that are in keeping with current cultural paradigms, and participate within these paradigms. Technology benefits education directly because of this. It offers media effects that are both familiar and necessary, as well as the media ground upon which our culture is presently evolving. Some studies have shown that students actually prefer to take technology-mediated courses over traditional face-to-face courses.

Throughout the use of technology is the necessity for establishing standards. This applies equally to the evolution of "revolutionary pedagogies" (see Trifonas, 2000) that use new technologies to reinvent and reinforce new ways of learning and living in digital culture, as well as to the evolution of these new technologies themselves. The establishment of technological and pedagogical standards will ensure that there is seamless integration of technologies within the digital pedagogies of contemporary culture. These evolving technological and intellectual standards contribute to the redefinition of learning and the establishment of a technologically-enabled life-long learning culture. As Privateer points out, this requires bold institutional change using the ground of ICT use in education as a change agent in the effects of education itself: "One suggestion for carving out a different strategic path is to think of instructional technologies as tools for re-engineering and reinventing curriculum" (1999, p. 64). The redefinition of education as a process is enabled by ICT: "When the classroom is networked to the outside world, the teacher shifts from being 'the only expert' to being a facilitator of the active work of learning" (Harrison & Vekar, 2000, p. 3). The teacher models learning as process.

In order to more seamlessly integrate online technologies within learning structures, it is essential to implement technological transparency with respect to the media used to access educational networks. While the technology can never truly be rendered transparent—as if it is not there—the notion of technological transparency refers to that media which becomes an accepted part of communication. For example, people pick up a telephone to make a call without considering whether there will be a dial tone; they are in fact surprised if there isn't one. The telephone in this case is transparent, as the person has already thought past the actual dialing of the number (in most instances) and is already thinking about what they wish to say to the person they expect to answer the phone. Bolter and Grusin (1999/2000) call this process "remediation, "an 'interfaceless' interface, in which there will be no recognizable electronic tools—no buttons, windows, scroll bars, or even icons as such. Instead the user will move through the space interacting with the objects 'naturally,' as she does in the physical world. Virtual reality, three-dimensional graphics, and graphical interface design are all seeking to make digital technology 'transparent.' In this sense, a transparent interface would be one that erases itself, so that the user is no longer aware of confronting a medium, but instead stands in an immediate relationship to the contents of that medium" (pp. 23–24; see also Levinson, 1997, pp. 104–14). While this notion of pure transparency may be unattainable, it does apply to the idea of digital literacy and using media to access online learning networks. Digital literacy requires rendering the computer transparent, as well as the operating system, dialup/Internet connection, and web interface. All must be seamlessly integrated into the user's sense of experience in order for this medium to be fully exploited for educational purposes. Within the learning of these new networked systems, new users are integrated within the expert community via a process of 'doing' and indoctrination of the FAQs of online living (see, for example Arias & Bellman, 1995; Berthold et al., 1998; Bromberg, 1996; Chen & Gaines, 1998; Croissant, 1998; Doyle

& Hayes-Roth, 1998; Harasim et al., 1995; Smith, McLaughlin, & Osborne, 1998; Turkle, 1995). Digital literacy would teach these skills while using them, using the apprenticeship model of learning; as the user becomes comfortable with the incidental skills required to operate a computer in order to get at the educational network and material, concepts of critical media literacy can be introduced into the curriculum.

Telepresence and the Virtual Real[i]ty

Concomitant with the idea of transparency is telepistemology—the nature of learning and knowing within telepresence, or learning to learn online within remote and virtual communities. There are many important issues currently being debated within this scope, ideas of telepistemology, the nature and production of online space, and the development of community that are problematising the distinction between the real and the virtual (Goldberg, 2000; Rheingold, 1991, 1993; Turkle, 1995). Ideas of community as it relates to telepresence are still evolving, and the text-based nature of most online communication requires an undue reliance on literacy without the visual cues that normally constitute interpersonal communication (Rheingold, 1993; Ito, 1998). As bandwidths increase and technologies get more sophisticated, we will be forced to engage these issues head on as we take technologically-mediated communication and education past the provision of static material and the interaction of participants amongst themselves, to the interaction with learning material and sophisticated artificial intelligence tutors. This will further enhance the idea of telepresense, the establishment of a sense of shared space among individuals who are working on a common task but are not in physical proximity. Incorporating other modes of communication within online education will enhance the overall educative experience and create a sense of place online within hypermediated learning environments. Encouraging "heteronomous learning, the pedagogically substantiated combination and integration of two or more modes of presentation means that multimedia teaching of content can be offered on a multisensory basis, thus enabling precise close overlapping of stimuli whereby better learning can be prepared, effected and strengthened. In addition, much higher levels of activity and interactivity can be achieved" (Peters, 2000, p. 16). Research into haptic and multisensory feedback has begun to explore this potentiality.

Technology is expanding the mind's eye of continuing education, reformatting the nature of communication and education to the extent that we have the opportunity to reconfigure the program and goals of education. An important distinction to make here is the idea that digital pedagogies can shape the direction of technology, rather than technology shaping how we see education. Shifting terrains of identity and community formation within online learning spaces will foster and enhance global consciousness, which in turn will help to generate the critical media skills necessary to living the virtual life. This life will be a schizophrenic one, in that it will simultaneously accept media as a ground of communication, while questioning critically this ground and its concomitant effects. Within this conception of learning, it is necessary to view technology integration in a holistic fashion, to create "information ecologies" as a framework for understanding the position of learning and living within the networked space of flows (see Nardi & O'Day, 1999). The evolution of digital pedagogies within this framework for life-long learning will shape the broader learning culture in which we live.

References

Arias, A. A., & Bellman, B. (1995). Networked Collaborative Research and Teaching. In E. Boschmann (Ed.), *The Electronic Classroom: A Handbook for Education in the Electronic Environment* (pp. 180–185). Medford, NJ: Learned Information, Inc.

Berthold, M., Sudweeks, F., Newton, S., & Coyne, R. (1998). It Makes Sense: Using an Auto-associative Neural Network to Explore Typicality in Computer Mediated Discussions. In F. Sudweeks, M. McLaughlin, & S. Rafaeli (Eds.), *Network and Netplay: Virtual Groups on the Internet* (pp. 191–220). Menlo Park, CA, Cambridge, MA: AAAI Press/The MIT Press.

Bolter, J. D., & Grusin, R. (1999/2000). *Remediation: Understanding New Media.* Cambridge, MA: The MIT Press.

Bromberg, H. (1996). Are MUDs Communities? Identity, Belonging and Consciousness in Virtual Worlds. In R. Shields (Ed.), *Cultures of Internet: Virtual Spaces, Real Histories, Living Bodies* (pp. 143–152). London: Sage.

Castells, M. (1996). *The Rise of the Network Society, The Information Age: Economy, Society and Culture* (Vol. 1). London: Blackwell.

Chen, L. L.-J., & Gaines, B. (1998). Modelling and Supporting Virtual Cooperative Interaction Through the World Wide Web. In F. Sudweeks, M. McLaughlin, & S. Rafaeli (Eds.), *Network and Netplay: Virtual Groups on the Internet* (pp. 221–242). Menlo Park, CA, Cambridge, MA: AAAI Press/The MIT Press.

Croissant, J. (1998). Growing Up Cyborg: Developmental Stories for Postmodern Children. In R. Davis-Floyd & J. Dumit (Eds.), *Cyborg Babies: From Techno-Sex to Techno-Tots* (pp. 285–300). New York: Routledge.

Doyle, P., & Hayes-Roth, B. (1998). Guided Exploration of Virtual Worlds. In F. Sudweeks, M. McLaughlin, & S. Rafaeli (Eds.), *Network and Netplay: Virtual Groups on the Internet* (pp. 243–264). Menlo Park, CA, Cambridge, MA: AAAI Press/The MIT Press.

Dusick, D. (1998). The Learning Effectiveness of Educational Technology: What Does That Really Mean? *Educational Technology Review* (Autumn/Winter), 10–12.

Fanning, J. (2000). Expanding the Definition of Technological Literacy in Schools. *Mid-Continent Research for Education and Learning* [Online]. Available: http://www.mcrel.org/products/noteworthy/noteworthy/jimf.asp.

Fusch, G. (2000). Breaking Down Perceived Barriers to Lifelong Learning. *Educational Technology & Society* [Online], 3(1). Available: http://ifets.ieee.org/periodical/vol_1_2000/fusch.html (accessed 1 December 2000).

Giroux, H., & Simon, R. (1989). Popular Culture as a Pedagogy of Pleasure and Meaning. In H. Giroux & R. Simon (Eds.), *Popular Culture, Schooling and Everyday Life* (pp. 1–29). Toronto: OISE Press.

Harasim, L., Hiltz, S. R., Teles, L., & Turoff, M. (1995). *Learning Networks: A Field Guide to Teaching and Learning Online.* Cambridge, MA: The MIT Press.

Harrison, J., & Vekar, J. (2000). New Learning Technologies: Applications, challenges, and success stories from the front lines. Available: http://www.telelearn.ca.

Harrison, L. (2000). Accessible Web-based Distance Education: Principles and Best Practices. Available: http://www.utoronto.ca/atrc/rd/library/papers/accDistanceEducation.html.

Hricko, M. (2000). Designing Accessible Web-Based Courses. *Indian Journal of Open Learning, 9*(3), 393–402.

Ito, M. (1998). Inhabiting Multiple Worlds: Making Sense of SimCity 2000 in the Fifth Dimension. In R. Davis-Floyd & J. Dumit (Eds.), *Cyborg Babies: From Techno-Sex to Techno-Tots* (pp. 301–316). New York: Routledge.

Kellner, D. (2000). Multiple Literacies and Critical Pedagogies: New Paradigms. In P. P. Trifonas (Ed.), *Revolutionary Pedagogies: Cultural Politics, Instituting Education, and the Discourse of Theory* (pp. 196–221). Routledge: New York.

Langford, L. (1998). Information Literacy: A Clarification. *From Now On: The Educational Technology Journal* [Online] (October). Available: http://emifyes.iserver.net/fromnow/oct98/clarify.html (Accessed 19 October 2000).

Levinson, P. (1997). *The Soft Edge: A Natural History and Future of the Information Revolution.* London and New York: Routledge.

Lyotard, J. F. (1979). *The Postmodern Condition: A Report on Knowledge* (Trans. G. Bennington and B. Massumi). Minneapolis: University of Minnesota Press.

McLuhan, M. (1962). *The Guttenberg Galaxy: The Making of Typographic Man.* Toronto: University of Toronto Press.

McLuhan, M. (1964). *Understanding Media: The Extensions of Man.* New York: Signet Books.

Nardi, B. A., & O'Day, V. (1999). *Information Ecologies: Using Technology With Heart.* Cambridge, MA: The MIT Press.

Nolan, D. J., & Weiss, J. (In press). Learning Cyberspace: An Educational View of Virtual Community. In K. A. Renninger & W. Shumar (Eds.), *Building VIrtual Communities: Learning and Change in Cyberspace.*

Porter, L., & Treviranus, J. (1998). Journal of Haptic Applications to Virtual Worlds. Available at http://www.dinf.ne.jp/doc/english/Us_Eu/conf/csun_98/csun98_082.html.

Privateer, P. (1999). Academic Technology and the Future of Higher Education: Strategic Paths Taken and Not Taken. *The Journal of Higher Education, 70*(1), 60–79.

Rheingold, H. (1991). *Virtual Reality.* New York: Simon & Schuster.

Rheingold, H. (1993). *The Virtual Community: Homesteading on the Electronic.* Reading, MA: Addison-Wesley.

Simerly, R. (1999). Practical Guidelines and Suggestions for Designing and Implementing Technology-Enhanced Education. *The Journal of Continuing Higher Education* (Spring), 39–47.

Smith, C., McLaughlin, M., & Osborne, K. (1998). From Terminal Ineptitude to Virtual Sociopathy: How Conduct is Regulated on Usenet. In F. Sudweeks, M. McLaughlin & S. Rafaeli (Eds.), *Network and Netplay: Virtual Groups on the Internet* (pp. 95–112). Menlo Park, CA, Cambridge, MA: AAAI Press/The MIT Press.

Trifonas, P. P. (2000). Technologies of Reason: Toward a Regrounding of Academic Responsibility. In P. P. Trifonas (Ed.), *Revolutionary Pedagogies: Cultural Politics, Instituting Education, and the Discourse of Theory* (pp. 113–139). New York: Routledge.

Turkle, S. (1995). *Life on the Screen.* New York: Simon & Schuster.

Waddell, C. (1999). The Growing Digital Divide In Access For People With Disabilities: Overcoming Barriers To Participation In The Digital Economy. Available: http://www.icdri.org/the_digital_divide.htm (accessed 20 October 2000).

Walshok, M. (1999). Strategies for Building the Infrastructure that Supports the Engaged Campus. In R. Bingle, R. Games, & Malloy (Eds.), *Colleges and Universities as Citizens* (pp. 74–96). Needham Heights, MA: Allyn & Bacon.

11

"TOMORROW WE GO BOWLING"

Covert Intimacy and Homosocial Play in the *Grand Theft Auto IV* Series

Marc Ouellette

The interactions among the male characters in the controversial but extremely popular video game, *Grand Theft Auto IV*, and its *The Ballad of Gay Tony* expansion pack, effectively provide a ritualized series of explorations of homosocial bonding within the context of otherwise traditional forms of masculinity. Indeed, the situation of the routines within familiar paradigms may ultimately be a key factor in the undoing of the incumbent masculine privilege, especially since befriending and defending openly gay characters figure in the central stories and operations of the game. The main character, Niko Bellic, regularly behaves in a manner consistent with Robert Connell's (1995) definition of "hegemonic masculinity": he resorts to violence, he resists conversation, he reduces women to objects, he relies on Machiavellian logic (p. 131). Rather than offering a linear narrative which becomes a celebration of the hypermasculine, *GTA 4* regularly exposes the contradictions and the ambivalence of hegemonic masculinities and even of its own audience and genre. Although the game's kernel story remains true to the formula of following a thug's progression from bit player to master criminal, in this iteration Niko's success depends upon regularly socializing with the other male characters in the game. These outnumber the women Niko must date by a wide margin. Dating was a feature added to the previous game, *San Andreas*, and not only was it required in order to complete the central plot, successful dates bestowed the avatar (and by implication, the player) with bonuses, required items and gifts which made finishing the game easier and/or possible.

The most recent games work on a similar pattern and so build on player familiarity with the system. However, most of the dating involves Niko courting other men through dinner, darts, pool, bowling and trips to clubs. Moreover, Niko unabashedly defends his friend, Florian Cravic, a.k.a. Bernie, from gay bashers in a series of missions leading to a key episode, "Hating the Haters," in which the infamous and predictable *GTA* drive-by takes out homophobic blackmailers. In *The Ballad of Gay Tony* expansion pack, the protagonist, Luis Fernando Lopez, is the chief henchman and confidant of Gay Tony, a crime and nightclub boss. Luis frequently defends his boss from any number of threats. Depending on one's perspective, *GTA 4* not only confronts players with a surprising perspective on masculine relations but also provides a place for exploring and for negotiating—i.e., for playing—the homosocial. Indeed, the play of the game and of the homosocial cannot be easily separated into the purely ludic or the purely narratological realms that seem to demarcate the critical imperatives incumbent in game studies.

Therefore, the game demands an approach which integrates rather than delineates the available readings to show how the game's ergodic, or "work path," dimension occasions and even encourages the homosocial (Aarseth, 1997, pp. 1–2). That *GTA 4* belongs to a game franchise assailed for its overall content makes Niko, Luis and the player's negotiations of masculine behaviours more extraordinary since this genre traditionally relies on hypermasculine modes, often to the exclusion and even detriment of women and minorities. Paradoxically, though, it is the fidelity to what Steve Neale (1981) would call its "generic verisimilitude," or its relationships and resemblances to others in its class, that the game can make such a striking intervention (p. 25). As Neale explains, attention to generic fidelity allows for considerable manipulation of fantasy within the bounds of generic credibility. Social transgressions, then, can be more easily accommodated than might be managed within more realist texts. As much as *GTA 4* was lauded (and lambasted) for its enhanced realism, the generic verisimilitude situates the game as a location for playing with possibilities that realism alone might render untenable.

The action within Liberty City could be described as primarily being homosocial—that is to say, dominated by same-sex relations (like male bonding) that have no explicitly sexual component. Eve Sedgwick (1985) observes that it is precisely on the register of the homosocial that the boundaries between the heterosexual and the homosexual are contested (p. 2). The homosocial can thus be understood as the liminal range of alternatives between heterosexual and homosexual oppositions. Yet, as Sedgwick argues, the homosocial may be constituted by that which is not sexual and is distinguished from the homosexual. It does not exist independently of the erotic and is deeply infused with desire. To describe the workings of *GTA 4* as homosocial is not to deny its desire or its sexuality. Undeniably, the game is riddled with a surfeit of sophomoric humour, including the in-game television show featuring mixed martial arts legend, Bas Rutten and its frequent jokes with sexual and/or generally homophobic content in the variety of radio commercials. These include the game's drink, Sprunk, the omnipresent "Rusty Brown's ring donuts," whose radio ads promise plenty of "creamy white" discharge, and of course the roadside hot dog and hamburger stands whose umbrellas proclaim "You can't beat our meat." The game also relies on a seemingly limitless string of feminizing insults, allusions to penetration, and myriad conquests to remind any observer that boys can be boys. The humour alternates among parodic, satiric, juvenile and banal, which makes locating the game's appropriative or critical force incredibly imprecise, if not impossible. That said, the laddish humour represents a key component of the generic verisimilitude that forms the safety net that facilitates the progressive transgressions of the games' queer friendly stance.

However, if we subscribe to the notion that pop cultural productions fall into three broad categories—who we are, what we hope for and what we fear—then the *GTA 4* games offer an intriguing example of texts that incorporate all of these facets into a diegetic world, but does so via the metonymic sign vehicle of Luis and Niko's male friends. Niko's cousin Roman is an eternal optimist who boasts and overstates the wealth of his taxi company. He represents the naive hopes and dreams upon which the American dream is built. Roman is all about a fantasy world. He regularly exaggerates in emails and in conversations about his life in the big time and his conquests of women. Stolen car dealer Brucie Kibbutz and club owner Gay Tony stand for who we are, especially given the likely intertext of the latter with the former owner of New York's infamous Studio 54. They are narcissistic and contradictory. Brucie appears homophobic either because he will not admit he is gay or because he does not yet know that he is gay. Regardless, these two are all for show. They are fake and superficial, as is drug dealer Playboy X, whose sexuality may also be indeterminate. Little Jacob, a Jamaican gun runner, worries about respect and loyalty. Niko tells Florian quite simply, you should be free to be yourself—the ultimate expression and contradiction of life, liberty and the pursuit of happiness. Not everyone is free to be who they are. Packie Mcreary, a street thug whose family includes both a gang leader and a police captain, clearly represents and reminds Niko of the disintegration of the family. Niko does not speak about his brother. In contrast, Dwayne obsesses about the past, the drug dealing, the betrayals, and fear not mattering and regrets making terrible decisions. Similarly, Luis' childhood friends Enrique and Armando offer a series of reminiscences about their past and moments in which they express how much they miss each other. Importantly, the variety of character types in the games provides multiple entry points for bonding to occur. Each links to a different facet of the protagonist which means expanded opportunities for the exploration of the homosocial.

"I suck at life, but I bowl like an angel": The Gameplay Function and the Homosocial[1]

As mentioned earlier, considering the combination of homosocial interaction and video games, this chapter takes two theoretical cues. The first of these lies quite obviously within game studies, but the second draws from the only roughly analogous location which offers a similar engagement with play and the homosocial within an otherwise purely hypermasculine context of violence, sexism, homophobia and sophomoric humour: sports talk radio. Like the dating routines in the *GTA 4* games, sports talk radio provides a safe platform for explorations of the homosocial. Michael Messner adopts the term "covert intimacy" to describe men's tendency to hide intimacy within superficially hypermasculine endeavours to avoid the discomforts and suspicion that obvious bonding efforts might entail (1992a, pp. 92–93). Time and space do not currently allow for a third, based on the work Christine Gledhill, Janice Radway and Elaine Rapping (among others) have done to analyze the contradictions and even complicity of the three levels of community which galvanize around soap operas, weepies and romance fiction. In the first regard, Gonzalo Frasca explains that the "potential of games is not to tell a story but to simulate: to create an environment for experimentation" (2003, p. 225). In a later article, Frasca expands upon this notion when he writes, "In temporal terms, narrative is about what already happened while simulation is about what could happen. [...] The potential of simulation is not as a conveyor of values, but as a way to explore the mechanics of dynamic systems" (2004, p. 86). This is more of a defense of games against the critical commonplace of "media effects" complaints than it is a statement against values being present in games. It must be established, then, which dynamic system is being explored in a given simulation and how this occurs. Here, the homosocial networks and the alliance with openly gay characters and causes provide the material for the experimentation within the (relatively) safe and familiar environment of an established video game series in an established video game genre.

However, Frasca's original position has much in common with a branch of Game Studies that seems to have almost New Critical bent. For example, Espen Aarseth has famously and categorically proclaimed that "games are not intertextual [...] games are self-contained" (1997, p. 48). As many games add a tactile or kinesthetic element (at the very least via dual shock controllers) not present in other fictive modes, Aarseth's statement should be taken as more of a call to arms for scholars intent on establishing Game Studies as a discipline before it is subsumed by the kinds of opportunism and empire building that beset other emerging disciplines and co-opted them into institutional agendas. That said, Aarseth's otherwise admirable statement still somewhat underestimates the work and/or the capacity of the imagination. At its extreme, it could be taken to overlook relationships among games in series, among games using the same engine and among games repurposing elements of other games. In this regard, it is important to acknowledge the debts *GTA 4* owes to its RockStar sibling, *Bully* both in terms of its mechanisms, physics but also in terms of its occasional surprise social networks and allegiances. For example, the onscreen map, the save routine and the AI routine used to mimic police pursuits are nearly identical in both games. The much-maligned *Bully* actually spends most of its time evading or redressing the actions of bullies, including gay bashing. It almost seems as if *Bully* serves as a sacrificial lamb or a test case given its relatively poor sales. These were due in part to its intense demonization by parents groups and mainstream media and the resultant knee-jerk reactions from fearful vendors. The very same vendors likely did well with *GTA 4*, which was among the top selling games of 2008. Although *Bully* really broke the ground in terms of its storyline and execution requiring the player to side (at least long enough to complete the game), it is *GTA 4*'s widespread popularity and contingent demographic coverage which makes its repurposing of the basic elements more significant than the original.

In anticipation of the progression of video games to include more complicated situations, Frasca hypothesizes what he calls "videogames (sic) of the oppressed" and posits that "videogames (sic) could indeed deal with human relationships and social issues, while encouraging critical thinking" (2004, p. 85). Even so, Frasca was not particularly optimistic about the potential for video games to explore "sacred moral codes [...] or for making moral statements" (p. 86). Simply put, the current figuration and location of video games and their players places them in an always already position of marginalization, infantilization, or both. In this regard, game makers are implicated as much as mainstream critics. However, even before Huizinga's (too) often cited *Homo Ludens* considered the value of play, Piaget recorded as play as essentially being "children's work" (Woolfolk et al., 2009, p. 47). Understood this way, play provides rehearsal, preparation, practice and possible scenarios. Here lies the importance of Neale's earlier cited observation regarding the transgressive potential to be found in generic verisimilitude. The combination of familiar features and similar structures which map onto the game genre makes the insertion of potentially problematic subjects something entirely within the realm of expectations. This is significant because it is hardly original or insightful to note that in any version of the *GTA* world, nothing is sacred. This makes it a terrific place to consider weighty issues.

Indeed, criminality is the order of business. Criminality is, in fact, the way to go in all versions of *GTA*. Ian Bogost writes of *GTA 3* that "those who argue that one can 'do anything' in Liberty City are mistaken; the game constantly structures freeform experience in relation to criminality" (2006, p. 157). Nobody is immune. The politicians are figured as corrupt, the police are corrupt and even America's favourite action hero, Jack Howitzer, is figured as a pervert. The in-game Internet includes a reference to "Little Lacy Surprise," Howitzer's early advertisement extolling his love for little girls' panties. Everyone is on the graft. Therefore, the fact that the Bernie missions leading to "Hating the haters" places a defense of GTA's first truly "out" character, Florian, within the context of a beating and a drive-by effectively situates the GLBTQ friendly satellite story within the normative diegetic and play structures. *The Ballad of Gay Tony* expansion pack offers a similar structure in the kernel of the erstwhile satellite story. For example, Luis regularly warns Evan, Tony's spendthrift philandering boyfriend, that Tony deserves better treatment. Luis also turns down opportunities to hang out—i.e., to date—his friends so that he can spend time with Tony. Unlike Niko, Luis eschews long term relationships with women, again because they take away from his time with Tony and their business together. In other words, defending the gay man, especially through the usual (violent) means by which the player (and avatar) metes out justice and righteousness, becomes a good thing within this diegetic world. The cut scene at the end of the last mission in the sequence, in which Nico tells Florian that he should be free to live as he chooses, reinforces the choice. As well, *GTA 4* introduces a feature which alters the storyline based on the player's decisions in a string of "who live and who dies" moments. These shape not only the story but also the ways the player can operate within the game because they affect Niko's subsequent interactions with his circle of friends and associates. Some of these are strengthened by the choice between friends, while some friendships are strained by the survivor's seeming realization that he was a hair's breadth from the same fate.

Thus, *GTA 4* does include what Frasca calls "manipulation rules," which allow the player to have the ultimate say, but within certain confines (2003, p. 231). One of the most important such decisions occurs when the player chooses between childhood friends turned rival drug dealers, Playboy X and Dwayne Forge, and again between feuding brothers, Francis and Gerry Mcreary. The latter choice is complicated by the fact that Francis is a crooked police captain and Gerry is an IRA supporting gang leader. However, in its reward structure— what Frasca calls its "goal rules"—however, the game's moral choices do have significant impacts on the game's outcomes, including the results of its homosocial play (2003, p. 231). If, for example, the player chooses to kill Playboy X, the result is an opportunity for friendship with Dwayne.[2] Regardless of one's moral basis for the choice to keep Dwayne, the reward is clear and also exists entirely within the rubric of criminality. If the player pushes Niko to a 79% "like" rating with Dwayne, the latter suddenly calls the cell phone and offers his eternal support. From that moment, backup, in the form of two of Dwayne's thugs, will be available with one simple phone call. In GTA there are few greater forms of love than sending one's "homies" to help a friend commit a felony. This is a tremendous reward and reveals a tremendous amount of loyalty. Although Dwayne rewards Niko, the ruthlessness with which he acts is recognized at the completion of the set of missions. Dwayne gives Niko an apartment and the use of thugs but he fades away as the plot progresses. In contrast, Niko's negotiation of the Mcreary family's squabbles brings him into increased contact with the youngest brother, Packie, and the boys' sister, Katie. The latter is significant not only because Niko dates Katie, but also because their relationship remains tentative largely due to an aloofness in Katie which stems from her experiences with her brothers. Conversely, Packie not only calls Niko regularly for "dates," he is quite revealing in his chatter during (stolen) car rides to hang out spots. He tells Niko the family history in detail, discusses his feelings on a variety of subjects and solicits Niko's opinion. More than once Packie comments that theirs is a relationship analogous to dating. In a more traditional narrative, one might argue that Packie encourages Niko's romance with Katie as a substitute or surrogate for his own affections. Certainly, that is the effect.

As the moral choice feature plays out in *GTA 4*, it seems to agree by disagreeing with Espen Aarseth's position that video games are "constrained by the story in unrealistic ways. What makes such games playable at all, and indeed attractive, is the sequence of shifting, exotic, often fascinating settings (levels), where you explore the topography and master the virtual environment. The gameworld is its own reward" (Aarseth, 1997, p. 51). As I have argued elsewhere, I see Aarseth's dilemma as mapping onto the Saussurean dialetic of *langue* and *parole*: "Saussure focused on *langue*; one could argue that ludologists concentrate on *parole*. The latter is the language of the individual text and—as Aarseth would have it—is imminent and particular. The former is the more conventionalized, codified system which is prior to the subject" (Ouellette, 2008). In *GTA 4*, as in the previous games in the series, the gameworld as (a) reward and as its own reward does play out to a great extent. Even the expansion pack takes time to ensure that the avatar and the player receive a tour of the city. However, the game also inheres because of its predecessor texts. Just as novels are understood by analogy to other novels, *GTA 4* is understood by analogy to other games. For example, a key *GTA* in game reward is increased access to all three dimensions of the game map through particular achievements. Every game map is made up of a series of islands and access to them serves as a reward for completing a specified number of missions. In the expansion packs, the islands are all accessible, but missions include races, chases and helicopter escapes to offer views of the city. More importantly, dating emerged in *San Andreas* as a key means of acquiring guns, cars and entry to certain locations. *GTA 4* and *The Ballad of Gay Tony* expand on these with the caveat that the routines of nights on the town occur primarily with other male characters. In fact, the dating mechanism replaces many of the more tedious skill building routines in *San Andreas*. In the previous game, there were several "schools"— for driving, for flying, for motorcycles, for boats—for training the player and to "power up" or "level up" the avatar's abilities. In contrast, the *GTA 4* games use the dating or the relationship building missions to accomplish the same thing. As mentioned earlier, the game borrows not just from earlier *GTA* entries, but also from its RockStar sibling, *Bully*. It is not a stretch to argue that the Marnie missions, in which Niko befriends a runaway and helps her to return home, and "Hating the Haters" could easily be dropped into *Bully* without any break in the generic verisimilitude.

Similarly, there are rewards for good healthy relationships with other characters. Little Jacob, for example, provides his own rolling "Ammunation" store with the full complement of weaponry not only appearing on-demand but also at a discounted price. Even Roman, at least initially, can send a taxi to pick up Niko and drive him anywhere. In this regard, the relationship's rewards are multiple and simultaneous: Niko has few friends at the beginning of the game, he has little money, and like the player has little knowledge of the city. Said another way, the early encounters with Roman–via bowling, darts, drinking and eating–comprise Nico's training as well as the player's training. Brucie, the most obviously ambiguously gendered character, eventually offers Niko helicopters, boats and cars at any time. These offer crucial means of escaping the police and help the player reach the all-important 100% completion in a number of ways. This includes providing access to the pigeons and sea gulls the player must exterminate in Liberty City, practice with vehicles, places to hide, places to look and general sightseeing. Brucie also provides Niko with access to a virtually limitless supply of money through performing the game's eponymous task. First, Niko steals cars for Brucie, who then recommends Niko to Stevie, a (stolen) auto exporter. After completing Stevie's list of cars, Niko can bring any car to the chop shop at any time. In *The Ballad of Gay Tony*, Brucie's older brother, Mori, reminds players of Brucie's ambiguous gender through taunts aimed at the younger sibling. Mori also has a more pronounced version of every one of Brucie's compensatory masculine behaviours. These are compounded by Mori's smaller stature and bigger boasts. Nevertheless, befriending Mori, listening to his problems and responding to his needs, results in rewards for the avatar and in turn for the player.

"Finally, someone wants to play!": Homosocial Experimentation[3]

Although the game and its expansion pack occasion and, more importantly, reward the player/avatar for the homosocial bonding and for siding with openly gay characters, it is the nature and the substance of these moves which make the *GTA 4* series more remarkable. The story arcs and game structures adopt and employ discourses of masculinity in ways that reveal the contradictions upon which the gender formation rests. Chief among these is a particular kind of masculine humour. Poking fun at masculinity has always been a *GTA* staple. David Nylund argues that sports talk radio, the second strand entry point for analysis of the homosocial experimentation in *GTA 4*, reflects a common social practice for many men–the desire to earn the homosocial approval of other, more powerful men, especially through proficiency in particular forms of banter and humour (2004, p. 147). Like Nylund, I would argue that humour also functions as one of the rules of the game. Certainly, in its various guises humour is omnipresent in Liberty City, from the names of streets to the various radio rants. In more specific terms, there are several purely masculine variations, as well, most notably, the trips to the strippers and the comments made in the strip club. Brucie is a frequent source and target of the humour, in large part because of his obsession with his own masculinity. In one emblematic exchange, Brucie tells Niko that they have to get serious. Niko responds, "If you want my advice, the only way you're going to get your balls back to normal is if you stop juicing [taking steroids] or get implants." The exchanges between Niko and Brucie, as well as those between Brucie and Mori, are loaded with barbs and taunts, coaxing and cajoling about the signs of masculinity the brothers project. The locations in which the discourse occurs all provide familiar outlets for male bonding within dominant hegemonic masculine paradigms. Sport sociologist Mike Messner explains that such fora allow men to share and to express what he calls a "covert intimacy [...] an intimacy that is characterized by doing together, rather than by mutual talk about their inner lives" (1992b, p. 232). This type of indirect bonding fosters a further bonding through shared understanding of a topic or experience of mutual interest. Messner differs from (most) previous and (some) subsequent scholars in recognizing the beneficial and even transformative potential of such discourse. On the surface the barbs, boasts and banter seem irrelevant at best and homophobic, violent and sexist at their worst. In delving deeper, Messner finds that men use this mode of discourse not only to establish a hierarchy but also as a prelude to more substantive, revealing discourse. It also becomes a cover for that discourse should the masculinity be questioned. As Nylund puts it, this bonding "can bring for genuine moments of closeness and should not necessarily be pathologized or seen as completely negative" (2004, p. 149). Taken this way, Packie's history of the Mccary family, including the fact that his sister witnessed several traumatic events, functions as this type of intimacy. It is kept covert by Packie's familiar ending to the story, which is his admission that he stays drunk and stoned to avoid thinking about any of it.

Thus, it is no surprise when Packie delivers the admission of his perpetual drunkenness in the form of a joke, as he and Niko are returning from a night of crime and of bowling (or darts or pool). In fact, Packie ends most of his confessions with a witty, self-deprecating comment. While the avatar laughs when Packie or others make these kinds of statements, some of them seem reserved for the player. For instance, Niko teases Roman almost every time they are together, but with no discernible effect. Niko occasionally chuckles at his comments and at his cousin. In short, the laughs are left to the player (as audience). More to the point are many of Gay Tony's comments about his network of gangster associates, especially Rocco. Very early in the game, Tony expresses confusion regarding Rocco's sexuality. The confusion stems from the "pent up suburban he-man angst [and] the fake tan and muscles." Nobody in the game world laughs, and so the humour is ironic both in the sense of the ambiguities of compensatory hypermasculinity and in the sense of the audience rather than the other characters being aware of the situation. In both cases, these asides recur throughout the game. Not only do Niko and Tony share "intimate" moments with the other characters, the intimacy is extended to the player. The player participates in, witnesses and also receives the intimacy.

Further covert intimacy comes from Dwayne Forge, who talks about the poverty he knew while growing up and which led him to crime. Niko always has a worse tale, including "After you walk into a village and you see fifty children, all sitting neatly in a row, against a church wall, each with their throats cut and their hands chopped off, you realize that the creature that could do this doesn't have a soul." Niko does not share this level of detail with everyone. In fact, he reveals different portions of himself to each person he dates in the game. Intriguingly, he talks about Roman to Little Jacob but not to the others. This may be because Jacob has a similar partnership with the aptly named Bad Man. Although they argue frequently, Niko and Roman eventually reveal that each admires the other. Niko admires Roman's gentleness and optimism; Roman admires Niko's strength and loyalty. As much as Niko appears to be an extraordinarily hardened hypermasculine figure, his frequent car rides and nights out provide a wide range of intimate glimpses into his past. To be sure, these must be gleaned from the taunts and barbs. The latter are a necessary part of the process and their presence can be a clue or a confirmation of the process that is taking place in the game. As Nylund further explains, men in groups tend to "define and solidify their boundaries through aggressive misogynistic and homophobic speech and actions. Underneath this bonding experience are homoerotic feelings that must be warded off and neutralized through joking, yelling, cursing, and demonizing anybody who does not conform to normative masculinity" (pp. 149–50). In *GTA 4*, the masculine behaviours take place in defense of and alongside Florian—who is out, and changes his name to Bernie after coming out—and Brucie—who is clearly in denial. Moreover, Florian/Bernie is the first person Niko calls after the Darko incident in which Bernie's relationship with a political candidate offers a target for blackmail.[4] Florian echoes Roman's sentiments that Niko should be proud, he did a good thing and offers to celebrate: "I say spa day!"

Since it follows the expansion pack format, with fewer scenes operating as satellites or hubs around the main story arc, *The Ballad of Gay Tony* begins with the game world already fully unlocked for the player and for the avatar. There are still a few missions to remind of and to reward with the sights and sites of Liberty City. Even so, the format has two key effects. First, the preliminary bits have been eliminated so that most of the relationships are long-standing and prior to the story. Second, the shorter story arc results in more compressed intimacy since the relationships are established ones. "Corner Kids" is a mission that illustrates these structures. Its completion has key rewards, in the form of twenty-five added side missions whose completion brings money, weapons and more contact with friends. When the mission begins Armando and Enrique harangue Luis, their friend since childhood, for moving uptown to work with Tony. The exchange is punctuated with two homophobic taunts and some predictably emasculating postures. Yet, once the crew moves from the street corner and its visibility to a car and its confined space, Armando admits, "Hey, I miss you, man." Later in the ride, Luis tells his co-conspirators that he will help them move up the ladder as he has. After explaining his plan for the eventual series of drug wars, Luis adds, "I love you guys." Not surprisingly, there are jokes about the confession; surprisingly, the focus turns to Armando and his relationships in prison. In this way, not only are the homoerotic feelings of the characters warded off, they are also warded off for the player. It is, however, the fact that the issue "needs" to be displaced at all that makes the incident significant. Displacement could not occur if homosocial experimentation were not instantiated as a possibility with palpable cognitive and affective responses of the sort that occasion such a vehement response.

One of the biggest areas of commonality between sports talk radio and a game like *GTA 4* is in the kinds of moral commentaries and/or criticism they receive. A critical commonplace suggests that the "media industry, therefore, often mobilizes pleasure around conservative ideologies that have oppressive effects on women, homosexuals, and people of color. The ideologies of hegemonic masculinity, assembled in the form of pleasure and humor" (Nylund, 2004, p. 148). In contrast, Nylund suggests that some sports talk radio programs which offer participation in the form of fax, email, text messages and phone calls provide a space where men can "play" in a homosocial world, engage the contradictions of masculinity and experiment with homosocial play. The best example Nylund analyzes is the *Jim Rome Show*, which superficially replicates the humour, sexism and hypermasculinity one also finds in *GTA 4*. The show is unique in that the host has a very well articulated and often repeated GLBTQ friendly stance. As the host, Jim Rome gives his listeners an ultimatum. They can listen or turn off his show if they do not like his positions. The video game only offers a modicum of that effect. Certainly, the much sought after 100% completion is impossible without going through the missions discussed. Nylund also highlights the role of talk radio, sports and sports talk radio in the process of creating "a homosocial institution that functions to assuage men's fear of feminization in current postmodern culture" (p. 149). These are all facets, including play and interactivity, involved, remediated or repurposed in *GTA 4*. The analogy hold because of the centrality of play—either in sport or in video game—in the process. Play is not only the antithesis of work. As mentioned earlier, it is a forum for experimentation. This is the stock and trade of Rome and of *GTA* games. However, what makes these productions more notable is the way in which masculinity functions as the justification for participation. Rome challenges his listeners to "man up" and to "have a take and don't suck" several times each day. For *GTA*, the challenges are issued by the games but also by their overwhelming popularity. Hence, a nearly one-third of the responses to the YouTube videos of the missions is "who cares if Bernie is gay, he gives you the Infernus." Admittedly, preferring ends over means is a hallmark of hegemonic masculinity in many of its forms. However, this only cements the relationship by making hegemonic masculinity complicit in the process of homosocial experimentation that is so central to the game.

Conclusions

Even if all of the analysis and considerations of homosocial play and the support of gay characters were stripped away and the game only means what it means, one irreducible fact remains. The games' kernel stories cannot be accomplished without assisting Bernie, supporting Tony and hanging out with innumerable male friends. Next, if only Aarseth's logic applies so that the game is its own reward, then Bernie's gift of an Infernus is still a key one: it can win races, it can outrun the police, it can be sold and it is fun to drive. More important, *GTA 4* relentlessly and thoroughly mocks and critiques the insatiable bloodlust, greed and intolerance of "post-9/11" America. Nowhere is this more pronounced than in the preferred masculine mode of the era. As well, American parents, especially overbearing, neurotic and narcissistic parents eager to offer their kids as status symbols while blaming others for the effects of the resultant neglect, bear a large part of the force of the satire and criticism in every installment since *GTA 3*. In short, *GTA 4* more than any other iteration of the franchise stands against the kind of reactionaries who protest the violence in video games but support the "war on terror," who fear their kids seeing gay men holding hands but voted twice for a regime that employed homophobic torture. A radio ad in *The Ballad Gay Tony* raises this very point. In any *GTA* world, parents are not just metonymic for a kind a parent. One could extend the metaphor so that parents are metonymic for America. If Baudrillard (1994) was correct in concluding that Disney World is America, then it may be the case that Liberty City is Disney World.

In the introduction to the premier issue of *Games and Culture*, Toby Miller (1981) offers some still poignant provisos for the future of game studies: "Social concerns about new technologies have led to a primary emphasis on the number and conduct of audiences to audio-visual entertainment: where they came from, how many there were, and what they did as a consequence of being present [...] new communication and cultural technologies and genres offer forms of mastery that threaten [...] the established order" (pp. 6–7). As has been noted with regard to other media which have received negative, sensational and often reductive attention from non-participants and those who watch only highlights, if at all, including rap music and professional wrestling, some video games include nods, responses and anticipations of their critics.[5] Every *GTA* game include in-built satiric responses to its (anticipated) critics. In this regard, it is well worth pointing out that *GTA*'s self-aware humour runs the risk of reinscription.[6] There is likely no better example than the series of negative gubernatorial campaign ads in *GTA 4* which proclaim a rival candidate's predilection for teenage boys in the country whose war he managed to avoid. These purportedly parodic elements fall into the rubric of the "ironic" humour found in what have become known as "lads' magazines" such as *Maxim*, *Details*, *FHM*, and others. The dominant strain of humour in these magazines seem to believe that saying the most offensive thing imaginably can be excused quickly and easily by saying, "Well, that's not how I meant it. I was being that offensive to show how absurd such offensive material really is." Of course, this relies on forgiveness being easier to obtain than permission as well as readers who are not predisposed to assume and to conclude the straight, as it were, reading of the text.

Any sense of a predisposition, then, depends entirely on the composition of the producers and to a much greater extent on the consumers. Nina Huntemann puts a very masculine face on video games, video game players and video game designers. Her data indicate that the top magazines have upwards of 90% male readership (2004, p. 4). Similarly, she cites data from *Interplay*, a leading trade publication, which show 95% of game designers as male (p. 5).[7] Huntemann then goes on to cite violent male relationships, games with violence and, based on Children Now's tautology regarding video games and violence, draws her own tautology that games with male characters reproduce a phallic economy based on hypermasculine performance, violence and the phallic order. Without masculine violence, *Grand Theft Auto* does not exist. However, every one of the games includes paramedic missions, firefighter missions and a host of other benevolent tasks. Since *San Andreas*, the requirement to forge relationships has been part of this list, too. Yet the basis of Huntemann's view still predominates in the popular and in the mainstream academic literature. At the same time, can *GTA* be read as consistently being on point or does it vary and contradict itself both intentionally and otherwise?

However, *Grand Theft Auto 4* is incredibly—perhaps, too much so—aware of itself as a text, as a member of a franchise, and as an intertext. In fact, this process began much earlier in the *GTA* series with the introduction of radio advertisements for the Degenatron in *Vice City* and the variety of games included within *San Andreas*. The responses themselves condition and produce the text. This is a poignant reminder of work that has been done elsewhere, especially by Christine Gledhill, Janice Radway and Elaine Rapping, on soap operas, the weepie, the romance and other so-called women's genres. These involve three levels of community: the one on-screen involving those acting out the fantasies and other situations; the one between the screen and the community which allows viewers to place themselves; finally, the community off-screen involving the viewers sharing their experiences with and because of the show. Despite the sexism, violence and hypermasculinity, this obviously applies to the sports-talk genre. Indeed, Nylund relies on its presence even as it remains unexamined in his study. Gamers clearly participate in such communities and have been doing so for some time. YouTube, XBox Live, fanzines, etc. formalize the layering rather than produce it. As mentioned earlier, the comments on YouTube confirm this progression.

In his own quest for an entry point for analysis, Nylund follows the premise that interactive and/or participatory media tend to personalize and particularize instances of intolerance. Thus, the discourse not only remains in line with neo-liberal discourse, the tendency also serves to foreclose the discussion, let alone analysis, of systemic and institutionalized aspects of homophobia (2004, 152). In other words, the assumption is that bigots are treated as isolated cases rather as reflections of societal structures. On the surface, the conversations between Niko and Bernie/Florian seem to support the conclusion that a neo-liberal, if not libertarian ethos applies. Niko repeats the familiar phrase that it should be "nobody's business" who is dating whom and the "not that there's anything wrong with dating you." These imply a semi-tolerant worldview that still clings to a homophobic system. The observant and the glass half-empty crowd will recognize the unspoken portion of the homophobia which completes the sentence, "You can date whomever you want, but I don't want to know about any of it." As many scholars observe, the determinism of the now-familiar, even trite, coming out narrative unproblematically presupposes that people who have same-sex desire need to reveal their sexuality—both from the pro and the con side of the issue and from the intelligent and from the bigoted—and become visible, while simultaneously and contradictorily reinscribing the myth of a universal gay subject. In this context, coming out, as Nylund suggests, becomes "a contested privilege, a 'right,' and the natural logical next step in achieving 'health' and an 'authentic life.' This identitarian narrative is supported by many people and institutions, including the mental health industry, straight allies, and in particular, by the dominant discourses of the urban gay community" (p. 156). Here I would argue that *GTA 4* differs significantly if only because of the "turn it off" factor having a diminished capacity as a response, effective or otherwise, within the gaming world. Completing the game cannot be accomplished without a relatively thorough involvement both in the dating routines and in the support of Bernie. Furthermore, the entirety of *The Ballad of Gay Tony* puts these issues front and centre. Sales charts from any of the established magazines show that it is one of the top selling expansion packs in history. If there is a "turn it off" factor, it rests among those who see games as another mindless medium.

At the time of writing, hegemonic masculinity seems under threat. Indeed, this provides the cover story of *Newsweek* for the week of 27 September 2010. Changes in global capital and in technology have brought changes in the work force and in the modes of its labour. It is arguable that an effect of these disruptions has been a backlash against the advances of GLBTQ liberation. For example, the Assistant Attorney General of Michigan was removed from office in the fall of 2010 after it was revealed he was stalking and harassing the openly gay President of the University of Michigan Student Union. The 2010 campaign of New York gubernatorial candidate Carl Paladino was dogged by his seemingly limitless stream of offensive remarks about gays. While the Obama administration has ended the "don't ask, don't tell" policy of the U.S. military, the Republican "Tea Party" members of Congress opposed the move with a retrograde discourse laden with long ago debunked myths. Clearly, a tremendous amount of work remains to be done either to destabilize hegemonic masculinity or to achieve equity for GLBTQ groups. On its own GTA 4 was by every measure the biggest selling game in history as of the end of 2009. In this iteration, Rockstar Games turn their longstanding confrontational and sensational approach to an ongoing engagement with hegemonic masculinity, homosocial bonding and alliances with GLBTQ characters. The timing, the content, but especially the medium make the games significant cultural objects and objects of study. While contemporary television shows such as Glee are applauded for their allegedly groundbreaking content, video games bring the added element of play. This adds participatory and experimental dimensions to the fold. Moreover, the context means that the structures of hegemonic masculinity are being deployed in their own reformation. Thus, there are significant impacts not only on gender but also on the study of video games, in general.

In a much discussed article entitled "Bowling Alone: America's Declining Social Capital," the political scientist Robert Putnam observes that "more Americans are bowling today than ever before, but bowling in organized leagues has plummeted" (1995, p. 70). He takes this to be illustrative of a widespread trend toward increasing social disengagement in many areas of contemporary American life. Video games and Grand Theft Auto, in particular, have been seen as contributors to this trend. Indeed, Miller's earlier cited article contains a response to Putnam, and the title of this chapter owes as much to that position as it does to Niko's nights of bowling. Strangely, the industry and some scholars almost seem to foster or to enjoy this view because it ensures that games remain outside institutional discourses. For example, Hilary Goldstein's (2008) review of GTA 4 for the important online journal, IGN, praises the centrality of the relationships but ignores their substance entirely. She delights in "cringe-worthy conversations, where you see Niko being sucked into the depravity of these peoples' lives to earn a few bucks or gain a long-sought revenge. That's a credit to the writing, to make what would normally just be some thug you're doing missions for earn your contempt. That's a mark that you care for Niko; that the story has gotten to you. There aren't many games that can pull that off" (p. 3). She writes of the relationships in terms of their benefits and nothing else. Even so, Goldstein never mentions Bernie or even Brucie. Somehow, Gay Tony is only a club owner on Grand Theft Wiki. Similarly, GameSpy's satellite site, Planet GTA, excludes Bernie on the page devoted to "The Characters of Grand Theft Auto IV." Perhaps it is the fear of alienating the core constituency with the proverbial elephant in the room that prevents even those in the game industry from considering the potential of the content in these games. Quite simply, *GTA 4* and *The Ballad of Gay Tony* really offer a corrective to the oft-repeated suggestion that video games and their component parts—i.e., solitary play, especially of debased digital games—increase cultural alienation. These games demand the recognition of the broader contexts of even traditional solo games and the expanding opportunities these entail for multi-player encounters. Presumably, this includes stealing a car to go bowling with your cousin.

Notes

1 This is one of the comments Niko makes if he wins a game of bowling.
2 In what came down to a moral choice for me, Playboy X had to go because he was the one pushing for the choice. He was a little too hungry. While there is no "correct" choice, there are advantages to this one.
3 If anyone in the *GTA* world commits an offence in view of a police officer, this is one of the automated responses that accompanies the resultant police brutality.
4 I chose to let Darko live the first time I played through the game.
5 Perhaps the best examples of this practice come from World Wrestling Entertainment, formerly the World Wrestling Federation. In one case, radical feminist groups joined a protest against the company's depictions of women only to discover not only that the protest was a hoax, it was led by the boss's daughter as part of the storyline for her takeover of the business.
6 For all of its potential, *GTA 4* contains so many contradictory elements that it is difficult to ascertain whether it is satiric or parodic at all. Although I have attempted elsewhere to consider this in detail, the results are still unsatisfactory (Ouellette, 2010).
7 Huntemann lists *Computer Gaming* at 95% and *Electronic Gaming* at 96% as two of the larger culprits.

Works Cited

Aarseth, Espen. *Cybertext: Perspectives on Ergodic Literature*. Baltimore, MD: Johns Hopkins University Press, 1997.

Baudrillard, Jean. *Simulacra and Simulation*. Trans. Sheila Faria Glaser. Ann Arbor: University of Michigan Press, 1994.

Bogost, Ian. *Unit Operations: An Approach to Video Game Criticism*. Cambridge, MA: MIT Press, 2006.

Connell, Raewyn W. *Masculinities: Knowledge, Power and Social Change*. Berkeley: California University Press, 1995.

Frasca, Gonzalo. "Simulation vs. Narrative: Introduction to Ludology." *The Video Game Theory Reader*. Eds. Mark Wolf and Bernard Perron. New York: Routledge, 2003. 221–44.

———. "Videogames of the Oppressed: Critical Thinking, Education, Tolerance and Other Trivial Issues." *First Person: New Media as Story, Performance, and Game*. Cambridge, MA: MIT Press, 2004. 85–94.

GameSpy. *Planet GTA*. Available at http://planetgrandtheftauto.gamespy.com/

Goldstein, Hilary. Rev. of *Grand Theft Auto 4*. IGN.com. 25 April 2008. Availabel at http://xbox360.ign.com/articles/869/869381p1.html.

Grand Theft Wiki (2006). Available at http://www.gtawikia.com (accessed Jan. 2010).

GTASeriesVideos (2009). GTA IV Mission #66—Hating the Haters. YouTube. Available at http://www.youtube.com/watch?v=Zi6FF-TQFKg (accessed 23 May 2010).

Huntemann, Nina B. "'Play Like a Man': Masculinity in Video Games." Mediacritica.net. 2004. Availabel at http://www.mediacritica.net/lectures/lectures.html.

Messner, Michael. *Power at Play: Sports and the Problem of Masculinity*. Boston: Beacon, 1992a.

————. "Like Family: Power, Intimacy, and Sexuality in Male Athletes' Friendships." In *Men's Friendships*. Ed. Peter M. Nardi. Newbury Park, CA: Sage, 1992b. 215–38.

Miller, Toby. "Gaming for Beginners." *Games and Culture*, 1:1 (2006): 5–12.

Neale, Steve. *Genre*. London: BFI, 1981.

Nylund, David. "When in Rome: Heterosexism, Homophobia and Sports Talk Radio." *Journal of Sport & Social Issues*, 28 (2004): 136–68.

Ouellette, Marc. "'I Hope You Never See Another Day Like This': Pedagogy & Allegory in 'Post 9/11' Video Games. *Game Studies*, 8:1 (2008). Availabel at http://gamestudies.org/0801/articles/ouellette_m.

————. "Removing the checks and balances that hamper democracy": Play and the counter-hegemonic contradictions of *Grand Theft Auto IV*. *Eludamos: Journal for Computer Game Culture*, 4:2 (Fall 2010): 197–213.

Putnam, Robert. "Bowling Alone: America's Declining Social Capital." *Journal of Democracy* (Jan. 1995): 65–78.

Sedgwick, Eve Kosofsky. *Between Men: English Literature and Male Homosocial Desire*. New York: Columbia University Press, 1985.

Woolfolk, Anita, Winne, Phil H., & Perry, Nancy. *Educational Psychology* (4th Canadian edition). Toronto: Pearson, 2009.

Games Cited

DMA Design (2001) *Grand Theft Auto III*. Rockstar Games (PlayStation 2).

Rockstar North (2004) *Grant Theft Auto: San Andreas*. Take Two (PlayStation 2).

Rockstar North (2008) *Grand Theft Auto IV*. Take Two (XBox 360).

Rockstar North (2009) *Stories From Liberty City: The Ballad of Gay Tony*. Take Two (PlayStation 3).

12

FROM GREEK SCHOOL TO GREEK'S COOL

Using Weblogs in a Greek Heritage Language Program

Themistoklis Aravossitas

Introduction

My children, a 16-year-old boy and a 13-year-old girl, spend most of their leisure time each day in front of a screen, as do most young adolescents today. My son is primarily concerned with participation in games where he communicates while playing with his friends through groups that collaborate via the Internet (Gee, 2003). My daughter, on the other hand, shows a greater interest in social networking sites, primarily Facebook, where along with 500 other million users, she manages her online profile and socializes with her friends by exchanging text messages (Barnes, Marateo, & Ferris, 2007).

My decision to allow my children to use these communication and entertainment tools was not a decision that my wife and I made lightly. We weighed the pros and cons of this modern adolescence (and beyond) mania. I understand that there is a good chance for my children to meet their future partners through their "games". They may be people of different ethno-cultural backgrounds, perhaps individuals who live currently hundreds or thousands of kilometers away from them. I also realize that my children spend more hours in front of electronic environments than in front of their books. Indeed, I notice that they read by far more electronic than written texts. They write less and they use their keyboards more. Their electronic world is conveniently transferred from their games' consoles and PC screens to laptops, "smart" e-agendas and their mobile phones.

As a parent and educator, I often appear annoyed by the dependency of my children on electronic devices. Nonetheless, I must admit that I have often seen my arguments shattered one after another by my children, as exemplified in the exchanges below:

Observing my daughter, I comment, "Again playing with your computer, Matoula?"

She replies, "I am not playing. I am working on a group project that my teacher gave us at school."

"And where are the other members of your group?"

"Online ... I am talking to them dad ... right now we discussing the project ... we are working on it ... I am sending Mary the video that I took of the flowers in our garden, and she adds her own pictures ..."

And, turning to my son, I ask, "And you, Andreas, why don't you do some work for your Greek school?"

His response is similar: "But that's what I am actually doing!"

"Playing with your PlayStation?"

"But dad, the game we play is about Greek mythology; that's the chapter we are in at school ... you should see it, it is so cool ... I am Hercules and I am trying to navigate the Aegean islands."

This family interaction is typical, I think, of similar discussions that take place in millions of homes or schools between "troubled" parents and teachers on one side and "glued" children or students on the other. The world of my children is different from the world I grew up in, but that does not mean that mine was necessarily better. My children can certainly learn more things through their games than I had imagined. As I did decades ago, they also do their homework. The difference is that they use images, audio, video and graphics instead of the "boring" pencil and paper or the black and white book of my own generation. Another difference is that they gather with friends not only in the basements or yards of their homes but also in electronic environments.

I am tired of wrangling with my children about their new work habits, cyberspace playgrounds and learning environments. Rather than fighting against them and their technology, I have decided to join them. I recently transferred my energy and my interest in heritage languages (Duff & Li, 2009) and the teaching of Greek language and culture in Canada to an environment similar to the one used by my children. I created a blog through which I can write and read, listen to music, watch videos, display pictures, interact with friends, colleagues, and often with my students not only as teacher but as a learner too.

Now my children and I squabble about who is first in line to use the computer, and I spend more time in the same environment with my children. Not only do I combine my work with fun, but I also feel less isolated from the modern mainstream.

Blogging for My School

Every blog has a certain orientation that reflects the philosophy and the interests of the author–blogger (Penrod, 2007). The texts and all forms of posts serve specific ends that, in my case, were multifaceted. As I designed and developed a blog for a heritage language school which operates in Canada under certain limitations (Cummins & Danesi, 1990; Burnaby, 2008), I aimed to achieve simultaneously several outcomes:

- To present the school announcements to parents, teachers and students instead of overwhelming them with tons of photocopies. Those announcements were in relation to events, the school's program, the curriculum, etc.
- To introduce articles, books and various sources concerning the teaching of the language, history and culture, thus providing support material that could be optimized by other teachers and students in the classroom or at home. My basic concern was the composition of authentic texts (Cummins et. al., 2008) that would offer the possibility of practicing reading comprehension and familiarization with the Greek language through topics that, contrary to a lot of school texts that we were using, would be related to the interests of the students and the educators. Those texts had to be relevant to the Canadian social and cultural reality and not just the Greek one, which is unknown or unfamiliar to many of our students.
- To update the school community on current issues (e.g., national, religious celebrations) and news or articles pertaining to our interests and the Greek-Canadian identity.
- To provide links to sources for educational or even recreational purposes.
- To outline utilities to support the work of teachers, sources related to their teaching modules: photos, videos or songs.
- To provide a platform for students to present their interests and their work in whatever medium they choose (text, combining text and photo, video, PowerPoint presentation, etc.)
- To provide a forum for teachers to showcase their work and their own interests, exhibiting and sharing lesson plans and teaching ideas open and accessible to all.
- To give parents the opportunity to monitor what their children learn at school and to inform them through various posts and blog sources.
- To allow the posting of homework activities, to inform students who are absent from school about their upcoming due dates for handing in projects and to allow observers (such as parents) to familiarize themselves with the school.
- To offer the opportunity for representatives of the community and its members, who support our school morally and financially, to get an idea of our activities and our school life.
- To allow stakeholders to have access to the school.
- To demonstrate the methodology of educational research through the posts; the sources used for each subject-post are outlined; different versions or views are presented and bibliographical references are available for further exploration of each topic.

- To provide methods of safe Internet navigation for those seeking their own sources.
- To provide entertaining educational games (puzzles, quizzes, etc.) and musical or amusing videos, enabling users to take a pleasant break while reading the posts or using the tools provided by the blog.
- To record the history of the school, through the presentation of events and all activities concerning the school-communal life.
- To open a permanent channel of communication with other schools or universities that also maintain blogs or websites, to investigate ways of further cooperation and communication with interested individuals or institutions, on a regular or occasional basis.

In summary, I could say that my objective through blogging was, on the one hand, the exploration and demonstration of our identity and the activities of the school, which included not only the students but also the teachers and parents (Gramston & Wellman, 2000) and on the other hand, the provision of support in our educational program, by offering access to tools that could enrich the program and foster the teaching and learning of our language and culture beyond the narrow boundaries in which we had been functioning (Feuerverger, 1997).

Sources available through the Internet are increasing daily, as are free services that can be used for training and education purposes. For a school and a program, such as ours, with limited resources and infrastructure, developing a blog that is updated continuously to include a variety of media could be beneficial to the curriculum and the teaching methods applied by the teachers.

Weblog

The term "weblog" was coined by John Barger in 1997 (Blood, 2000), and shortly thereafter, it was simplified to "blog" (Merholz, 2002). Peter Scott, a Canadian expert on blogs, has developed a commonly accepted definition of blog as "a Web page containing brief, chronologically arranged items of information" (Scott, 2001), but that is up to where common acceptance stands. Some speak of blogs as personal websites with frequent row of information, personal experiences, analyses, comments and links, which are managed by one person. This is partially true as not all blogs are personal pages, anymore. Schools and businesses, clubs, and organizations create different types of blogs all the time.

Apart from the common characteristic of all blogs, which is the reverse chronological order so that the newest post always appears first, other features like personal administration, the hyperlinks to other blogs, posts' archives and free, public access and comments on their content, may differ from blog to blog. Some blogs have a group of administrators working together or alternatively;

others are not accessible to the public without a password or do not allow unregistered users to comment on the postings (the blog content).

Blogs appeared in the late 1990s. For many observers, their appearance was marked by the blogger weblog development software by Pyra Labs in 1999 and the following statement of the *Guardian's* journalist, Neil McIntosh: "It is not often you can say a website has changed the face of the web, and had an impact far beyond the confines of its own domain. But, for many, Blogger is such a site. For a little over two years now, Blogger has brought its 'Push button publishing for the people' to the net ..." (2002).

Kevin Werbach wrote that, although personal pages have appeared since the early days of the Internet, the first sites self-identified as blogs joined the World Wide Web in 1997 (2001). Others consider this "entrance" a bit earlier. Ancestors of the blogs, according to Dylan Tweney (2002), are the online diaries such as "Justin Hall's Links from the Underground" (1994). Depending on everyone's definition of blogs, we get contradictory stories about their birth, but we all agree that blogs became known and started to flourish when the first free software for their creation was allocated in 1999.

The evolution of blogs and their impressive development is related to the practice facilities that they provide. It is the only way that any writer can publish directly. Also, these new "tools" require no special knowledge of software programming and application and do not require a new set of skills.

Through blogs, ideas can travel with the click of a mouse to a global audience that has the ability to consider them, read and comment on them, to research and analyze or even influence them. The theory of social networks gives us a clear explanation of why blogs have such a powerful social impact (Granovetter, 1973). Through these tools, people can shape and influence their social networks, and this facility, in turn, is something that can influence their own happiness (Christakis & Fowler, 2009).

Web 2.0 Tools

Blogs, along with the opportunities that they carry, are currently placed in the category of Web 2.0 tools. These applications, interactive features and tools allow users to run interactive communication and to create and share information, using the Internet as platform. In other words, we have a flow of information in multiple directions. This information current can be created and shared by many. The world of Web 2.0 is, however, fickle in terms of applications and forms (Kelly, 2010). There are systems of participatory content, such as blogs and wikis, services, social sharing (e.g., del.icio.us, Slide share), communication tools, social networking sites like Facebook, tagging, mushups (combination of two services), RSS feeds, and so on, acting as glue that connects all departments together. All these tools—together with search engines such as Google, Wikipedia, and the blogosphere—provide teachers with a bridge to the generation of the Internet, while offering a vast array of new ways and opportunities to teach them (Barnes, Marateo, & Ferris, 2007).

It must be stressed, however, that the tools of the Web 2.0 generation cannot teach or replace the dynamic interaction of students and students and students and teachers. Based on the theory of collaborative and experiential learning, and the theory of constructivism and scaffolding learning, those features and capabilities of Web 2.0 means can be used as educational tools (Vivitsou et al., 2007). Their usefulness for learning depends on how well students are prepared to use their critical thinking in order to address problems associated with the vast supply of sources of content which may be educational, informative, dangerous or just promotional. How many videos on YouTube, for instance, are purely promotional, and how many have an educational potential? The role of the teacher as a mentor is not threatened, but upgraded in this seemingly practical but essentially vast and complex learning environment (Barnes et al., 2007).

Blog Features

In the few months that I have dealt systematically with blogs, I cannot say that I am still able to understand and operate them at full capacity. The reason is simple. New functions (most of them free of charge) are added daily, and as mentioned earlier, no explicit software analysis knowledge for processing and development is required. It is simply a matter of how much time the interested blogger has available to experiment with the new applications. Even though some applications may preoccupy an inexperienced administrator, there are open groups in the form of online communities, including the "Blogger Help", where fellow-bloggers are ready to clarify everything at zero time. Some of the most common and useful features of blogs are:

- Weblog archives: the posts are kept in the blog after the removal of the current page. Records may be searched by posting dates of by content trough a keyword.
- Weblog search engine: it can be done either by the title-theme of related topics or by the author's name, if many authors are contributing postings to one blog.
- Webcam: fixed or mobile camera connected to the Internet can provide picture, images from an event in evolution such as conference presentations, or a lesson that is presented in a classroom.
- Opinion polls: some blogs conduct polls/surveys to their readers, often concerning issues of interest to the blog and its audience. Thus interactivity is encouraged and a synthesis of viewpoints among participants is presented.
- Permanent links: a permanent connection allows the provision of identity URL for every single post with a code that was given to it when it was first published. So every posting may be accessed on the Internet independently.

Edublogs

The first educational blogs or "edublogs", as they are known, are indicated by the records of the Wayback machine to be published on the website edublog. com in May 2001.The name of these blogs refers directly to their usefulness. These blogs are created for educational purposes, such as the cooperation and information exchange between teachers and students or between teachers and parents, or between individual or groups of students.Today, there are many platforms for multiple developers and users of educational blogs, such as: Free Edublogs (with more than 500,000 members), Edu Spaces, Twitter, Teach for Us, Teacher Lingo, etc.

While blogs did not start off for educational or training purposes, it can be said with ease today that they are cut and sewn for education depending on how we use them; they may provide a faithful application of educational principles widely accepted, such as the theory of constructivism (Vygotsky, 1978).

By facilitating language and text, not necessarily presented in a written form, educational blogs enable a student or any member of a learning community to share ideas with others. The possibility of the commentary of these ideas, allow interested parties to participate in the social construction of meanings and knowledge. The constructive process of negotiating meanings is fostered when, for example, the author of a post accepts the comments of others and returns to his original idea to rethink it.

The amazing element is that in this process, the roles can be reversed. As you accept comments on your posts, you might also comment on posts of others. The teacher can comment on posts of students and vice versa. This feature sets a paradigm of critical dialogue between those who teach and those who are taught (Freire, 1973) and allow blogs to go beyond formal education policies by providing a unique field for critical pedagogy practice. "As blogs enter mainstream public consciousness from the margins of the Internet where they originated, they bring a hidden and newly awakened army of interactive participants who may be experiencing the kinds of unsettling (to the powers that be) critical consciousness that is within the goals of an increasingly democratized culture such as Paulo Freire as an educator sought to foster ..." (Boese, 2003).

We will examine next, in detail, the advantages of using blogs in relation to different pedagogical theories and we will consider them both as mechanisms for literacy enhancement and as tools for building learning communities, such as the one of the Aristoteles Greek Heritage Language School in Toronto, Canada.

Blogs for Literacy Enhancement: The Theoretical-Pedagogic Framework

From Literacy to Multiliteracies, Communities of Praxis and Transformative Pedagogy

With the rapid development of Information and Communication Technologies since the last decade of the past century, and the dramatic strengthening of the phenomenon of human mobility, the concept of school literacy education had to be reviewed. In 1996, New London Group, a group of scientists from different areas of education, coined the term "Multiliteracies" as a concept that attempts to combine two adjacent changes.

The first change relates to the importance of linguistic and cultural diversity and differing versions, new ways of speaking and writing, even within the same language. With globalization (economic and social) and the intensity of the migration phenomenon, linguistic diversity and multilingualism acquires local dimensions.

The second change relates to the nature of the new technologies of communication and transmission of meanings, in multimodal settings (visual, audio, territorial, etc.) which weakens the traditional dependence of the meaning on the grammar of written texts (Cope & Kalantzis, 2000).

Multiliteracies as a new approach to the substance and pedagogy of language and literacy emphasize the friction of the students with a wide range of textual types, linguistic and cultural resources and connect the learning process with the development of a critical meta-language that enables learners to understand the cultural and social dimensions of texts. On this basis, those involved in the learning process are required to understand the historical and social dimensions of designing texts in order to be able to redesign and to regenerate them, creating out of them a new meaning which includes self-perspectives.

The teaching procedures that are described in the Multiliteracies pedagogical orientation are incorporated into four phases which are not to be presented as successive stages (New London Group, 1996, p. 86).These phases are:

- the "situated practice", which refers to the use of available genres and text forms through the experiences and the different points of view of the learners;
- the "overt instruction", a systematic, detailed and conscientious approach to the sense of understanding of the design process in different cultural environments;
- the phase of the "Critical Framing", which invites students to distance themselves from the object of study and its cultural surroundings; and
- the "Transformed practice", as the phase where the meaning produced can be transferred to different contexts and cultural environments

As part of the Multiliteracies framework, literacy is associated with new technologies, new forms of text that are emerging, visual communication cultivated by the modern multi-media, and new social requirements and business conditions, such as the need for continuous learning and assessment, as well as problem solving practices, leading all to an overall goal of individual development that can be achieved through education and literacy. This new theoretical approach to literacy and the practical applications of Multiliteracies, occurring in different cultural and educational contexts (Cope & Kalantzis, 2000), has opened new avenues in education and provided examples of various pedagogic approaches through new technologies. Later on we will see how these applications can be adapted to educational blogs.

If Multiliteracies help us realize the new opportunities and demands for the connection of education to new social-cultural and communication environments, the theories of scaffolding-constructive learning and transformative pedagogy provide a framework to integrate our teaching in this "new world" and create a balance between where we should go and how we should get there.

Scaffolding learning is based on the socio-cultural model of co-constructivism and stems from positions expressed by scholars such as Vygotsky, Rogoff, Bruner, Hillocks, and Dewey (Wilhelm, Baker, & Dube, 2001). When asked how students learn, the theorists of behaviourism (Phillips & Soltis, 2003), such as Skinner, Pavlov and Thorndike, indicate that the answer lies in the transfer of knowledge from teacher to student, both of which are passive carriers and receivers of curricula. Progressive "cognitivists", notably Piaget, Rousseau, and Chomsky, describe learning as a natural process, achieved through the activation of students, who are using their teacher's assistance to overcome biological limits that determine how and when learning is achieved.

In the socio-cultural model of co-constructivism (Wells, 1999), knowledge is described as a product of social and cultural integration. How and what students learn depends on the opportunities that "experts" (such as parents and teachers) provide to them. This process is interactive and not a given or a "natural" phenomenon. The roles of student and teacher according to the three above mentioned pedagogic-learning models are quite different. For the behaviourists, the role appears as passive because it all depends on the curriculum, while for the cognitivists, it is more active, as the student is required to reach the construction of knowledge within an environment created by the teacher, in such a way that will allow individual development into concrete steps. According to representatives of the socio-cultural model of co-constructivism, the student enters a collaborative process with the participation of the teacher who should observe the students individually and in groups and assist learning through their Zone of Proximal Development (Vygotsky, 1978). The teacher's obligation is to adapt the curriculum to the needs of his or her students and cultivate an environment of critical inquiry.

As the theoretical background of the three "schools" and the roles that each one provides for students and teachers vary, so do their proposed teaching methods. In the case of behaviourism, the teacher teaches (orally or in writing), and the student is required to learn by memorizing the material on which she will be examined. For the progressive cognitivists, the student has choices in the sense of choosing the texts to be read or the type of work to be undertaken in order to discover knowledge. The socio-cultural model calls for the creation of small and large groups, working under the supervision and support of the teacher who guides, records and analyzes the progress of each student and provides individualized assistance to achieve the maximum results.

Finally, we come to the question of who is to blame if the student's progress is unsatisfactory. The answer for the first two "schools" is common: the student. In the first case, it is because he or she failed to meet the demands and pace of the curriculum, and in the second, because there is an "evolutionary delay"—a failure/weakness, or because he or she is not ready for this school/program and the causes can be sought frequently in family or other social conditions.

In the third case, the responsibility lies with the "experts" (parents, teachers, administration, and so) and is attributed to the failure of close observation of the student to overcome difficulties met in different stages of the learning pathways, or failure on the part of the "expert"-administrator in selecting an appropriate teacher for every student, for not making informed decisions or due to the inability of the expert to properly prepare the student.

If, as an active teacher, I am called to answer the question of which of these three "schools" of pedagogy I believe is appropriate for the current educational conditions, I will reply that the socio-cultural, co-constructivist model best fits the current circumstances in (let us say) a Canadian, American or European school context. But I could not reject the possibility of coexistence of these models and their complementarities within a broader framework that includes all three, or some aspects of each approach.

Before addressing this model of synthesis of pedagogical approaches, I should point out a shortcoming found in the theoretical formulation of the above teaching concepts. This is the social element, the question of identity of those involved in the educational process (Cummins, 2001), whether students or teachers, that according to the new circumstances discussed earlier, as we outlined the Multiliteracies pedagogy platform, appears nowadays very important to education.

The question of the identity of students and teachers is one aspect of the education process which is very important in the case of this thesis, as the teaching and learning of heritage languages is inextricably linked to notions of identity and its continued negotiation at all levels—in the relations developed at school, in the family or in the society at large. As identities are shaped at an individual level (e.g., between teacher and student) or at a group level (among communities), relationships and forces are developed that are either authoritarian, with the dominance of one party over the other, or balancing, characterized by mutual understanding and mutual respect (Cummins, 2001).

In any case, these relationships are not static. Thus, we must take them under serious consideration on the quest for a fuller picture of ideal contemporary pedagogical practices. While we have been preoccupied with whether learning depends more or less on the teacher, the student or the environment, current conditions require us to understand that the learning process occurs within a community, composed of and influenced by many interested parties.

Rogoff, Matusov, and White (1996) refer to a learning community as an environment that includes both the active learners and their more mature or expert partners, usually adults, who will guide and encourage the less experienced (as proposed by Vygotsky). In such an environment, everyone cooperates in what evolves metaphorically into a community of praxis, which is described as "reflection and action upon the world in order to transform it" (Freire, 1970). In these communities, members attempt not only to create meaning but also to be activated and learn how to apply their knowledge in order to solve problems as in "real world" circumstances.

Within these communities, learning goes beyond the context of transfer and acquisition. Rather, it is produced as a result of a transformation process. As students are supported and their representation evolves, their role is transformed, turning them into more active members of the community who will eventually undertake, in turn, the role of the experts. Similarly, the roles of the experts (teacher-specialists) are also transformed, as they have to adapt their participation according to the progress of students or as new ways of cooperation to achieve the common goals are searched and identified.

Having outlined the concept of transformation, in relation to participation in a dynamic educational environment, we can complete the notion of the synthesis of behaviourist, cognitive and constructivist pedagogical approaches, including the transformational aspect, which is essential because as we are about to explore the implementation of educational blogs in the Heritage languages context, participation in learning communities is one of the most fundamental points. The synthesis of such pedagogical orientations is shown vividly in "Promoting Academic Achievement in Multilingual School Contexts through Transformative Multiliteracies Pedagogy" (Skourtou, Kourtis-Kazoullis, & Cummins, 2006). The traditional pedagogical approach is one of directly transferring knowledge to students. Here, the pedagogical value is limited to the re-establishment of previous knowledge on the part of students and the development of learning strategies but learning occurs in specific units and no opportunities for expansion of knowledge and motivation for critical inquiry occurs.

A progressive socio-constructivist approach, which includes the use of higher mental functions by the students and the participation in an exploratory learning process, is theoretically based in Vygotsky's views on the construction of knowledge through collaboration between the teacher-expert and the student.

A transformative approach can expand the horizons of our pedagogical quest beyond the transmission of knowledge, based on the implementation of curricular requirements and the construction of knowledge with scaffolds provided by experts to consider the need for student understanding of the connections between knowledge and power relations. Transformative pedagogy builds on collaborative critical inquiry in order for the student-learner to be able to understand and explore the social conditions and the coercive relations in her community and her life. The student is required to develop skills of critical literacy to gain personal perspective in relation to issues such as social equity and justice. Transformative pedagogy is influenced by the work of Freire and Vygotsky (Cummins, 2000) and effectively introduces the social relations factor to the act of teaching. This is an important addition to the procedures of transfer, construct and integration of knowledge as the aim of education is not only to pass on knowledge but to make the student an active member of society.

Applications on Educational Blogs

Next, we will examine how the use of educational blogs can incorporate a variety of teaching approaches, and in particular, how it can provide the appropriate environment for transformational pedagogical practices, which in combination with Multiliteracies can be described in a framework of five key principles:

1. Transformative Multiliteracies Pedagogy constructs an image of the child as intelligent, imaginative, and linguistically talented; individual differences in these traits do not diminish the potential of each child to shine in specific ways.
2. Transformative Multiliteracies Pedagogy acknowledges and builds on the cultural and linguistic capital (prior knowledge) of students and communities.
3. Transformative Multiliteracies Pedagogy aims explicitly to promote cognitive engagement and identity investment on the part of students.
4. Transformative Multiliteracies Pedagogy enables students to construct knowledge, create literature and art, and act on social realities through dialogue and critical inquiry.
5. Transformative Multiliteracies Pedagogy employs a variety of technological tools to support students' construction of knowledge, literature, and art and their presentation of this intellectual work to multiple audiences through the creation of identity texts. (Cummins, 2009, pp. 38–56)

My particular interest is to explore how the above principles can be practically expressed and implemented through blogging.

Discourse, according to Gee (1990), involves more than issues of syntax, phonology and vocabulary. It includes the element of identity which is being constructed by members of a learning community through an interaction of principles, personal attitudes and social practices.

In the environment of a classroom, student texts (in all different forms) are presented to a limited audience, mainly consisting of teachers and classmates, but in the blogosphere, talented readers can judge a student as a writer for his or her views and the means he or she chooses to use in order to communicate. If the comments are positive, feedback empowers the student as a talented writer-researcher and communicator. However, even a negative comment might be a reason for the student to be more careful the next time, concerning the information sources used or the development of arguments (Penrod, 2007).

In blogs, every learner has the opportunity to work on topics of individual interest, using the means with which he or she is comfortable. Therefore, learners can create posts on their favourite sport or the music that represents them—or even on a particular school subject that excites them. Their passion for the subject-topic of their choice, and the sense that through the blog (which is a "real" environment) they can teach the world, may have greater meaning as a learning incentive than a weighty written project that they have to present in the classroom.

Especially in the major educational issue of cultivating writing skills, blogs may be quite successful for two reasons. First, blogging is a pleasurable activity (Penrod, 2007, p. 7), so student-writers consider posting on blogs not as academic writing but as an extracurricular activity, which results in their view of writing in this case as "fun." Additionally, students often spend more time in posting than in doing other writing work because of the practical, self-directed, enjoyable and creative nature of dealing with blogs.

In blogging, the theory of Lev Vygotsky's "Zone of Proximal Development" finds a perfect application field because an experienced mentor (who may be a teacher, a parent or a classmate) taking advantage of the practical possibilities of current technology available in blogs, can create the basis on which every student, with minimal assistance, can develop various skills (Penrod, 2007, pp. 31–32). The expert has the opportunity to keep a distance and observe this development process as the student goes through a continuous dialogue with members of the community. The mentor monitors the student who may eventually assume the role of the expert as he or she becomes comfortable with content and technology, and as new, inexperienced users are entering the community.

Here the possibilities of collaborative learning are enormous, since learners can work in groups or pairs where each member has different levels of expertise, be it more technologically proficient or better in writing, and so on (Penrod, 2007, pp. 21–22). They can collaborate in researching sources, in familiarizing themselves with new software and applications. It is also important to note that they can engage in these learning activities at their own pace and on chosen time, beyond the restrictions of a classroom environment.

As a collaborative action, blogging teaches students that writers depend on their readers and readers on the writers. The performance of a reader or a writer depends greatly on the other part. Communication requires a transmitter and receiver or, as in the case of blogs, the writer and the reader. Students as bloggers, begin to develop the feeling that the writers should be careful in building a relationship with their readers to ensure an accurate understanding of their message.

In the process of blogging, the appearance of a student or any special needs of the student-writer are not important (Penrod, 2007, p. 25), since in such an environment the discrimination factor is absent. Through blogs, students can bridge cultural, social, economic, emotional and spatial gaps. Thus, they can take control of the learning process.

With their versatility and the plethora of instruments or genres that can be used for posts, students who write on blogs can take advantage of their particular skills (e.g., the comfort of synthesizing rap music lyrics, or familiarity with graphic arts) to develop and present an illustrated text. At the same time, the bloggers/authors have the incentive of immediate and tangible feedback. They see their text being published at once and anticipate comments as recognition of their efforts (Penrod, 2007, p. 22). When they are satisfied with the action of writing, they tend to write more and pay more attention. Student-bloggers practise research both for the use of appropriate means of expressing their ideas and for the identification of resources that will help them look informed and intelligent to their readers. The exchange of comments in which they get involved, frequently with audience far beyond the boundaries of a class or a school, locates them in actual social dialogue settings.

Bloggers consider critically the nature and accountability of the information that they are about to present as well as the methods/means of presenting their ideas and messages. Since those messages are intended for a broad public audience, bloggers should take into account social, cultural, emotional and political dimensions of their texts and whether their writings will challenge or cause the response of readers.

As they construct a blog and create content, students are concerned with the quality of their posts (audiovisual material, articles, images, etc.) to keep their readers interested. This process of research, analysis, synthesis and final selection, is a process of genuine critical inquiry that mimics the situation that "real authors" have to go through.

In the case examined by this thesis, the use of weblogs for teaching and learning a heritage language, studies demonstrate that blogs can support students with such second-language learning needs (Penrod, 2007, p. 30). The dialectic element which is evident in blogs empowers students to practice their writing skills (with written posts) or their oral communication skills (with audio blogging, podcasting). As many students of second/foreign language are reluctant to express or share their oral and writing abilities with native speakers, blogs allow the practice in which, for example, the experienced and the inexperienced can work together, creating their own community, before opening to more "central" language activities. Through blogs, students can narrate their own stories, display their cultural wealth, share photos or videos from their home, their interests, and combine written text (which they may not have comfort with) with audio-visual material.

In conclusion, through participation in an educational blog, learners can engage alternatively or in succession in the role of the writer and the reader-commenter. They can expose their talent and build on prior knowledge, using the instrument/means they have the greatest comfort with. Initially, their efforts may be supported by experienced instructors. Then, they assume this role for themselves. They can practise just their writing skills or use the enormous blog development opportunities to apply multimodal communication of meanings. Bloggers who are familiar with new applications of Information Technology actually get the chance to teach those skills to others, members of their learning community, and get empowered by such a role shift. As a result, they become active participants in knowledge construction within their community.

In brief, blogs are excellent tools, the proper mechanisms for transformative and Multiliteracies pedagogy's applications, given that they are used sufficiently with adequate support on the basic stages by experienced mentors who can help users overcome any initial fears and difficulties, thus minimizing the risk of early disappointment.

Application of the Framework "Literacy-Engagement and Literacy Attainment" in Toronto's Aristoteles Greek Heritage Language School Blog

In promoting the use of new Information and Communication Technologies, and in particular the opportunities offered by the development of educational blogs for Heritage Language schools, especially for teaching the Greek language and culture in Canada, I requested the collaboration of students and teachers of the Aristoteles school during the school year 2009–2010. A Grade 10 student (intermediate class), a third-generation language learner (Suarez, 2007), expressed an interest in contributing to the school's blog by submitting a post on one of the books she had recently read.

The process evolved as follows. The student had already read the book in her native language (English), thus she was familiar with the content and she created simple sentences in English, which included the key elements of the book (author, case, space-time context, characters, plot). Using her prior knowledge of the Greek language, she attempted to translate her sentences into the target language (Greek). A teacher provided support for her to correct some errors in spelling and syntax and to turn the sentences into a text form. Via e-mail, her text reached the blog administrator who searched for images/pictures and proposed a text layout. The student added her personal comments, stating the reasons why she liked this book and specifying the elements that made it interesting and enjoyable. Before publishing the document, the student had the opportunity to observe it again from a distance, as an integrated posting display. She proposed further changes by adjusting her content to the comprehended skills of the readership. At this stage, she demonstrated awareness of the reading capabilities of her less experienced readers, that is, her classmates.

The original text, comprised of simple sentences in English and comments on a book previously read by the student, became a literature presentation article written in Greek, in a text format enriched with visual material. Through the experience of publishing a blog post-article (book review), the student used her initial writing skills (creation of simple sentences) and expressed different aspects of her talent and identity, as a reader and book reviewer. Later on, she found her own way to further develop her skills (within her Zone of Proximal Development) by creating a grammatically correct and conceptually comprehensive written text. Feedback was an important factor since the publication of her post was recognized first by the teacher and classmates and then by each visitor-viewer of the blog.

The student was empowered not only by the idea of getting positive responses but also through the collaboration of at least two experienced mentors (the teacher and the administrator) who acknowledged her efforts, worked with her by editing her text and by providing assistance for spelling and grammatical corrections. In addition, there were several written communication opportunities between the collaborating individuals, as text messages and e-mails (between the student and the experts) were exchanged. Support and empowerment was even stronger for the student in finding out that with her work she established an example. In fact, it was right after her publication that students of the Grade 12 (senior-advanced) class collaborated with another teacher and the blog administrator in posting their comments in the target language about films they had recently watched.

Based on the five principles of Transformative Multiliteracies Pedagogy, as presented above, the following results were evident:

1. The student was recognized as smart, imaginative and linguistically capable. The idea to present a book through a blog review post was original since it was implemented for the first time in the Greek school blog where she had the opportunity to show her abilities in the target language as a reader as well and as a writer of a specific genre.
2. Her cultural capital and her prior knowledge were acknowledged. The ability to read a book in English and to analyze it (the reader's talent) was recognized by the experts and classmates as well as the fact that she

managed to present her content in the second language, in a comprehensive written manner (two more aspects of her talent acknowledged; the writer and the language learner since a skill was acquired in one language and transferred to another).

3. She developed the cognitive capacities to writing a new genre, and she had the opportunity to present aspects of her personal identity by explaining what it was that she liked in the book, what she found interesting and entertaining.

4. She took the risk to express her opinion, to critique a literary work, and through the dialogue which developed with the comments of her classmates, the teacher, the administrator and users of the blog, she exercised the skill-concept of critical inquiry, in practice.

5. Rather than limiting the presentation within the classroom's narrow range of audience, using a draft text written by hand, she published her text as a blog post, which allowed her to develop electronic text composing skills (using audio-visual material), and she addressed a potential worldwide audience, thus she overcame the fear of public exposure, quite characteristic of the holdbacks that language learners experience.

If the whole process had been reduced to the traditional pedagogical model approach, the student would be invited to read a book offered by the teacher, memorize it and face assessment (on her memorizing skills). If we had followed the progressive cognitivist model, the student would have the option to read a book of her choice and to select the method of presentation. The teacher would still reinforce her efforts at every stage, but the audience would have remained restricted to the classroom level. However, using the school blog and the implementation of the socio-cultural model of constructive learning and the principles of Transformative Multiliteracies pedagogical approach, the benefits were greater.

The student produced "fun" work because her prior knowledge and talent was recognized. She realized her self-development as a language learner, as she evolved from the initial stage of writing simple sentences in English, to translating in the target language and publishing a comprehensive text which included the use of new technologies.

Furthermore, she engaged, through the process of her article preparation, in dialogue with other members of the school community (the teacher and administrator) and saw her role transformed, from the stage of a student-observer of the blog to an active member-author and mentor of her classmates. The post did not limit her to merely inform others about a book that she read. She offered an example of blogging as a means for the cognitive development of students and for literacy enhancement in a collaborative learning environment.

With her critical stand, she assumed the risk of expressing her personal thoughts and ideas and she received comments from other members of the learning community which was extended far beyond the confines of a school classroom. Through the student's blog posting experience and as her role evolved, it became obvious how such a community can be transformed into a community of collaborative practice. Skills from different cultural backgrounds were used in parallel and constructively. The assessment process was automatically initiated, as comments and observations of those who read this particular post prompted the student to self-evaluation of her work and encouraged her towards further improvement. The example of a simple student posting on a school blog became a point of reference for other teachers and students in adapting new, more creative forms of school work.

Finally, it revealed to the broad community, an aspect of the work done in an isolated, to date, educational program which claims recognition and upgrading.

Conclusion

Along the path of this chapter, I attempted to describe the theoretical context in which a weblog can be used to promote pedagogy and literacy at a heritage language school of a particular ethnic cultural community in Ontario, Canada. I presented some aspects of the blogosphere and of new IT tools, and I attempted to prove the great potential of applying them in marginalized educational programs where students can only be engaged if their identity is recognized and appreciated (Cummins, 2001; Skutnabb-Kangas, 2000). I investigated the pedagogical implications of such an application and gave an example of the synthesis of progressive teaching directives, in student blog postings.

I believe that the educational use of blogs highlights the enormous potential of students and teachers in heritage language programs (Valdes, 2001). The rapid expansion of the new media has opened new avenues, as they give room for the submission of modern teaching methods that can foster the creation of learning community networks, bridging students, teachers and people interested in the development of heritage languages and the preservation of cultures. The educational blog that was created on an experimental basis is now becoming a step for a qualitative upgrading of our program.

It was founded and developed according to the principles of Transformative Multiliteracies Pedagogy and can exploit the possibilities of literacy enhancement and other advantages that social and knowledge media obtain through the rapid evolution of ICT in the contemporary digital era.

The space of the Internet is ever-expanding, multicultural, and global. The World Wide Web is larger than our school, our community and our city. In this vast, limitless environment, Aristoteles has a distinguished address. Online, we are housed in www.easterngr.blogspot.com, and this site, our electronic home, remains always open. There, everyone can see what we do, what we learn and what we are concerned about. There, anyone has access to our identity.

References

Barnes, K., Marateo, C., & Ferris, S. (2007). Teaching and learning with the Net generation. *Innovate Journal of Online Education*, *3*(4). Retrieved July 3, 2010, from http://innovateonline. info/pdf/vol3_issue4/Teaching_and_Learning_with_the_Net_Generation.pdf

Blood, R. (2000). Weblogs: A history and perspective. *Rebecca's Pocket*. Retrieved June 17, 2009, from http://www.rebeccablood.net/essays/weblog_history.html

Boese, C. (2003, March). The spirit of Paulo Freire in blogland: Struggling for knowledge-log revolution. *Into the Blogoshere*. Retrieved August 1, 2010, from http://blog.lib.umn.edu/ blogosphere/the_spirit_of_paulo_freire.html

Burnaby, B. (2008). Language policy and education in Canada. In S. May & H. N. Hornberger (Eds.), *Encyclopedia of language and education: Language policy and political issues in education* (Vol. 1, 2nd ed., pp. 331–341). New York: Springer.

Christakis, N. A., & Fowler, J. H. (2009). *Connected: The surprising power of our social networks and how they shape our lives*. New York: Little, Brown.

Cope, B., & Kalantzis, M. (2000). *Multiliteracies: Literacy, learning and the design of social futures*. New York: Routledge.

Couros, A. (2010). *The networked teacher*. Retrieved August 1, 2010, from http://www.squidoo. com/edublogs#module13132739

Cummins, J. (2000). Biliteracy, empowerment, and transformative pedagogy. In J. V. Tinajero & R. A. DeVillar (Eds.), *The power of two languages* (pp. 9–19). New York: McGraw-Hill. Retreived July 11, 2010, from http://www.iteachilearn.com/cummins/biliteratempower-ment.html

Cummins, J. (2001). *Negotiating identities: Education for empowerment in a diverse society*. Los Angeles: California Association for Bilingual Education.

Cummins, J. (2009). Transformative multiliteracies pedagogy: School-based strategies for closing the achievement gap. *Multiple Voices for Ethnically Diverse Exceptional Learners*, *11*(2), 38–56.

Cummins, J., Bismilla, V., Chow, P., Cohen, S., Giampapa, F., Leoni, L., et al. (2008). Affirm-ing identity in multilingual classrooms. In F. Shultz (Ed.), *Multicultural education* (14th ed., pp. 116–119). New York: McGraw-Hill. (Reprinted from *Educational Leadership*, September 2005, 38–42).

Cummins, J., & Danesi, M. (1990). *Heritage languages: The development and denial of Canada's lin-guistic resources*. Toronto, Ontario, Canada: Our schools /Our selves Education Foundation.

Duff, P. (2008). Heritage language education in Canada. In D. Brinton, O. Kagen, & S. Bauckos (Eds.), *Heritage language education: A new field emerging* (pp. 71–90). New York: Routlege.

Duff, P. A., & Li, D. (2009). Indigenous, minority, and heritage language education in Canada: Policies, contexts, and issues. *The Canadian Modern Language Review*, *66*(1), 1–8.

Feuerverger, G. (1997). On the edges of the map. *Teaching and Teacher Education*, *1*, 39–53.

Freire, P. (1970). *Pedagogy of the oppressed*. New York: Continuum.

Freire, P. (1973). *Education for critical consciousness*. New York: The Seabury Press.

Garmston, R., & Wellman, B. (2000). *The adaptive school: Developing and facilitating collaborative groups*. El Dorado Hills, CA: Four Hats Seminars.

Gee, J. (1990). *Social linguistics and literacies: Ideology in discourses*. New York: Falmer Press.

Gee, J. (2003). *What video games have to teach us about learning and literacy*. New York: Palgrave Macmillan.

Granovetter, M. (1973). The strength of weak ties. *American Journal of Sociology*, *78*(1), 1360–1380.

Kelly, B. (2010). *UK Web Focus*. Retrieved August 1, 2010, from http://ukwebfocus.wordpress. com/

McIntosh, N. (2002, January 1). *A tale of a man and his blog*. Retrieved August 1, 2010, from http:// www.guardian.co.uk/technology/2002/jan/31/internetnews.onlinesupplement

Merholz, P. (2002). *Play with your words*. Retrieved June 17, 2009, from http://www.peterme. com/archives/00000205.html

New London Group. (1996). A pedagogy of multiliteracies: Designing social futures. *Harvard Educational Review*, *66*(1), 60–92.

Penrod, D. (2007). *Using blogs to enhance literacy: The next powerful step in 21st century learning.* Toronto, Ontario, Canada: Rowmann & Littlefield Education.

Phillips, D., & Soltis, J. (2003). *Perspectives on learning.* New York: Teachers College Press.

Rogoff. B., Matusov, B., & White, S. (1996). Models of teaching and learning: Participation in a community of learners. In D. Olson & N. Torrance (eds.), The *Handbook of Cognition and Human Development* (pp. 388–414). Oxford, UK: Blackwell.

Scott, P. (2001). *Blogging: Creating instant content for the web.* Retreived, May 6, 2009, from http://library.usask.ca/scottp//112001/definition.html

Skourtou, E., Kourtis Kazoullis, V., & Cummins, J. (2006). Designing virtual learning environments for academic development. In J. Weiss, J. Nolan, & P. Trifonas (Eds.), *International handbook of virtual learning environments* (pp. 441–467). Norwell, MA: Springer.

Skutnabb-Kangas, T. (2000). *Linguistic genocide in education or worldwide diversity and human rights?* Mahwah, NJ: Erlbaum.

Suarez, D. (2007). Second and third generation heritage language speakers. *Heritage Language Journal.* Retrieved July 6, 2010, from http://www.international.ucla.edu/languages/heritagelanguages/journal/article.asp?parentid=72420#back_app

Tweney, D. (2002). *Weblogs Make the Web Work for You.* Retrieved July 6, 2009, from http://dylan.tweney.com/writing.php?display=295

Valdes, G. (2001). Heritage language students: Profiles and possibilities. In J. Peyton, D. Ranard, & S. E. McGinnis (Eds.), *Heritage languages in America* (pp. 37–80). Retrieved July 11, 2010, from http://www.nflc.org/reach/documents/valdes.pdf

Vivitsou, M., Gikas, A., Minaoglou, N., Konetas, D., Economacos, H., Lampropoulou, N., et al. (2007). *Weblogs as learning and collaborative tools in the framework of the online community of Greek educators of the Panhellenic School Network.* Retrieved June 18, 2009, from http://www.intelligenesis.eu/nikiweb/pubdocs/07/07/Vivitsou-et-alEEEP-07+.doc

Vygotsky, L. (1978). *Mind in society.* Cambridge, MA. Harvard University Press.

Wells, G. (1999). *Dialogic inquiry: Towards a sociocultural practice and theory of education.* Cambridge, England: Cambridge University Press.

Werbach, K. (2001). *The triumph of the weblogs.* Retrieved January 15, 2006, from http://www.eadventure.com/conversation/article.afm?Counter=7444662

Wilhelm, J., Baker, T., & Dube, J. (2001). *Strategic reading: Guiding students to lifelong literacy.* Portsmouth, NH: Heinemann.

13

THE DIGITAL GAME AS A LEARNING SPACE

Peter Pericles Trifonas

The introduction of digital and electronic representation and communication technologies in the arts and sciences, popular culture and education has evoked strong and often oppositional reactions with respect to learning and literacy. Some have welcomed the educational challenges of digital culture and emphasize its possibilities for individual emancipation and social transformation in the new media information age. From this perspective, the traditional cultural consumer and educational subject before the digital revolution is perceived more or less as a "passive" recipient and reader of static and finished cultural products that promoted a formal type of end-oriented learning and literacy through books, paintings, or films with discrete themes, meanings, and ideologies. Interactive digital cultural objects such as websites, DVDs, or online gaming environments are welcomed as unique learning environments where meaning is negotiated and constructed because users can manipulate, enter, explore, perform or even partially create their own forms of literary and representational content (e.g., blogs, *Wikis, YouTube, Facebook*). Other reactions are more critical.

Because of its sophisticated techniques of multi-medial simulation and immersion, digital culture is accused of absorbing its recipients in an all-pervasive "virtual world" of visual representations experienced and understood by individual users as "all-consuming environments" instead of digital simulations offering up a shared cultural space that requires the negotiation of meaning among the constituent members of a learning community. Digital culture is believed to obliterate the distinction between reality and fiction by presenting the user with already "finished" images of a possible world. The fear is that the engagement and activation of the faculties of creative imagination and critical literacy are suppressed with the instant satisfaction of thrills and a delusional wonder of the educational subject in simulations. This diversity of opinions suggests that digital technologies are generating a profound change in the way we engage with the educational environments of cultural objects such as digital games that instantiate and require new forms of literacy through which we learn to read and interact with others and the world around us.

Since the 1960s, new digital techniques for the creation, processing and distribution of text, images, and sounds have been applied to existing "popular" and "high" art forms and genres, and have profoundly changed their appearance, impact, and the ways we engage with representations and texts as educational environments. Digital technologies have enabled the rise of new forms of art and entertainment predicated on the possibility of interactive educational environments that often synchronize with the participants' movements or interventions, epistemological interests and aesthetic desires. Digital culture has become the means for enacting forms of public pedagogy through which we learn to read and engage others and the world around us. The way in which the attention of public spectatorship is triggered by the educational potential of digital media environments and the kind of engagement that is solicited in the way we decode and respond to its representations seems to have changed likewise due to the proliferation of a digital culture: nowadays even visitors to traditional institutions that perform a public pedagogy like museums are asked to *do* as much as to look and listen and read, and to *experience* as much as to interpret and reflect on objects and texts.

Digital technologies have transformed cultural perceptions of learning and what it means to be literate. An important cultural phenomenon, the digital game, is as yet sufficiently understood as an "educational environment." New media techniques mobilize audiovisual simulations and kinesthetic representations to teach by enveloping the user in digital educational environments. The rapid sophistication and convergence of digital communication channels such as email, the Internet, video conferencing, and instant messaging have introduced the possibility of real time involvement of the audience in otherwise unidirectional forms of cultural mediation and information dissemination and have given rise to new enter forms of representation like multi-user online games, in which the participants are co-creators of fictional gaming worlds. New concepts such as *interactivity* and *immersion* have attempted to describe the nature of human perception and cognitive participation inaugurated by the technological innovations of digital media. But these concepts have been as elusive and problematic as they are suggestive in attempting to explain the phenomenology of user responses; therefore, their usefulness for understanding the effects of our engagement with digital media as a form of learning and literacy has been limited. For example, the term *interactivity* was initially used with regard to computer interfaces that allowed for user input and control while running a program (in contrast to computers, which process preloaded data without interruption). The concept of *interactivity* in fact applies to all uses of modern human computer interfaces and has very little analytical value for understanding the effects of technology on the forms and structure of our cognitive and affective responses: how we decode representations within the medium, what we learn from them, and the ways our learning is affected. *Interactivity* suggests the possibility of an equal exchange between a digital interface, its programmed textual representations, and the user; whereas, many so-called "interactive media objects" merely allow the user to choose between several pre-determined paths or react to the movements of the cursor, without having genuine control over the form or content of the digital domain. On the other hand, proponents a theory of *interactivity* have presumed that reading a novel or viewing of a painting or film is a passive learning experience—a form of spectatorship and not interaction. As theorists of reading response have pointed out, interactions with traditional narrative could not function semiotically without the active imaginative and cognitive "construction" of a mental text by the reader in the role of meaning maker. So, far from being the most distinctive feature of digital technology, the theory of *interactivity* amounts to very little insofar as it allows us to understand the unique complexity of the educational effects of digital technology upon us as literate beings and how we read *the* medium, read *in* the medium.

The same kind of skepticism has been voiced with regard to the concept of *immersion*. Embodied forms of learning and entertainment like flight simulators, digital games, IMAX films or Computer Assisted Virtual Environments may give the spectator the feeling of *being in* the image and may exceed traditional media in terms of sensorial impact. Yet when one takes a closer look at the novelty of these new forms of digital representation and the genres they have invented, the impact of digital technologies appears to be not so radical after all, even though it may be technologically revolutionary. Older forms of commercial amusement in the nineteenth and early twentieth century like circuses, panoramas, magic lantern shows and dramatic spectacles relied on the same sensorial immersion of the participant audience and forms of reading. It would be too hasty, however, to conclude that forms of representation used by digital and electronic communication technologies have made no difference in the way we learn to interpret and understand how to relate to real world phenomena and to each other. When considering the large scale effects of digital media on us locally and globally as educational environments, there has been a cultural transformation in the ways we have come to redefine learning and literacy. Many small shifts in our experience of digital representations and media have, in their cumulative combination, amounted to a qualitative transformation of the experiential field of learning and literacy. This research area is still in its infancy. Often accounts of the educational cultural consequences of digital technologies as forms of learning and literacy are based on what are believed to be new media's inherent possibilities and future promise rather than on analysis of actual practices.

The heading "digital game" comprises all kinds of video games: P.C. games, console games, arcade games, games that are played offline or online, single-player and multi-player games. Digital games are highly interesting research objects for several reasons. The strong cultural reactions evoked by new media in general are evoked even more vehemently by digital games, as is evident in the recent discussions of their supposed stimulation of aggressive behavior. Digital games use very sophisticated techniques for enhancing both the player's agency and sense of immersion, and thereby exemplify new media culture's structures of engagement on the level of individual game-play. On the level of the culture as a whole, digital games are both an exponent and a vehicle of cultural transformation. Not only do they form a rapidly growing part of the popular culture industry, they also instigate transformations in other cultural domains such as education. Played in a multi-player fashion online digital games engender new forms of social relationships and new forms of shared participation in cultural literacy and modes of learning. As games are used for instructional purposes in schools, industry, and the army or air force for training purposes, the playing of games is no longer constricted to a sphere outside normal adult life, but forms part of the "serious" world of production and consumption, knowledge and education. This suggests that digital technologies may have changed the characteristics and cultural significance of learning and what it means to be literate—not to mention the nature of play itself. This significance may be broader than the acquisition of cognitive skills. Through the act of play, computer games prepare and "train" the general public for a "culture of real virtuality" in which we require digital literacy skill for decoding and understanding media simulations in our environment and how to relate to them as public forms of learning or public pedagogy. Digital games constitute a strategic research site because they exemplify the transformations in perception and participation that are characteristic for digital culture of learning and literacy. However, what these transformations are seen to consist of, depends on what aspects of gaming are foregrounded and with what non-digital cultural phenomena digital games are compared.

Digital media technology has transformed the nature of toys, games, and playing, and the way in which players interact with and participate in them. The increasing technological sophistication of toys has changed the way in which we play and what we play, and the way in which toys, games, and play are valued in general since the late eighteenth century. This historical line intersects with historical processes like urbanization, industrialization, and the birth of various specifically child-related sciences. Against this historical background, the varied and rich tradition of reflection on the cultural and social meaning and significance of games and playing has to be surveyed in order to be able to consider how *digital* technology has changed what we play and how we look upon play. Extant theories of games and playing based on non-digital games are still useful when investigating digital games. Because digital games combine an innovation in the world of games with an innovation in the world of media technology, they do not only challenge current theories of the social and cultural significance of games and playing, but also prevailing theories of technology. What makes the participation and interaction in playing a digital game different from that in a non-digital game? And what is the role of technology in shaping this difference? Digital games have changed tremendously since their initial introduction in the fifties. They've become more and more complex, popular, and contested. To illustrate this, the so-called "classic" digital games can be compared with contemporary digital games. Questions to consider are: What has changed in the scope of the fifty years since we know digital games? How do players participate and interact with a basic, black-and-white game such as *Pong* (1972) compared to a full-color, highly complex, narrative-motivated, irony-laden, hours-consuming game such as *Grand Theft Auto: Vice City* (2003)? And how have the cultural appreciation and position of digital games shifted during the last decades? One of the central changes that is taking place, for example, concerns the way in which digital games are interlaced with institutions such as the army, education, museums, policy making, commerce and industry. It is clear that there is a growing tendency to use the complex technology used for creating very realistic, immersive, and engaging game worlds outside the domain of entertainment. Different disciplinary approaches to digital games have erupted recently in artificial intelligence, cognitive psychology, media studies, philosophy, and critical theory, for example. What are the effects of this growing use of game-based simulations outside the world of entertainment, e.g., as a training facility or as a new way of producing knowledge or goods, on the valuation and place of digital games in culture and society?

The digital game "interface" encompassing the technology, user, and the socio-cultural milieu of both human and machine, as the performative site of game-play that enacts a public pedagogy through its means of educational and cultural transformation.

Comparing forms of user engagement with digital games and other forms of textual, aural, haptic, and visual representation—e.g., participation and spectatorship with cultural objects such as books, paintings, music, cinema—can reveal the complex phenomenological structure of user participation and perception to analyze and understand the way players' engagement with digital games is structured as a digitally mediated form of learning and literacy. The interface is the *sociotechnical site* imbibing the intricate and complex relations between the social and the technological fields of the players' experience. When the concept interface is not limited to the hardware and software interfaces, but taken to include the player and the (social) environment in which the game is situated as well, it constitutes an outstanding subject matter to evaluate the theoretical perspectives used in the study. Constructivist theories of technology, in so far as they elucidate the engagement of the player with digital gaming technologies, examine technical tools in their concrete materiality and actual use, foregrounding the ways in which they transform actions and goals and are themselves transformed in practice. Any analysis must seek to complement those conceptions of the effects digital technology with analyses of the cognitive constitution of user responses that position the spectator in relation to internal textual or codic mechanisms of digital games and the interaction between these textual structures, the technological objects that represent them, and the social context. Concepts from phenomenology and models from semiotics and poststructuralism allow us to foreground the analysis on the intentionality and embodiment of the subject and the role technological mediation plays in the relations therein.

A focus on the *perceptual* aspects of digital games is tantamount to an analysis of the relation between immersion and agency in the construction of the gamespace, elucidating the cultural transformations at stake when comparing digital games with earlier forms of (audio)visual representation and spectatorship, such as perspective painting and cinema. Investigating the complex phenomenological structure of participation and perception in digital culture requires us to focus on the spatial dimension of new media objects such as digital games. While spatiality has been the subject of much speculation and criticism in new media theory, little attention has been given to the complexity of its actual experience and its conception by embodied spectators who are using digital media apparati as a form of literacy. The issue of content and structure within digital spectatorship and participation is far from resolved. It is expressed by the predominance of two accounts of the cultural significance of digital space that seem to oppose and to exclude each other. The first holds that, in comparison with more traditional spatial representations such as perspective painting and cinema, the space of digital media invites a sense of total absorption, as it positions the player/spectator *in* the space of representation and requires participant attention and activity *within* the space of the image to such a degree that the player/spectator is completely immersed in the virtual space and oblivious of the real world outside. The second account emphasizes the spectator's distance and control. Where traditional spatial representation relied on the willingness of the spectator to conform to a constructed point of view, spatial representation in digital culture allows the spectator the freedom to act, to move around, to make choices, and to manipulate or even construct the spectatorial positions suggested by the representation. Both accounts are too one-sided. Playing digital games seems to rely on the tensions and exchanges between the interface and user freedom to move within it. New media theorists still show a tendency to overlook this complex phenomenological structuring of spectatorship because they focus on the virtual reality experience (VR). VR seems to promise that the virtual and the real could become one and that the illusion of immersion could be complete. Thereby the material presence of the visible screen and its function to separate virtual from physical space would tend to lose its cultural significance. The continuing popularity of screen-based games shows that the opposite might be true. In spite of the technological possibilities to develop interfaces that go beyond the screen, digital game culture is still a "screen culture." In digital games the visual acknowledgement of the screen has even come to demand a pivotal role. This recognition allows us to trace both continuities and discontinuities between "analog" and digital media culture as the haptic elements of touch screens or haptic simulations (e.g., Nintendo *DS, Wii,* Sony *PSP*) are increasing sought after. Thus, while the experience of space by the film spectator is produced largely *in spite of* the spectator's reflection on the materiality of the screen, the unreality of the film, and active motor agency in relation to what is shown on the screen, the experience of space in digital games is produced *through* this active, embodied and reflective position outside of the image. The spectator engages with the game space by moving an "avatar," by handling the virtual camera, by manipulating items, and by attending and reacting upon two-dimensional displays onscreen. Each of these means immerses the spectator only on the condition of his or her active and deliberate participation of the visual interface to the bodily and sensorial experience of digital space by the flesh-and-blood spectator in relation to the developer's model addressee.

The *social* aspects of digital gaming relate to the construction of new types of shared cultural participation and communality. New media not only transforms old media and already existing practices, but also the users and subjects of these media and practices. New media certainly have changed means and practices of gaming in several respects, but most of all they have transformed the social setting and the physical environment in which game playing used to take place and have introduced new social practices and forms of game playing. Whereas in earlier offline computer games the human adversary had been replaced by the computer's "artificial intelligence," online computer games have replaced the direct, face-to-face contact with fellow players by electronically mediated communication through a global network.

Much has been written about the opportunities electronic communication media have provided for experiments with virtual identities and social life. In online gaming environments, players can literally hide their identities behind the mask of the avatar by assuming an identity that differs from their real-world persona in significant respects like gender, age, ethnicity, and social status. There is a growing body of research on online environments as places favored especially by adolescents to experiment with social identities: how online computer games supplement the "real" social lives of their players and the forms it can take: player identifications with online personae; players'; changes in players' social and communicative skills and behaviors in online gaming environments; players' problem solving skills; technical knowledge acquisition (e.g., programming skills); player sensitivity to cosmologies, ontologies, belief systems, languages, rules, or habits that are markedly different from those rooted in their own cultural and social morays. Some gaming individuals or communities have been observed "from within" virtual environments to gauge the differences between the politics of online identity construction and those acted out in everyday life. Ethnographic research on Internet-based communities offers alternative means and sources (e.g., archived discussions of chatrooms, newsgroups and discussion lists, as well as logbooks and, of course, email connections). Research dealing with online gaming practices has already demonstrated the usefulness and reliability of these and similar sources. A central role has been assigned to the relation of the interface to the bodily and sensorial experience of digital space by the flesh-and-blood spectator. Current theories and methodologies in the social sciences and humanities have not yet developed adequate categories to describe, analyze and interpret new media objects like digital games. Not only do digital games combine several media and involve all kinds of bodily and sensorial experiences, but they are events rather than objects, as they are not fixed once and for all, but change materially as a result of the interventions of their recipients, who may either act alone or in a social exchange with other players. The difficulty of intellectually grasping new media objects like digital games is exemplified in the recent debate around the narrative structure of games. Whereas the "narratologist" argument is that digital games can be analyzed in narrative terms, the "ludologist" argument claims that the crux of a game is the exercise of a range of cognitive, imaginative, and sensomotor skills, either for its own sake or in order to achieve a goal. An analysis of the digital game as a learning medium has to take this debate into account, and foreground other theoretical perspectives that in combination may allow for a deeper understanding of the ways in which players engage with and thereby modify the digital play. To account for the cultural impact of digital games as a virtual learning environments requires a new theoretical framework and vocabulary rooted in empirical research that can be used to construct a matrix capable of systematically representing cognitive an affective responses characteristic of user engagement with the new media interface of the digital game. Its intellectual and scientific potential lies in the examination of user engagement with the pedagogico-technical phenomenon of the digital game as a learning space of single and multiple users in order to understand the transformations regarding what it means to learn in the digital age of converging literacies.

CONTRIBUTORS

Themistoklis Aravossitas is a graduate of the University of Athens Pedagogic Department of Primary Education and the Ontario Institute for Studies in Education (OISE) of the University of Toronto, having received a Master of Arts in Curriculum Studies and Teacher Development. He is currently continuing his studies as a Ph.D. student at OISE/UT. After serving as a teacher in elementary education in Greece, he is now professionally involved in heritage language education in Canada, where he serves as the Director of Education for the Greek Community of Toronto.

Dr. Suzanne de Castell is Professor and Dean pro-tem of the Faculty of Education at Simon Fraser University. She's interested in relations between media and epistemology, between "knowing" and "tools of intellect," in relation to print literacy, new media studies, and game-based educational technologies. Her books include *Literacy Society and Schooling* (with Alan Luke and Kieran Egan), *Language, Authority and Criticism* (with Alan and Carmen Luke), *Radical Interventions* (with Mary Bryson) and *Worlds in Play* (with Jen Jenson). Her current work is on the ludic epistemologies of game-based learning, exemplified in several projects co-developed with Jenson: Contagion, a compelling game about public health, Arundo Donax, a gripping engagement with Baroque music, and Epidemic, a social networking site where your "friends" are contacts you manage to infect. She co-edits the Canadian Game Studies journal, *Loading*.

Dr. Michael Hoechsmann is an associate professor in Education at McGill University. His research interests are in the areas of media, new technologies, literacy, new literacies, youth, cultural studies and education. He is the author of *Reading Youth Writing: "New" Literacies, Cultural Studies and Education* (with

Bronwen E. Low; Peter Lang. 2008). For four years, he was the Director of Education of Young People's Press, a non-profit news service for youth 14–24.

Dr. Liisa Ilomäki is a leader and a researcher in the Technology for Education Research Group, Department of Psychology, University of Helsinki. Her research interest is focused on issues related to ICT and the consequences in education; especially on school level. Currently she co-ordinates a large EU-supported project Knowledge Practises Laboratory (KP-Lab). She has been responsible of two large local level evaluation studies about ICT in schools in Finland, and she has participated in several European research projects as the responsible researcher in UH (OECD study about Innovative schools, EU-supported projects CELEBRATE, Ernist, P2P).

Jennifer Jenson is Assistant Professor of Pedagogy and Technology at York University in the Faculty of Education. Her current research interests include gender and technology, cultural studies of technology, and the design and development of educational computer gaming applications. Jennifer has recently been awarded a Canadian Foundation for Innovation grant to study "play" as it relates to education and computer-based gaming and she currently is principal investigator on a SSHRC grant, "Education, Gender and Gaming" (EGG), which updates theoretical and practical work in the area of gender and technology, through a cultural studies approach to gender and video game playing. She is also is co-investigator of a SSHRC, Research Development Initiative grant (RDI) (with Dr. Suzanne de Castell) which looks to new digital technologies for data collection, analysis, representation and reporting. Finally, she has completed, with Drs. Brian Lewis and Richard Smith (Simon Fraser University) a Canada-wide study of technology policies and policy practices in K–12 schooling.

Richard Kahn is an Assistant Professor of Educational Foundations & Research at the University of North Dakota. The Chief Editor of *Green Theory & Praxis: The Journal of Ecopedagogy*, he is the author of *Critical Pedagogy, Ecoliteracy, and Planetary Crisis: The Ecopedagogy Movement* (Peter Lang); as well as the forthcoming *Ecopedagogy: Educating for Sustainability in Schools and Society* and *Education Out of Bounds: Cultural Studies for a Posthuman Age* (Palgrave Macmillan, co-authored with Tyson Lewis).

Minna Lakkala has a background in general psychology and computer science. She has an extensive experience of in-service teacher training in the educational use of information and communication technology. She has participated in several national and international research projects concerning the use of technology at schools and higher education settings. Currently she is a researcher at the Technology in Education Research Centre (TEdu) in the Department of Psychology at the University of Helsinki. Her main research interests relate to the issues of pedagogical design and students' scaffolding for technology-mediated collaborative inquiry and innovative knowledge practices.

Robert Luke, Ph.D., is Assistant Vice-President of Research and Innovation for George Brown College. He is also Chair of the Research Group of Poly-technics Canada. Dr. Luke is an experienced researcher and expert at work-ing effectively with diverse groups. His research focuses on the application of innovative technologies in healthcare and education, and the evaluation of out-comes associated with new technology development, adoption and adaptation.

Peta Mitchell is a lecturer in Writing in the School of English, Media Studies, and Art History at the University of Queensland. She is the author of *Carto-graphic Strategies of Postmodernity* and a number of book chapters and articles on critical theory, twentieth-century literature, and academic discourse. Her research interests include online publishing, new media technologies, spatial theory, and metaphor.

Marc Ouellette is Managing Editor of *Reconstruction: Studies in Contemporary Culture*. His works have appeared *Game Studies* and *Eludamos: Journal for Com-puter Game Culture*. Ouellette is an active member of the Learning Games Initiative.

John Potter is Programme Leader for the MA in Media, Culture and Com-munication at the London Knowledge Lab, part of the Institute of Education at the University of London. He is a member of the Centre for the Study of Chil-dren, Youth and Media directed by David Buckingham. John's recent research experience has been focused on younger learners as media producers of mov-ing image texts, animation and short digital video pieces. He has also worked with serving teachers and media students developing modules and research on blogging, including the uses of social software across learning contexts. He has presented widely at conferences and seminars and has been involved in a num-ber of research projects in the field of new media in education. Together with Neil Selwyn and Sue Cranmer he is the author of a study of the dispositions of younger learners with regards to new technologies and wider digital culture in formal and informal sites of learning. Before joining the IOE, John worked for a number of years in teacher education at Goldsmiths College and at the Uni-versity of East London. He was also an advisory teacher for ICT in Newham in East London and has taught throughout the age range in primary schools. In addition to academic research papers, he has published books for pre-service and in-service teachers on the uses of technology in primary schools.

Stuart R. Poyntz teaches Communications and Media Studies at Simon Fraser University in British Colimbia. His research interests include children, youth and media cultures, theories of the public sphere, with specific concern for the work of Hannah Arendt, and young people's historical thinking, particularly in relation to digital media technologies. He has extensive background in the history of media literacy, nationally and internationally, and has written on Canadian cinema and the relationship between film and historical representation.

Juha Suoranta is Professor of Adult Education at the University of Tampere, Finland. He has worked as Visiting Scholar in the University of Illinois and UCLA, and as Visiting Professor in the University of Minnesota. His latest books include *Children in the Information Society* (2004), *Education and the Spirit of Time* (2006), and *Wikiworld* (2009).

Dr. Peppi Taalas is the Development Manager and Vice Director of the Language Centre at the University of Jyväskylä. She has expertise in (language) learning technologies, new learning cultures and professional staff development programmes. Her research interests include change in learning and teaching cultures, multimodal pedagogies, teacher roles and attitudes in technology enhanced language learning settings. She has been an active member of various policy initiatives and development projects and continues her research on the changing teaching and learning practices in language teaching. She has also been a coordinator of the Finnish participation in various OECD and EU projects and initiatives in the area of ICTs in education.

Peter Pericles Trifonas is a professor at the Ontario Institute for Studies in Education, University of Toronto. His areas of interest include ethics, philosophy of education, cultural studies, and technology. Among his books are the following: *Revolutionary Pedagogies: Cultural Politics, Instituting Education, and the Discourse of Theory* (Routledge, 2000), *The Ethics of Writing: Derrida, Deconstruction, and Pedagogy* (Rowman & Littlefield, 2000), *Ethics, Institutions and The Right to Philosophy* (with Jacques Derrida; Rowman & Littlefield, 2002), *Roland Barthes and the Empire of Signs* (Icon, 2005), *Umberto Eco & Football* (Icon, 2005), and *Pedagogies of Difference* (Routledge, 2002).

Tere Vadén is Assistant Professor in Hypermedia at the University of Tampere, Finland. He has studied cognitive and social effects of new media, theories of information society, and free/open-source software. His latest books are *Rock the Boat* (2003), *Artistic Research* (2005), and *Wikiworld* (2009).

John Willinsky is Khosla Family Professor of Education at Stanford University and sometime professor at the University of British Columbia. He is the director of the Public Knowledge Project at Stanford, UBC, and Simon Fraser University, which has been working for a decade on improving the scholarly and public quality of research through the development of open-source platforms for journals and a research program studying the impact of this increased access to research on professionals and the public, as well as on the global dimensions of the academic community. Much of his work, including his book, *The Access Principle: The Case for Open Access to Research and Scholarship* (MIT Press, 2006), as well as the software for journals and conferences, is freely available on the project's website.

INDEX